Augsburg College
George Sverdrup Library
Minneapolis, Minnesota 55404

WITHDRAWN

D1264288

Land Reform in Taiwan

LAND REFORM IN TAIWAN

Chen Cheng

China Publishing Company

COPYRIGHT 1961 BY CHINA PUBLISHING CO.

First Edition

PRINTED IN TAIWAN, REPUBLIC OF CHINA

HD
1167
F75
C5

CONTENTS

67746

tttt

PREFACE

L AND REFORM achievements on Taiwan have attracted widespread attention. Countries of Southeast Asia, the Middle East, Africa, and Latin America have sent representatives to make on-the-spot inspections or have requested cooperation and the dispatch of Chinese personnel to help them solve their land problems. Foreign visitors have shown a keen interest in our program. Consequently, it is hoped that these pages will make a small contribution to better understanding of Taiwan land reform and serve as a reference for those who want to carry out similar projects.

A study of Chinese history for the last 2,000 years shows recurring patterns of war and peace. Many causes may be listed, but the most important is inability to maintain a proper balance between land and population for any length of time. Whenever population increased to a point where land was insufficient, violent uprisings broke out and civil wars ensued. But with resulting reduction of population and restoration of the land-population equilibrium, another period of social and political stability would begin. Lasting peace and stability are not possible until this vicious cycle has been ended.

We know only too well that the best way to effect changes in an agrarian economy is to develop industry and trade. However, in a country where the economy is predominantly agricultural, capital investment in land and the exploitation of human labor constitute great impediments to such development. We must begin by setting capital and labor free through land reform.

Not only that. Even to step up land productivity, land reform is necessary. Under an unreasonable tenancy system, farmers have neither the interest to increase production nor the ability to improve land utilization. When the author was Governor of Hupeh Province in 1939, a serious drought occurred. Curiously, farmers refused to cooperate with the civil and military personnel and students who were dispatched to help them pump water into their fields. We later discovered this was because they could enjoy the full fruits of their labor only by allowing the rice seedlings to wither and then planting drought-resistant crops in their stead. After the implementation of farm rent reduction on Taiwan in 1949, there was a steady increase in rice production. This was due to the fact that with increased income resulting from rent reduction, farmers have greater incentive and increased ability to boost production.

The author was appointed Governor of Taiwan Province in 1949. At that juncture the general situation on the mainland was deteriorating fast, the morale of the people on Taiwan was low, economic confusion and social unrest were rampant, and it looked as though anything might happen. To safeguard the island as a base of operations for national recovery, we required social stability, and the first prerequisite had to be satisfactory solution of the problem of the people's livelihood. Social and economic conditions of Taiwan still rested on an agricultural basis. Farmers constituted more than three-fifths of the population, and the number of tenants was more than two-thirds of all farm families. Social stability, improved people's livelihood and economic development could take place only through land reform.

In view of the unstable situation on Taiwan at the time, it was decided that reform should not be rushed but should be undertaken in a series of steps. As the first of these, rent paid by tenant farmers was limited to 37.5 per cent of the annual yield of the main crop. The successful implementation of this program can be attributed to three factors: (1) reasonable rentals which gave the tenant more income but caused relatively slight loss to the landlord; (2) correct classification of land categories and grades, leading to just and reasonable appraisal of the yield of the main crop; and (3) heightening of the farmer's incentive and productive ability in coordination with the government's policy to boost production of rice by 20 per cent. Consequently, the amount of the landlord's income was not diminished in spite of rent reduction.

At that time, about 21 per cent of farmland in Taiwan was public land. As a part of its rent reduction policy, the Chinese Government offered such lands for lease at reduced rentals in order to improve the livelihood of farmers. Once the rent reduction program had been successfully carried out, the government decided, in 1951, to offer these lands for sale to incumbent tenants, who were given all necessary protection and assistance.

By 1953, the rent reduction program had become solidly established and had produced excellent results. With this as a basis and with the experience gained from the sale of public lands, we decided to implement a land-to-the-tiller policy aimed at eradication of the tenancy system and the freeing of capital invested in land to promote industrial and commercial development and the transformation of the economic and social structure of the country.

Five principles were adopted. (1) We decided to carry out the program gradually and by peaceful means. Landlords were permitted to retain a reasonable maximum of tenanted land. Amounts over and above this limit were compulsorily sold to the government at fairly fixed prices for resale to tenants. Next, the government extended loans to the farmers to enable them to buy the lands retained by the landlord. (2) Both the compulsory purchase of land and its resale were effected through the government without direct contact between landlord and tenant so as to prevent abuses or disputes. (3) Care was taken to see that the buyer was the original tiller, that the land was the same he had been tilling, and that the way of operating the farm was unchanged. (4) For protection of other enterprises, limits were set to farmlands owned by educational, social, and economic undertaking and industrial and commercial plants, and such lands were exempted from compulsory purchase and sale. (5) Protection was given to owner-cultivators by preventing the transfer or lease of farmlands purchased under the land-to-the-tiller program before the price had been paid in full. A production loan fund was provided to encourage the farmer-purchaser to operate the land on a cooperative basis with improved techniques.

Successful implementation of the land-to-the-tiller policy was attributable to these principles and four other important factors. First, a firm foundation had been laid by the operation of the rent reduction program. Second, the prior implementation of the general landownership classification program had resulted in clear and accurate data on land categories, distribution of rights, actual condition of use, and identity and number of resident and non-resident landlords. Third, the compensation paid landlords by the government was fair and reasonable. Issuance of land bonds and stock shares of public enterprises as compensation guaranteed landlords against the risk of possible inflation. Fourth, the government induced landlords to engage in industry and assisted those with small holdings to take up other occupations.

Several conspicuous results have emerged from land reform on Taiwan, social unrest and confusion have gradually given way to stability. Social order is especially good in the rural areas. After the farmers acquired landownership, they became deeply interested in maintaining peace and order in the community. The farmer's productive capacity has been raised and economic development fostered. Increased income, a better livelihood and higher purchasing power have stimulated industrial and commercial development and economic prosperity. Gradual transfer to industry and trade of the capital originally tied up in land has led to a phenomenal development of trade and industry, transformation of the social and economic structure, and a big forward step toward an industrial society.

According to our experience, the implementation of land reform is not only basic to the betterment of the people's livelihood and the promotion of political and social stability, but also a motive force for furtherance of economic development and industrialization. The progress we have made in economic reconstruction is largely due to the influence of changes in agriculture.

As of today, our efforts are directed toward several goals. On the one hand, we have to preserve and expand the achievements of land reform and protect the interests of the farmers. On the other, we need to strengthen land utilization and make full use of the economic value of land in order to enrich the people as individuals and the nation as a whole. Meanwhile, we must accelerate economic development and foster industry. The author is convinced that with the implementation of land reform on Taiwan, we can break China's vicious circle of cyclical war and peace, and also fully develop our industry and trade so as to modernize the national economy and the people's livelihood, and to guarantee and develop political democracy through economic freedom. We may even say that land reform on Taiwan will mark an important change in the course of our history.

The situation on the Communist-controlled Chinese mainland is entirely different. There, in the name of agrarian reform, the Chinese Communists have deceived the people and created a reign of terror. As a result of Communist rule, Chinese farmers have fallen into the status of serfs. Years of farm failure have exposed all the people to starvation. The contrast with the situation on Taiwan is clear and indisputable.

We are sincerely sorry for our failure to carry out Dr. Sun Yat-sen's land-to-the-tiller ideal while we were still on the mainland. Though that failure may be partly attributed to internal disturbances and foreign invasion, it was due mainly to the selfishness of a small minority of people, to their shortsightedness and lack of courage. The achievements of land reform on Taiwan may compensate, to some extent, for that failure, but we cannot be satisfied with this limited accomplishment. We must make greater exertions to achieve still greater progress. We must be determined, on the basis of the experience gained on Taiwan, to put the land-to-the-tiller policy into effect on the mainland after its recovery. Our brethren there then may be delivered from starvation and slavery, and come to enjoy the freedom, stability, and happy life that they are entitled to.

Chen Cheng

Taipei, Taiwan
Republic of China
December, 1961

CHAPTER 1

INTRODUCTION

THE LAND PROBLEM

M AN cannot live without land, from which he derives his sustenance. Land is, as a matter of fact, the mainstay of human life. It must be observed, however, that while there has not been much change in the total area of land since ancient times, the increase of population, if unchecked, may have no limit at all. In primitive ages when there was plenty of land with few inhabitants, every person could have as much land as he wanted. Hence there was no land problem. But in later times, as land became scarce in proportion to increased population, the supply was insufficient to meet the demand. Land became an object over whose possession individual fought individual and nation fought nation. Thus the land problem gradually arose.

Though the land problem is complex, it may be said to consist of the following aspects:

1. Problem of land distribution: This arose as a result of the lack of proper regulations to govern the ownership of land and the enjoyment of its fruits. The feudal form of land distribution was unjust and objectionable. Unrestricted appropriation of land for their own benefit by big landlords must be considered outrageous. This was a phenomenon which Tung Chung-shu, an

eminent scholar of the Western Han Dynasty (206 B.C.-24 A.D.) bitterly lamented when he said: "The land owned by the rich stretches from one end to the other without a break, but the poor have no place even to stand upon."

2. Problem of land taxation: The system of taxation in China was not known as a sound one. This was true especially of taxes on land. As the farmers lived on land and could not easily evade tax payment, the Government depended mainly on the land taxes to defray national expenses. In view of the excessive levies imposed on them, the farmers suffered greatly. The tenant farmers, who were objects of exploitation by landlords, were particularly hard hit. The result was as Mencius described: "In years of plenty the farmers live a miserable life; in years of scarcity they cannot escape starvation and death." Owing to the fact that the tenant farmer did not till their own land, they had no incentive to step up production. Therefore, fields often lay uncared for and production was low.

3. Problem of cadastration: Cadastration was an immensely difficult task in China. It was made doubly so by the specially privileged classes that entrenched themselves in their own localities. Even under an enlightened monarch such as Emperor Kuang Wu of the Eastern Han Dynasty (25-220 A.D.) and at the beginning of a new dynastic era, to boot, it was discovered during a cadastral survey that, as the historian tells us, "the situation in Yingchuan and Hungnung is fairly good, but that in Honan and Nanyang is pretty bad." If such phenomena were to be found under the rule of an enlightened Emperor, the situation at other times can be well imagined. As a matter of fact, field boundaries long had been confused and attempts to refix them had not been taken seriously. The net result was that those having more land paid lower taxes and those having less land paid higher taxes. There were even cases in which those who had land did not pay any land tax and those who paid land taxes had no land at all.

4. Problem of land utilization: Our knowledge of land utilization was rudimentary and backward. We used to attribute natural disasters to the will of Heaven and thought that a plentiful or poor harvest had nothing to do with human effort. We were

contented with the status quo and would not exert ourselves to make progress. Nay, we even considered reliance upon Heaven for our bread and butter as true wisdom. The result was that though we were an agricultural nation, many people were still starving in the countryside.

As an ancient saying goes, "A nation depends upon its people, and the people depend upon food to keep themselves alive." In an agricultural society, to solve the problem of food for the people is the basic task of those who wish to regulate the family life, to order the national life, and to pacify the whole world. With the solution of this problem, all other problems can be easily solved. But if this problem is not solved, the spread of hunger and starvation can be expected to lead to disaster for the nation.

Ancient kings and emperors, ministers, and great statesmen in China all appreciated the importance of agriculture and were mostly physiocrats. As such, they regarded the development of farming and sericulture as the most important task. They also knew that land problems had to be dealt with carefully, and that if those problems could not be solved, it would be futile merely to develop farming and sericulture. Consequently, there have been plans for the solution of the land problem in the successive dynasties. In other words, there have been successive efforts at land reform throughout Chinese history.

The reforms, some proposed and some carried out, during the Eastern Han Dynasty (25-220 A.D.) by Usurper Wang Mang and by Emperor Wu of the Western Tsin Dynasty (265-316 A.D.) and during the Northern Wei (386-534 A.D.) and Tang (618-906 A.D.) Dynasties, were all progressive measures having to do with land distribution. Other measures carried out during the reigns of Emperor Wu (140-88 B.C.) of the Han Dynasty and Emperor Kuang Wu (25-57 A.D.) of the Eastern Han Dynasty and at the time of Prime Minister Wang An-shih (1018-1086 A.D.) of the Sung Dynasty also made great contributions to the solution of the land tenure problem. But it was a pity that most of these reform measures were implemented for only a short time, and even then not thoroughly implemented. We may therefore say that the land problem in China was sometime partially solved, but never wholly and permanently solved.

For this reason, the problem of food has never been satisfactorily solved in China, and hunger and starvation have always been with us. Desperate people facing hunger and starvation are likely to take advantage of all opportunities to make trouble and raise the standard of revolt. Students of Chinese history find that years of civil commotion arising out of a poor harvest far outnumber the years of peace. Eight or nine out of every ten such disturbances have been caused by our failure to find a thoroughgoing and permanent solution of the land problem.

As another Chinese saying has it, "What has already happened cannot be helped. Let us see what we can do for the future." In order to insure permanent and lasting peace for China, we must have a set of workable measures for the permanent and thorough solution of the land problem. This is a responsibility we cannot shirk.

To carry out our mission, we must first of all have a clear and accurate understanding of the current problem.

As the Chinese mainland is presently under Communist occupation, we shall leave it out of our discussion for the moment. Now let us take a look at the land problem in Taiwan.

SCARCITY OF ARABLE LAND

The general condition of the distribution of population and land in Taiwan may be described as follows:

(1) The land area of Taiwan Province as a whole is 35,961 square kilometers (13,881 square miles). In 1949 the population was more than 7,300,000 with an average population density of 205 persons per square kilometer (530 persons per square mile). Since 1958 the population has exceeded the ten million mark and the population density is approaching 300 persons per square kilometer (780 persons per square mile) and still increasing. If this situation is not changed, Taiwan eventually may become

one of the most densely populated regions in the world.

(2) According to statistics of 1949, the area of cultivated land in Taiwan Province was 842,301 *chia* (2,018,760 acres) and the agricultural population was 3,879,581. On the average, each individual could have only 0.2171 *chia* (0.5203 acre) of cultivated land. In the same year, there were 665,134 farm families, each of which could have on the average only 1.2663 *chia* (3.0351 acres) of cultivated land. From these figures it is evident that the area of cultivated land in Taiwan is too small. This is Taiwan's biggest land problem.

It is extremely difficult to expand the area of cultivated land. Though cultivated land in Taiwan is only about 23 per cent of the total area, nine-tenths of the other 77 per cent is mountainous and forest land, which either is unsuitable for cultivation or should not be cultivated for the good reason that mountains and forests are no less useful than farm land.

The following chart* shows changes in the area of cultivated land in Taiwan Province from 1948 to 1959. A glance at the chart will show how difficult it is to expand such an area.

CHART 1

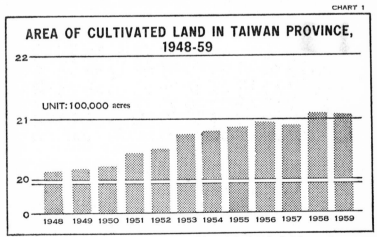

AREA OF CULTIVATED LAND IN TAIWAN PROVINCE, 1948-59

UNIT: 100,000 acres

Note: Owing to the fact that some of the cultivated land was washed away in the devastating flood of August 7, 1959, the area of cultivated land in that year was smaller than in the previous year.

* For detailed figures, see APPENDIX, Table 1, p. 307.

POPULATION PRESSURE

The island of Taiwan has a population density exceeded by few other countries. Further inquiry will show that the annual rate of population increase in Taiwan is astonishing. For recent years this rate is 33.5 per thousand, more than double the world average of 16 per thousand.

Though the populations of Venezuela, Mexico, and Malaya also are increasing at annual rates of more than 30 per thousand, they are large countries and have vast areas of land. The situation of Taiwan is not comparable.

The following chart* shows the increase of population in Taiwan Province from 1948 to 1959. The reader will note that in recent years the rate has even exceeded the average of 33.5 per thousand.

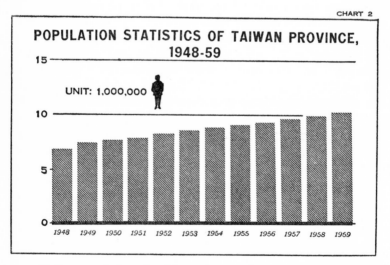

CHART 2

POPULATION STATISTICS OF TAIWAN PROVINCE, 1948-59

UNIT: 1,000,000

1948 1949 1950 1951 1952 1953 1954 1955 1956 1957 1958 1959

If the population should continue to increase at the present rate, it would double in thirty years. As land area remains relatively constant, the pressure of population on land can be well imagined.

* For detailed figures, see APPENDIX, Table 2, p. 307.

MALADJUSTMENTS IN LAND DISTRIBUTION

Next let us take a look at the actual condition of land distribution in Taiwan by noting the comparative number of tenant farmer and owner-farmer families.

According to statistics compiled by the Taiwan Provincial Department of Agriculture and Forestry and the Taiwan Provincial Office of Accounting and Statistics, the number of tenant farmer families was about 68.8 per cent (37.8% of tenant farmer families and 31% of part owner-farmer families) of the total number of farm families at the end of the Japanese occupation in 1945. According to figures for 1950, 1951, and 1952, there were 169,216 part owner-farmer families, who constituted 24 per cent of the total number of farm families; 242,754 tenant farmer families and 44,924 farm hand families, constituting 34.5 and 6.4 per cent, respectively, of the total number of farm families in Taiwan. Taken together, these part owner-farmer, tenant farmer, and farm hand families, which did not have enough cultivated land or no land at all, amounted to 64.9 per cent of all the farm families. In other words, there were only 35.1 per cent of owner farmers, totaling 247,675 families, who had enough land to till. This shows how land distribution has been maladjusted.

The following chart* shows the number of owner-farmer, part owner-farmer, tenant farmer, and farm hand families in Taiwan.

Next let us take a look at the breakdown of the area of cultivated land in Taiwan. According to statistics compiled at the time of the General Landownership Classification in 1952, the area of private cultivated land was 681,154 *chia* (1,632,536 acres), of which 427,197 *chia* (1,023,872 acres), constituting 62.72 per cent of all the private cultivated land, was owner-cultivated and 253,957 *chia* (608,664 acres), constituting 37.28 per cent of private cultivated land, was tenanted land. At the time of the General Landownership Classification in Taiwan, the rent reduction program was carried out over a period of three years during which many tenant farmers purchased large tracts of

* For detailed figures, see APPENDIX, Table 3, p. 308.

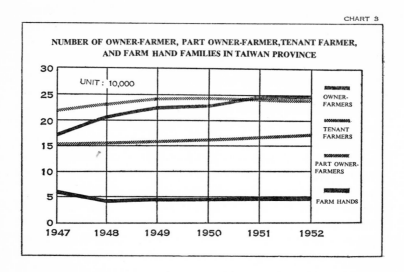

CHART 3

NUMBER OF OWNER-FARMER, PART OWNER-FARMER, TENANT FARMER, AND FARM HAND FAMILIES IN TAIWAN PROVINCE

cultivated land for themselves.   Even then, the area of tenanted land was still as high as 37.28 per cent.   This shows that there was still a very serious situation wherein large numbers of farmers did not own the land they were tilling.

Though the area of tenanted land was by no means large, the number of part owner-farmer, tenant farmer, and farm hand families was big enough to constitute 64.9 per cent of all farm families.   It is therefore clear that those having their own land to till accounted for only a small number of families and owned much of the land, and that those leasing the land of others accounted for a large number of families and cultivated only small areas.   This is clear evidence of the maladjustment in land distribution and land utilization.   The net result was that in the villages, the rich became richer and the poor poorer.   This was not only a rural economic difficulty but also a social and political problem.

WORSENING OF THE TENANCY SITUATION

The tenancy relationship on cultivated land in Taiwan was

widespread and the conditions were also harsh to the extreme. The land rent was generally more than 50 per cent of the harvest. It ran as high as 70 per cent in more fertile areas. In addition, there was a so-called "iron-clad rent," an arrangement by which, irrespective of good or bad harvest, or of natural or manmade disasters, the lessee was required to pay a certain amount of rent. There was also a rent on by-products, which meant that besides the regular amount, the tenant had to pay the landlord 50 per cent or more of the by-products he had produced through the application of additional labor or the investment of additional capital. Sometimes the rent on by-products was payable in the same ratio as the regular rent. Only a very few lease contracts were for definite periods of time, and most of them were oral, without any written document to back them up. Instances of subleasing by tenants to other tenants were also common. This led to a hierarchical form of exploitation. Extraordinary extortions in the form of security deposits, guarantee money, and payment of rent in advance were also demanded and caused the tenant farmer to suffer unbearable hardships.

Under such an unreasonable system, the tenant farmer not only had to pay high rentals and to suffer other forms of exploitation, but also had to agree to leases without any definite period of time and with no written contract to fall back upon. This enabled the landlord to evict the tenant at will and intensified his sufferings, without providing him with any security. How was it possible to expect an increase in farm production and to hope for the improvement and better utilization of farm land?

In tilling land that does not belong to him, the tiller feels no special love for the soil and has little interest in increased production. From the viewpoint of the national economy, such a state of affairs is a great loss. Not only that, but the tenant farmer has to live in misery in spite of the year-long efforts he has made in the fields, while the landlords could live comfortably without working. This contrast could have created serious conflict between classes. If this situation had remained uncorrected, it could have been a source of social and political trouble. History has provided one example after another of such an unfortunate turn of events.   For this reason, it was necessary for Taiwan to carry out land reform.

LAND REFORM

We shall not attempt a historical review of land reform in China.   In modern times Dr. Sun Yat-sen (1866-1925), father of the Chinese Republic, used the "equalization of land rights" as a revolutionary slogan in pre-republican days.   Since establishment of the Republic in 1912, the country has had an interminable series of civil wars and foreign encroachments, so that the policy of "equalization of land rights" remained regrettably unrealized at the time of the Communist take-over on the mainland in 1949. However, anyone who studies land reform in recent decades must begin with Dr. Sun's teachings.   We must say something about his views to make clear the origins of our reform programs.

When Dr. Sun went to Europe and America for the first time in 1896, the countries of the west were in the midst of a land reform movement.   Henry George was advocating the single tax in the United States.   John Stuart Mill's theory that all unearned increments of land should go to the public was receiving much attention in Britain.   Adolf Damaschke was organizing a land reform league in Germany.   The question of land nationalization was being discussed in Russia.   Australia was beginning to introduce a land value tax.   With an attentive ear and an open eye, Dr. Sun learned all the theories relating to the land problem.   At the same time, he was familiar with the history of land reform in China and knew the advantages and disadvantages of the various proposals that had been put forward by successive reformers. With all this knowledge as a background, he propounded the theory of "equalization of land rights" as a guiding principle for land reform in modern China.   On the establishment of the *Tung Men Hui,* an association of revolutionists organized by Dr. Sun in 1905, the "equalization of land right" was proclaimed to be one of the four main planks of the revolutionary platform.

Said Dr. Sun in the manifesto issued by the *Tung Men Hui:* "The blessings of civilization should be enjoyed by all citizens on an equal footing. The economic organization of society should be improved and the value of land throughout the country should be assessed. The current value of land should still belong to the original owner, but the increased value of land resulting from social improvements and progress after the revolution should go to the State to be enjoyed by all citizens in common. We shall build up a new society and nation in which every family and individual will be able to support themselves and no one in the country shall be destitute. If anyone should try to monopolize land and have a stranglehold on the life of the people, he shall be considered as a public enemy." From this it will be seen that the essential idea in Dr. Sun's theory of the "equalization of land rights" is his insistence that "the blessings of civilization should be enjoyed by all citizens on an equal footing." This idea comes pretty close to the theory of rent as enunciated by European and American scholars and fits in well, particularly, with John Stuart Mill's theory that all unearned increments of land should go to the public.

The *San Min Chu I,* or Three Principles of the People, propounded by Dr. Sun, has as its ultimate objective the realization of the Principle of People's Livelihood, which is conditioned upon the implementation of two fundamental measures, namely, "equalization of land rights" and the "regulation of capital." He was particularly emphatic on the first of the two and took pains to explain it on all possible occasions.

To quote from some of Dr. Sun's public speeches:

"The public ownership of land is founded on the very nature of things. There was land long before mankind came on the scene. Land will remain after mankind has disappeared from the surface of the earth. Land is common property. How could man call it his own?"—Speech to the Socialist Party at Shanghai, 1912.

"The nationalization of land does not require that all land be taken over by the State. It can be accomplished this way: if, in building roads or opening markets, it is necessary to pass through fields, gardens, or houses or to use certain pieces of land for the purpose, the land in question may be purchased by the Government from its owner according to the value he had declared in his initial application for a landownership certificate."—Speech on *How to Carry Out the Principle of People's Livelihood* delivered before newspaper reporters at Canton, 1912.

"Many scholars in various parts of the world are in favor of land nationalization, which is reasonable and may be adopted by us. But, in my view, not all land should be owned by the State, but only those parts of the land which are needed for public purposes." — Speech on *Concrete Measures for Equalizing Land Rights* delivered before Kwangtung Provincial Assemblymen and newspaper reporters at Canton, 1912.

These quotations show that, in Dr. Sun's view, land should be owned by the public, in principle, and should not be owned by any private individual. This is the fundamental theoretical basis for a new land policy. But in practice there is no necessity for nationalizing all the land, only those pieces that are needed for public use. The people may still own land. From this it will be seen that Dr. Sun is in favor of land nationalization only as a matter of principle.

"The biggest gambling in the world is land speculation, such as is being carried on in Canada today. It is a general law that where industry and commerce are developed, the value of land there will become higher and higher. This has happened in Hongkong and Shanghai where one *mow* (0.02451 acre) of land, formerly worth ten or 100 silver *yuan,* is now worth as much as thousands and tens of thousands of silver *yuan.* If the land value is not properly equalized in time, powerful capitalists will compete with one another in investing their money in land speculation after the further development of industries. If that should happen, it would spread all over the country in ten years and there would be a big economic crisis." — Speech on *The Equalization of Land Rights* delivered before newspaper reporters at Canton, 1912.

"The land problem is a big one. In order to prevent the

poor from becoming poorer and the rich richer through unregulated land relations, it is necessary to practice the Principle of People's Livelihood, which can be done only by beginning with the equalization of land rights as formerly advocated by the *Tung Men Hui.*" — Speech on *Concrete Measures for Realizing the San Min Chu I* delivered at Canton, 1921.

In other words, though land may be privately owned, the Government should exercise a high degree of control over the private ownership through the equalization of land rights in order to forestall speculative buying and selling and prevent the poor from becoming poorer and the rich richer.

"Every county, at the beginning of self-government, shall first assess the value of private land in the whole county, which value is to be declared by the owner himself. The local government shall tax private land on the basis of its assessed value and may purchase it at the same value. If, after this assessment, the land increases in value as a result of political advancement or social progress, such unearned increment should be set aside for the common benefit of the people in the whole county, and should not be kept by the landowner as private profit." — *Fundamentals of National Reconstruction.*

Such are the concrete, practical measures for implementing the equalization of land rights. They are simple and easy to carry out. If they are put into practice, the land problem will be fundamentally solved.

With respect to agricultural land, Dr. Sun also advocated "rent reduction" and "land to the tiller," both of which can go hand in hand with the "equalization of land rights."

Says Dr. Sun in his third lecture on the Principle of People's Livelihood:

"A large majority of the people in China are peasants, at least nine out of every ten, yet the food which they raise with such wearisome labor is mostly taken away by the landowners. What they themselves can keep is barely sufficient to keep them alive. This is a most unjust situation. If we are to increase the production of food, we must make laws regarding the rights and interests of the farmers; we must give them encouragement and protection and allow them to keep more of the fruit of their land . . . . When the Principle of People's Livelihood is fully realized and the problems of the farmer are all solved, each tiller of the soil will possess his own fields—that is to be the final goal of our efforts . . . . Although China does not have great landlords, yet nine out of ten farmers do not own their fields. Most of the farming land is in the possession of landlords who do not do the cultivating themselves . . . . Of the food produced in the fields, 60 per cent, according to our latest rural surveys, goes to the landlord, while only 40 per cent goes to the farmer. If this unjust state of affairs continues, when the farmers become intelligent, who will still be willing to toil and suffer in the fields? But if the food raised in the fields all goes to the farmers, they will be more eager to farm and production will increase."

This is Dr. Sun's "land-to-the-tiller" theory, which is an important message for the backward areas.

In the *Fundamentals of National Reconstruction,* Dr. Sun points out: "Annual receipts from the land tax, unearned increment, products from public land, the yield from mountains, forests, rivers and lakes, proceeds from the sale of mineral wealth and water power, all belong to the local government, and shall be used for the operation of public enterprises, for the care of the young and the aged, the poor and the sick, for the relief of victims of disasters, and for meeting other public needs." This means that with the realization of Dr. Sun's theory of land reform, not only would the land and peasant problems be satisfactorily solved, but social welfare and the well-being of the people would also be promoted.

In the light of Dr. Sun's teachings and in view of the seriousness of the problem, land reform was an urgent matter on Taiwan.

The reform that has been carried out on the island in the last ten years includes the following items:

1. Rent reduction on cultivated land.
2. Sale of public land.
3. Implementation of a "land-to-the-tiller" program.
4. Reclamation and full utilization of cultivated land.
5. Implementation of a program for the equalization of land rights in urban areas.

Of these five items, the program for the equalization of land rights in urban areas is comparatively new and will not be discussed in these pages. The other four items, however, have been carried out over a period of many years and have achieved excellent results. How they have been implemented will be presented in the following chapters. Here it only will be necessary to point out one basic principle that we have faithfully followed from the very beginning.

That principle is our determination to effectualize Dr. Sun's teachings on land reform and to carry them out in conformity with the time-honored ideals of government of, by, and for the people.

It may be objected that the private ownership of land is contrary to Dr. Sun's idea of land nationalization. But, as a matter of fact, it is not. As we have already pointed out, he was in favor of land nationalization in principle only. A nation is a collective entity. It is made up of individual people. There can be no nation without individuals. It is only through their hands that a nation or state can possess this or that. As the ancients have said, "Heaven can see only as the people see; Heaven can hear only as the people hear." Now if the omnipresent and omniscient Heaven can see and hear only as the people see and hear, how can the state possess anything without its going through the hands of individual men and women? In our view, Dr. Sun's idea of land nationalization should be properly understood to mean:

First, that the Government may, to meet public needs, purchase privately owned land and turn it into public land.

Second, that the Government may, according to laws enacted by representatives of the people, let private individuals have land ownership, and that such land under private ownership is as good as being publicly owned, because private individuals are by no means entirely free but are bound by the laws and regulations of the country.

Viewed in this light, Dr. Sun's theory of land nationalization does not rule out the private ownership of land, which, however, has to be based on public opinion and law, and cannot go beyond certain bounds. This is different from the Communist type of nationalization, which is aimed at the expropriation of all property.

Applying the principle of government by the people to matters relating to land, we find that under such principle the people are free to make use of their own land for productive purposes without outside interference, on condition that there be no conflict between private and public interests and that no harm be done to another person or persons. To harmonize private and public interests, landowners may select representatives to draw up or screen draft laws, or discuss and approve practical measures, in order to insure that all points of view are duly taken into consideration. Though the land reform implemented in Taiwan in recent years was initiated by the Government in the first instance, all the laws and regulations governing its actual operation first were screened and approved by the people's representatives at various levels and then enforced. Nor is that all. The basic structure for the implementation of land reform is the Farm Tenancy Committee, which with the exception of a few *ex-officio* members, is mostly composed of farmers' representatives. The farmers' associations and irrigation associations are also organized by the farmers themselves for the transaction of business affecting their personal interests. It thus can be seen that land reform in Taiwan has been carried out according to the spirit of government by the people.

As to the principle of government for the people, it is evident that this refers to the fact that all the products of land should, after the payment of taxes, water fees, and other necessary expenses, be enjoyed by the farmer himself. The land here referred to also includes that which is not under individual ownership. In the case of all lands, if their unearned increment is the result of social progress, that increment will be taken over by the Government to be used for public welfare. In this sense, the land reform in Taiwan is aimed at the promotion of government for the people.

The land reform that has been carried out in conformity with the principle of government of, by, and for the people also may be called a land reform in the spirit of Dr. Sun's Three Principles of the People, or the *San Min Chu I*.

A land reform in the spirit of the *San Min Chu I* should begin by letting the people have a decisive voice in the planning and execution of the reform measures and end by permitting them to enjoy all the fruits thereof. Likewise, the people also should be responsible for carrying out the reform program. These three aspects of the people's role are interdependent and none would be complete without the other two. The right of ownership serves as the basis of land reform; execution of the reform plans provides the motive power; and enjoyment of the fruits of reform is the final reward for all the exertions made by the people. Only in this way can the potentialities of land be completely utilized, the reform work be crowned with success, and the people obtain real benefits. Only in this way can theory be translated into fact and not remain a dead letter.

CHAPTER 2

FARM LAND
RENT REDUCTION

PROPOSAL FOR RENT REDUCTION IN TAIWAN

L AND reform in rural areas of Taiwan is aimed at realization of the "land-to-the-tiller" ideal. But in view of the inveteracy of the tenancy system on this island, that ideal could not be realized all at once. If it was to be realized at all, it had to be done by stages, of which rent reduction was the initial one.

The policy of rent reduction long had been one of the planks of the Kuomintang platform. A 25% rent reduction was introduced first in Kwangtung, and then in Hunan, Hupeh, and Chekiang provinces. But owing to a variety of obstacles which prevented smooth implementation of the program, no marked result was achieved. In 1930 the central Government promulgated the Land Law, which provided among other things that farm rentals should not exceed 37.5 per cent of the total annual yield of the main crop. That was how the program came to be known as a "37.5% rent reduction."*

With the outbreak of the Sino-Japanese War in July 1937,

*The two terms, 25% rent reduction and 37.5% rent reduction, really mean the same thing. By the former term is meant the taking of one quarter of the total annual yield as the tenant's share and then dividing

commodity prices began to rise in all parts of the country. Consequently, demands for the increase of farm land rentals and of security deposits became more and more insistent. This made the life of the tenant farmers more miserable than ever. As the author happened to be concurrently Governor of Hupeh at the time, he ordered the implementation of a 25% rent reduction throughout the whole province in 1940, and it succeeded remarkably well. An amendment to the Land Law in April, 1946, provided that the farm land rentals should not exceed eight per cent of the land value. But owing to practical considerations, this amendment was never put into effect. In the next year the original provision of a 37.5% rent reduction was restored. However, this also remained a dead letter and did not lead to any actual results.

As the author comes from a rural family, he knows the hardships and miseries of the people. Being a faithful disciple of Dr. Sun Yat-sen, he was sorry that he could not put Dr. Sun's teachings on the equalization of land rights into practice. As Governor of Hupeh, he tried to overcome all obstacles in order to enforce a 25% rent reduction to serve as a sort of example for other provinces. The details of that reform have been described in the *Reminiscences of My Public Life* and will not be repeated here. On his appointment to be Governor of Taiwan in 1949, he was acutely conscious of the seriousness of the land problem in this province. Benefiting by the experience he had gained in Hupeh, he began soon after assumption of office to enforce a 37.5% rent reduction on this island for the double purpose of carrying out the central Government's rent reduction policy, and of realizing one of his long-cherished ambitions.

In the previous chapter we have already touched upon the deplorable situation of the tenancy system in Taiwan. Some further explanation of it may be made here.

The most objectionable features of the tenancy system in Taiwan were insecurity of tenure and excessive rentals. Insecurity

the remaining three quarters equally between landlord and tenant. By the latter term is meant the assignment to the landlord of one half of the remaining three quarters, or 37.5 per cent of the harvest.

of tenure was caused by the lack of written contracts. Most of the contracts were made by word of mouth, and written contracts, amounting to only one in ten, were the exception. Furthermore, most of the leases were not for any definite period of time. The landlord might, for reasons of personal interest, evict the tenant at will. With no security of tenure, the tenant was always in danger of momentary eviction.

Excessive rentals was an old phenomenon. Since there was no security of tenure, competition between tenants was much keener. This gave the landlord an opportunity to evict the tenant and raise the rentals at will. According to an article on *Tenancy in Taiwan* in the *Taiwan Economic Yearbook,* Volume II, some farm rentals in the Hsinchu region were as high as 70 per cent of the harvest. Such rates are rarely found anywhere else in China; they are certainly the highest in East Asia. A survey conducted by the Chinese Research Institute of Land Economics showed that 1,439 tenant families in 43 districts and townships in the seven counties of Taipei, Hsinchu, Taichung, Tainan, Kaohsiung, Taitung and Hualien paid an average of 56.8 per cent of the harvest in 1948.

Another abuse is worth mentioning. Certain big landlords, with too much land or with land scattered in widely separate regions, would farm out their land to "land sharks" in order to avoid difficulties of management for themselves. These land sharks would then sublease the land to tenants, thus creating a form of intermediate exploitation. There were, in addition, many extra payments such as security deposits and advance rent payments which the tenant was called upon to make. If he had no ready money to effect such payments, he would be forced to borrow it from money-lenders at high interest rates. This would be an additional burden on the hard-pressed tenant. Other forms of exploitation by the landlord were the rendering of free labor service, tilling part of the land for the landlord, or the performance of other services for him, and the presentation of gifts to him on New Year's Day and other festivals. To allow the tenant farmers and farm hands, who, as pointed out in Section 1, Chapter I above, constituted 64.9 per cent of all the farm families in Taiwan, to groan under the exploitation of the landlords was not merely a land and economic problem, but a social and political matter. If this problem had not been solved in good time, it would have adversely affected the stability and very existence of the nation.

For this reason, the proposal to reduce farm rentals was a very timely measure.

IMPLEMENTATION
OF RENT REDUCTION

In carrying out the rent reduction program, the Chinese Government began to make the necessary arrangements in January, 1949. Actual enforcement started in April of the same year and was concluded in September. It took only a few months to finish an unprecedented and difficult task. The speed with which the work was completed and the smoothness with which it was carried out were, it must be confessed, entirely unexpected.

The following is a brief description of how the program was implemented.

COMPLETING THE LEGISLATIVE PROCEDURE

The Land Law and other related laws contain only general principles on the rental rates for farm land and on tenancy relations. There were no integrated legal provisions which could serve as the basis for rent reduction. In view of the complicated nature of the tenancy system in Taiwan, the adoption of unified laws and regulations, specific, concrete, and detailed, would be necessary for effective implementation of the reform measures. Such laws and regulations would have to take into account actual conditions and needs in Taiwan, besides conforming to the general principles contained in existing laws enacted by the central Government.

As the adoption of unified laws and regulations was an important task and might exert a decisive influence on the success or failure of the reform program, great care had to be taken in their initial drafting.   For this purpose, the views of local governments and the people were solicited.   Experts and scholars, related governmental authorities, responsible officers of civic bodies, representatives of the people, and members of the press were invited to take part in meetings for the discussion of all aspects of the problem.   Every conceivable difficulty and all possible conflicts were taken into consideration in the discussion meetings.   Finally, a set of Regulations Governing the Lease of Private Farm Lands in Taiwan Province was drawn up.   Upon approval by the Provincial Council, the Regulations were promulgated on April 14, 1949.

To facilitate execution of the program, the Taiwan Provincial Government drew up and promulgated sets of other regulations, including Detailed Rules for the Implementation of the Regulations Governing the Lease of Private Farm Lands in Taiwan Province, Important Points in the Registration of Private Farm Land Lease Contracts in Taiwan Province, Rules for the Organization of Rent Reduction Enforcement Supervisory Committees in Taiwan Province, and Rules for the Organization of Rent Reduction Enforcement Supervisory Committees in the Counties and Municipalities of Taiwan Province.   At the same time, all the counties and municipalities in Taiwan were instructed to enforce the program beginning from harvest of the first crop in 1949.

To strengthen the executive power for implementing the rent reduction policy, the Executive Yuan (Cabinet) of the central Government drew up a Farm Rent Reduction Bill which, after having completed the legislative procedure in May, 1951, was promulgated the next month.   At this point, all the legislation on rent reduction was complete.

Essential points of the rent reduction legislation include the following:

(1)   Reducing rental rates: It was provided that the farm rents the tenants had to pay to landlords should not exceed 37.5 per cent of the total annual yield of the principal product of the main crop; that if the rents originally agreed upon exceeded 37.5 per cent, they should be reduced to 37.5 per cent; and that if they

were less than 37.5 per cent, they should not be increased. At the same time, all extra burdens such as advance rent payments and security deposits were to be abolished. In case of crop failure caused by natural disaster, it was provided that rent reduction or remission in proportion to the degree of damage done to the crop might be permitted.

(2) Protecting the tenant's rights: It was provided that all farm lease contracts must be written and that the lease period should not be shorter than six years. For the duration of the contract, the landlord might not, except for legally specified reasons, terminate the contract. Even if the lessor should give up his right of ownership to a third party, the contract would remain valid with respect to that third party. If, at the end of the lease contract, the lessee should be willing to continue the lease, the contract must be renewed, unless the lessor should take back the land for his own cultivation, in accordance with legally specified procedures.

(3) Respecting the landlord's rights and interests: According to the farm lease contract, the tenant should pay rentals on time. The landlord's rights and interests were duly protected by the provision that he might terminate the contract if arrears of the tenant had totaled two years' rent. The fact that the landlords were represented on the various levels of Farm Tenancy Committees charged with the duty of conciliating disputes between landlords and tenants was further evidence that the rent reduction law had not been enacted for the sole benefit of the tenant, but that the rights and interests of the landlord also had been taken into full consideration.

ESTABLISHING SUPERVISORY AGENCIES

The authority for the execution of the rent reduction program in Taiwan was vested in the Land Bureau of the Department of Civil Affairs on the provincial level and in the county and municipal governments at their level. But as the task was entirely unprecedented and concerned with the interests of large numbers of people, it was feared that the Government would not be able to carry it out successfully singlehanded. It was therefore decided to set up supervisory and guidance agencies to supplement governmental efforts. These agencies were: a Committee for the Supervision of the 37.5% Rent Campaign for the province as a whole, a 37.5% Rent Campaign Committee for each county and municipality, and a Sub-Committee of the 37.5% Rent Campaign Committee for each district and township.

The Provincial Committee for the Supervision of the 37.5% Rent Campaign was composed of 17 members, including the Speaker of the Provincial Assembly, Chief Judge of the Taiwan High Court, five members of the Provincial Council, Director of the Provincial Land Bureau, Director of the Provincial Information Office, and eight civic leaders. The Committee was responsible for information, assistance, and supervision in the implementation of farm rent reduction.

The County or Municipal 37.5% Rent Campaign Committee was composed of 21 to 23 members, including the Magistrate or Mayor, Heads of the Land Office, Police, Social Affairs, Agriculture and Forestry, and Civil Affairs Sections, one representative each of the District Court, County or Municipal Council, and Farmers' Association, three to five high school principals, three civic leaders, and two representatives each from landlords, tenant farmers, and owner-farmers. The Committee was responsible for supervision, information, conciliation of disputes, appraisal of the standard amounts of the total annual main crop yield, and other matters relating to farm rent.

The District or Township Sub-Committee of the 37.5% Rent Campaign Committee was composed of the District or Township Chief, three to five principals and teachers of the primary school, chief officer of the police station, three civic leaders, one representative of the Farmers' Association, and two representatives each from landlords, tenant farmers and owner-farmers. The major functions of the Sub-Committee were rendering assistance to the enforcement of rent reduction, preliminary conciliation of disputes between landlord and tenant, and making of recommendations to the County or Municipal 37.5% Rent Campaign Committee in the light of actual local conditions.

The above-mentioned County and Municipal Committees and the District and Township Sub-Committees were abolished as soon as new form lease contracts had been signed. But in order to preserve the post-reform tenancy system and the achievements of the rent reduction program, County, Municipal, District, and Township Farm Tenancy Committees were later set up according to the provisions of the 37.5% Rent Reduction Act. These Committees were composed of two *ex-officio* members (who were Chief of the Land Section of the County or Municipal Government and Chairman of the County or Municipal Farmers' Association in the case of counties and municipalities, or the District or Township Chief and the Land Officer of the District or Township Office in the case of districts and townships), five representatives of tenant farmers, two of owner-farmers, and two of landlords, a total of 11 members. These members who represented tenant farmers, owner-farmers, and landlords were separately elected from among themselves by secret ballot. The method of election was this. First of all, the tenant farmers, owner-farmers, and landlords of the various villages and precincts elected their own delegates, who then proceeded to elect from among themselves members who would represent their respective groups on the District and Township Farm Tenancy Committees. Next, these members would elect from among themselves delegates who would represent their respective groups in the final election of members of the County and Municipal Farm Tenancy Committees.

The principal functions of these Farm Tenancy Committees were:

(1) Information, assistance, and supervision in the implementation of farm rent reduction.

(2) Appraisal of the standard amount of the total annual yield of the principal product of the main crop on farm lands.

(3) Investigation of crop failures and decision on measures for the reduction or remission of farm rent in such eventuality.

(4) Conciliation and re-conciliation of disputes over the lease of farm lands.

(5) Investigation of or advice on matters relating to farm rent reduction that were referred to the Committees by the Government.

The functions of these Committees were expanded during the implementation of the Land-to-the-Tiller Program in 1953 to include the power to make decisive recommendations on such matters as the retention and sale of cultivated land, the assessment of the value of buildings that were purchased by the Government together with the land itself, and the assessment of the value of land retained by the landlord but which the tenant wanted to purchase later. From this it will be seen that though the land reform carried out in this province was sponsored by the Government, much of the work was done with the enthusiastic support of and on the initiative of the people themselves. This was an instance of land reform through popular effort.

SIGNING OF FARM LEASE CONTRACTS

The signing of farm lease contracts was both the most important and the most complicated task during the execution of the rent reduction program. It is quite understandable that in the case of verbal contracts, which constituted the great majority of all pre-reform lease contracts, it was impossible to determine which party was right and which party wrong whenever any disputes arose. Even in cases in which there had been written contracts, the documents contained so many loopholes as to be useless for the settlement of disputes. Hence the signing of new lease contracts was a complex affair.

The signing of the contracts in this province was done in the following ways:

(1) The form for all farm lease contracts was uniformly prescribed by the Government, giving in detail the rights and obligations of lessor and lessee, including all particulars of the land to be leased and the amount of rent payable, so that no possibility of dispute might ever arise. This form was to be used

by the landlord and tenant in signing a new contract.*

(2)   Every farm lease contract was to be signed in triplicate: one copy to be kept by the lessor, one copy by the lessee, and the third copy by the District or Township Office.

(3)   Before signing a new contract, the lessor and lessee had to apply for it.   They were not allowed to conceal the relationship which existed between them.   If, owing to the absence of the landlord or other exceptional circumstances, no joint application could be made, one of the parties might make a unilateral application.   In that case, the other party would be notified by the District or Township Office to come to complete the required procedure.

(4)   The signing of a new farm lease contract had to be witnessed by the Chief of the District or Township Office, and the contract had to bear the official seal of such Office.

The work of signing new farm lease contracts began on a province-wide scale in May, 1949, and was completed by mid-June. For the province as a whole, 302,000 farm families signed 393,000 lease contracts involving 256,000 *chia* (613,000 acres) of cultivated land divided into 841,000 plots.

With the implementation of the Land-to-the-Tiller Program in 1953, more and more tenanted farm lands were purchased by the tenants and converted into owner-operated lands.   By the end of 1956, the total area of tenanted farm lands in the province as a whole was only 96,000 *chia* (230,000 acres); the total number of tenant farmer families was reduced to 156,000 and the total number of farm lease contracts was only 183,000.   There was a sharp drop in all aspects of tenancy relationship.

INSPECTION AND RECHECKING

In order to insure the effectiveness of the new farm lease contracts for the double purpose of rent reduction and protecting the tenant farmers, provision was made for province-wide inspec-

* For a sample of the new contract, see APPENDIX, Figure 1, p. 315.

tion and rechecking, which began in the various counties and municipalities as soon as they had completed the signing of new contracts. The province was divided into five areas, namely: Northern, Central, Southern, Kaohsiung and Eastern. To each area the Provincial Government sent supervisors to oversee the actual inspection and rechecking by county, municipal, district and township inspectors. The work began in July, 1949, and was completed in September.

Inspection and rechecking were carried out by two methods: examination of written records and holding of conferences and interviews.

Duplicate copies of the newly signed farm lease contracts and the applications filed by landlords and tenants were examined to see if there were any irregularities. If any irregularities were discovered, the duplicate copies were corrected and both the lessor and lessee were notified to come to make the necessary corrections in their copies. This aspect of the inspection and rechecking was done by personnel of the District and Township Office under the eye of the provincial supervisors.

The holding of conferences and interviews was aimed at finding out whether any black-market rentals had been paid, advance rent payments had been made, and landlord or tenant had failed to sign a new lease contract, and whether there had been any other illegal acts in violation of rent reduction laws and regulations. This was done through:

(1) Village meetings and owner-and-tenant meetings, in which the participants were encouraged to expose all illegal collections of farm rentals and all failures to sign new farm lease contracts. Once any illegal action was exposed, it could be immediately corrected.

(2) Personal interviews with tenant farmers to see if there were any black-market farm rentals or other illegal rent payments. If anything of that kind was discovered, it would be immediately corrected.

The village meetings and owner-and-tenant meetings were

usually held with the provincial supervisors in the chair and with the participation of the District and Township Chiefs and all the officers in charge. The meetings were enthusiastically attended by both landlords and tenants. Many grievances were exposed in the course of the meetings and duly redressed. Personal interviews with tenant farmers were conducted by county and municipal personnel under the supervision of provincial supervisors. These also resulted in the correction of many errors and illegal practices.

Altogether, 34,817 cases of illegal eviction, black-market farm rentals, failure to sign new farm lease contracts, incorrect registration of land categories and land grades, and incorrect water charges were discovered in the course of inspection and rechecking, and all were satisfactorily settled.

With the coming into force of the new lease contracts, all verbal contracts were wiped out and no illegal exaction by the landlord remained possible. In this way the rights and interests of the tenant farmer received effective protection.

TENANCY PROBLEMS
AFTER RENT REDUCTION

It was something of an anomaly that there should be more, instead of fewer, tenancy problems after the implementation of rent reduction. This was due to a variety of causes. Some problems arose out of changes in the land itself; some out of the landlord's unwillingness to give up his former rights and interests; some out of the farmer's ignorance or misunderstanding; and some out of weaknesses in laws and regulations. Let us see how the different kinds of problems were handled.

DISPUTES OVER LAND
CATEGORIES AND GRADES

There had been occasional changes in the categories and grades of farm land in Taiwan. Up to the end of World War II, when Taiwan was retroceded to China, there had been four province-wide readjustments, if we exclude still earlier changes. The readjustments were made at about ten-year intervals. The last one, made from 1942 to 1944, resulted in the division of paddy field and dry land into 26 grades each.   The readjustment of land category for individual pieces of land in the postwar period followed the same procedure as before the war.   But when dry land was converted into paddy field, the owner often would not report it to the authorities in order to evade the payment of taxes.

In implementing rent reduction in 1949, the Government relied upon the old land records for information on land categories and grades as a basis for the assessment of the total annual yield to be used as a standard for the collection and payment of rentals after rent reduction.   However, owing to the passage of time, much of the information on land categories and grades contained in the old records did not conform to the actual situation.   That was why some people held that pending the further readjustment of land categories and grades, there should be no rent reduction. There was sound reason for this view.   Therefore, the Provincial Government in 1950 undertook a regional readjustment of the categories and grades of those lands that had been registered. For this purpose a set of Measures for the Readjustment of Land Categories and Grades in Taiwan Province was drawn up and promulgated for the observance of all counties and municipalities. These measures provided for the following steps:

(1)   Delimitation of readjustment areas: On the basis of relevant data and the results of on-the-spot investigations, areas where changes had occurred would be marked out as unit regions where readjustments would be made.   For each of these unit regions, a definite category and grades would be assigned to the land lying within it and these items would be duly entered in the Check Sheet for Regional Changes in Land Categories and Grades. If the changes that had occurred in any given unit region had been widely different, it would be divided into still smaller regions.   To each of these, definite category and grades would be similarly assigned for all the land.

(2)   Method of readjustment: The readjustment of land categories and grades was to be separately made in each of the

unit regions that had been marked out as described above. In respect to categories, all lands that no longer could be put to their original use as a result of permanent improvements or serious natural disasters, or all lands that had been used by public utility, communication, or water conservancy enterprises, were readjusted in the light of actual conditions. In respect to land grades, all lands whose productivity had undergone changes as a result of permanent improvements or serious natural disasters were readjusted in the light of actual conditions by comparing them with adjacent lands which had remained in their original condition and had not been affected by improvements or disasters. If there had been any change in land categories in any given unit region, the land grades there also were readjusted. On the other hand, in cases where there had been change only in land grades but no change in land categories, only the land grades were readjusted.

(3) Evaluation and approval: When the proposed readjustment of land categories and grades had been worked out, the County or Municipal Government would notify those tenant farmers, owner-farmers, and landlords who had been affected by the changes to choose their respective representatives to attend an Evaluation Meeting to discuss and pass on the proposed readjustment. The results of the Evaluation Meeting would be subject to review by the County or Municipal Government, which would send officers to make a sampling recheck and to correct errors, if any. Then the proposed readjustment would be submitted to the Provincial Government for approval.

(4) Revision of farm lease contracts: The farm land affected by this readjustment comprised 160,518 plots amounting to 70,746 *chia* (169,558 acres), scattered in 305 districts and townships throughout the province. Of this total, 73,803 plots amounting to 30,580 *chia* (73,292 acres), were paddy fields, which constituted 45 per cent of all the plots and 43 per cent of the total area subject to readjustment. The owners and tenants of all the farm lands lying within the regions subject to readjustment and regulated by the rent reduction lease contracts were separately notified by the County and Municipal Governments to have their original lease contracts properly revised and the farm rental rates

fixed anew in the light of the readjustments just made.

Disputes over land categories and **grades** arose out of changes in land itself. As soon as such changes had been checked and readjusted, these disputes were settled.

TERMINATION OF LEASE CONTRACTS

With the implementation of the rent reduction program, both the advance collection of rent and collection of rent in excess of the prescribed amount were prohibited by law. But in order to evade the clear-cut provisions of the lease contract, some tricky landlords did not hesitate to use coercion or inducements to make the tenant sign a written statement saying that he was willing to terminate the lease of his own free will. When a landlord had such a statement in hand, he could offer it as evidence to show that the tenant wanted to give up the lease and that, therefore, he himself could take the land back for his own use.

From the beginning of 1950 to the end of June, 1951, there were 16,349 cases of this kind of lease termination. Twelve months later, the number had increased to 35,313. The situation was quite serious and careful handling was called for.

The inducements landlords offered to the tenants to extort from them a promise to terminate the lease usually took the form of cash, useful articles, or small pieces of land. These bribes, or gifts, if you will, were known as "monetary considerations in exchange for privileges and rights," which the tenants, in the face of the landlord's prestige and social influence, had to accept willy-nilly. After the land was taken back by the landlord, he seldom cultivated it himself but secretly leased it to another person at black-market rates. In other cases, he might either sell the land outright or hire farm hands to cultivate it for him. In any case, he would be keeping illegal gains for himself.

To cope with such cases, the Government in March, 1951, set up a regular supervisory and inspection system for the settlement of questions of lease termination that had already arisen as well as for the prevention of similar questions in the future.

For this purpose the entire province was divided into seven regions, to each of which the Provincial Government sent a supervisor to be permanently stationed there. Several inspectors were selected from among the county and municipal land officers by the Provincial Government, and each of them was assigned to serve in a particular locality. Altogether, there were 62 such inspectors for the province as a whole. The duties of the provincial supervisors as prescribed for them by the Provincial Government were popularization of governmental policy; exposition and explanation of laws, regulations, and rules; investigation of cases of lease termination and tenancy disputes, both actual and potential; study of their causes and possible methods of solution; settlement of such cases in cooperation with County and Municipal Governments; and prevention of their recurrence. Working under the direction of the provincial supervisors and the County and Municipal Governments, the inspectors made regular calls on landlords and tenants in their respective localities, furnished information and assistance to the local people, and cooperated with the District and Township Offices in helping to settle disputes between landlords and tenants. In addition to the provisions contained in the rent reduction laws, regulations, and rules, the Provincial Government issued executive orders and instructions for the guidance of the provincial supervisors in the handling of problems on the spot. By the end of June, 1952, 95 per cent of the above-mentioned cases of lease termination had been satisfactorily settled and the remaining five per cent were being settled one by one. Since then, similar cases have seldom occurred. Such cases as do occur usually are settled quickly by the local County and Municipal Governments.

It need hardly be pointed out that all the cases of lease termination arose because the landlords were unwilling to give up their vested rights and interests.

TENANCY DISPUTES

The number of tenancy disputes involving lease contracts was greatest; those involving rent payments came second. Disputes involving lease contracts included those relating to refusal to sign lease contracts, illicit changes in the wording of lease contracts, subleasing the land and mistakes in lease contracts.   Cases of this kind amounted to 45 per cent of all tenancy disputes.

Disputes involving rent payments included those concerning the amount, kind, quality, and standard of the farm rent in kind, its conversion rate, and the date and place of its payments as well as the repayment of arrears and the remission and reduction of rent due to crop failure.   The most common type of dispute had to do with the kind of crops to be used for the payment of rent, especially in those areas where the three-year rotation fields were located.   Disputes of this kind easily arose, because the actual crops grown by the tenant, who was governed in the choice of crops by such considerations as irrigation facilities and the price of farm products, might not be exactly the same as was stipulated in the lease contract.

Disputes involving arrears of farm rent were also rather complicated.   Most of them arose out of arrears for the period before the implementation of the rent reduction program, for it had been the practice then neither to sign written contracts nor to give written receipts to tenants for rents they had paid, nor to provide for fixed amounts of rent.   Since the enforcement of rent reduction, the landlord would ask for the payment of such arrears or even go so far as to take current payments to offset past arrears.   On the other hand, the tenant would say that he had never owed the landlord any overdue rent, because there had been a crop failure in the season or seasons in question and that he had, therefore, been entitled to a remission or reduction of rent.   Even after the enforcement of rent reduction, there were still many instances of the non-payment of the reduced rent, either because of the landlord's refusal to refund the security deposit, or because of differences of view as to the proper percentage of remission or reduction to be applied in a case of crop failure, or because of the tenant's inability to pay.

Though there was a regional readjustment of land categories and grades in 1950, that had not put an end to disputes of this kind, because the annual productivity of lands of the same category

Officials check actual conditions of farm tenancy

Committee settles disputes arising from tenancy reform

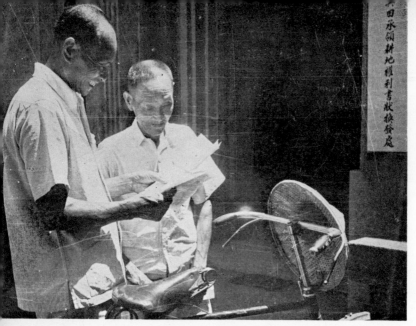

New owner-farmers receive their land certificates

Former landlords attend stockholders' meeting. They received corporate shares instead of cash

and grade in the same county or municipality might not be exactly equal.   Other disputes involved the refusal by the landlord to refund the security deposit, the use of farmhouses and their sites, etc.

In handling all these disputes, the competent county and municipal authorities based their actions on the provisions of laws and regulations wherever there were laws and regulations to fall back upon.   But in the absence of clear-cut legal provisions, they would bring the opposing parties together and try to effect an amicable conciliation.   The greatest difficulty was encountered in cases in which the landlord would not accept any conciliation but appealed directly to a court of law, thus causing endless trouble for the tenant.   This difficulty was removed with the establishment in June, 1952, of the County, Municipal, District and Township Farm Tenancy Committees charged with the function of effecting conciliation in tenancy disputes before they were brought to the attention of the judicial authorities.

Tenancy disputes arose mostly out of failure to conform to lease procedures in violation of laws and regulations.   As soon as disputes occurred, they caused inconvenience to both the authorities and the individuals concerned.   The people in Taiwan are noted for their law-abiding spirit.   Violations were not due to willful violation of laws and regulations, but because of incomplete knowledge of them.

SPECIAL PROBLEMS

Problem of the prior right of purchase.   In order to realize the land-to-the-tiller ideal as soon as possible, the Government provided that the incumbent tiller of leased land had prior right of purchase.   But disputes frequently arose owing to the following circumstances:

(1)   In offering his land for sale, the landlord purposely raised its price and compelled the incumbent tiller to buy it at that price.

(2)   The landlord would not notify the incumbent tiller of

his desire to sell his land, but would sell it to a third party.

(3)   The incumbent tiller would not, in the period prescribed by law, express his willingness to buy the land or would refuse to acknowledge the receipt of the landlord's written notification of his desire to offer the land for sale.

(4)   The incumbent tiller would, in the period prescribed by law, express his willingness to buy only a part of the land and not the whole of it, or purposely delay the signing of a purchase contract.

In order to deal with these circumstances, the Government laid down the following principles:

(1)   If the landlord purposely raised the price of his land, the incumbent tiller could submit arguments and evidence to the County or Municipal Government with the request that it fix the price in the light of the price of land of the same category and grade in the same locality and notify the landlord to sell his land to the incumbent tiller at the assessed price.

(2)   In the future the purchase and sale of land were to be made at prices calculated according to the rate used in the sale of public land by the Government.   If the purchase price was to be paid in installments, the purchaser would be exempt from paying the farm rent beginning from the year and season in which the purchase was made and should at the same time begin to pay the land tax.

(3)   In offering his land for sale, the landlord should send a written notification to that effect to the incumbent tiller through the District or Township Office.   If, at the end of 15 days, the incumbent tiller did not express willingness to buy the land, the landlord might immediately sign a purchase and sale contract with a third party.   If the landlord should fail to follow this procedure and should secretly sell his land to a third party, the incumbent tiller could appeal to the court of law and demand the payment of damages by the landlord.

(4)   If the incumbent tiller should be unwilling to buy the land or should fail to make any concrete commitments either way

in the period prescribed by law, he would be considered to have waived his prior right of purchase and the landlord could then sell the land to another person. But if the landlord cut the price and again offered the land for sale, he should still notify the incumbent tiller according to the prescribed procedure.

(5) If the incumbent tiller should refuse to acknowledge the receipt of the landlord's written notification and should, at the end of 15 days, fail to make any commitments with regard to this matter, the landlord could sell his land to another person.

(6) Even if the incumbent tiller should express his willingness to buy the land but purposely delayed the signing of a purchase contract, he would be considered as having waived his prior right of purchase.

(7) In case the incumbent tiller could purchase only a part, or only the more fertile part, of several plots of land offered for sale by the landlord at any one time, the landlord could refuse to sell it to him if these plots formed one contiguous whole and their total area fell short of the minimum unit as prescribed by Article 31 of the Land Law. Otherwise, the incumbent tiller should be permitted to buy only the part or only the more fertile part he liked. In case the landlord should refuse to sell the plots separately, the matter might be handled according to the provisions of Article 33 of the Land Law. In case the incumbent tiller wanted to buy only the more fertile part, he should be permitted to do so if this would not interfere with the proper utilization of the adjacent lands.

(8) After the incumbent tiller had waived his prior right of purchase, his rights as a lessee would still remain unimpaired.

(9) In requesting registration of transfer of land ownership, the new landowner who had purchased the land according to law should present both a certificate issued by the District or Township Office showing that the incumbent tiller had waived his prior right of purchase and the new lease contract signed with the original tiller. Only then could the competent authorities proceed to screen the request for registration.

These principles were either approved by the Central Government or prescribed by the Taiwan Provincial Government in order to make up for the inadequacies of the original laws and regulations.

Problem of security deposit. The collection of security deposits had been a rather prevalent practice in tenancy relationships in Taiwan. It was particularly prevalent in Hsinchu, Taoyuan and Miaoli Counties. In spite of the provisions for coping with this problem in the rent reduction laws and regulations, disputes often arose over the conversion rates and refunding of security deposits in relation to the comparative value of the old and the new currencies. For this reason, further provisions for handling this problem were called for.

(1) Problem of the conversion rate for security deposits: Owing to changed economic conditions, it obviously would be unfair if the security deposits were to be refunded to the tenant by the landlord according to the amount originally paid by the tenant. It was, therefore, provided that all security deposits paid by the tenant according to lease contracts entered into in and before 1944 should be refunded in proportion to the rise in the local market price of paddy rice from 1944 to the time the security deposits were to be refunded; and that all security deposits paid by the tenant according to lease contracts entered into in and after 1945 should be refunded in proportion to the rise in the local market price of paddy rice from the time of the contract (the month being taken as the standard) to the time the security deposits were to be refunded. As to the actual local market prices of paddy rice in the different months of any given year, they would be ascertained and tabulated by the food authorities of the various counties for distribution to the various districts, townships and villages for ready use. All those landlords who had evaded the refunding of security deposits were found out and their misdeeds corrected.

(2) Problem of the refunding of security deposits: After being converted according to the standards described above, all security deposits in excess of one fourth of the total annual land

rent should be refunded. But in the Taipei-Hsinchu area, where past security deposits had been excessively high, some landlords were unable to refund the deposits all at once. This problem was eventually solved by providing for refunding over a period of years.

Problem of inheritance of tenancy rights and the signing of separate lease contracts. Though tenancy rights are one form of legal obligation and are legally inheritable, the landlords would generally try to take back the land after the death of the original tenant. They would refuse to sign separate lease contracts with the deceased's heirs for fear that the latter would divide the land into fragments for cultivation. This problem had baffled the authorities of the various counties, where it often happened that the original tenant had died long ago but his name continued to appear in lease contracts without any attempt being made to change it.

With a large number of dependents in a farm family, it was only natural that when several brothers divided their property after the death of their father, they would also divide the land which their father had leased from a landlord and on which the whole family depended for sustenance. But the landlord would regard this as a form of sublease and would refuse to sign separate lease contracts with the brothers. As a matter of fact, however, the brothers had already divided the land into separate portions for separate cultivation by themselves. Such an anomalous situation could easily give rise to disputes.

To deal with this problem, the Government made a two-point decision. It decided, on the one hand, that no farm land should be broken up into fragments smaller than the legally prescribed minimum unit area and, on the other, that the landlord should, in recognition of realities, sign separate lease contracts with his present tenants whose father, his former tenant, had died.

Problem of farmhouses and their sites. Though there is a provision for the use of farmhouses by the tenant in Article 12 of the 37.5% Farm Rent Reduction Act, it is not inclusive enough.

To deal with the disputes that arose over this matter, the Government made the following supplementary regulations:

(1) If the site to be used for the construction of farmhouses was not included in the farm land under lease, nor mentioned in the 37.5% farm lease contract, a supplementary lease contract for this purpose should be signed. If any fee had to be charged for the use of the site, it should be calculated according to the provisions of Article 97 of the Land Law.

(2) If the site to be used for the construction of farmhouses was included in the farm land under lease, no fee should be charged.

(3) In repairing farmhouses, the landlord should be responsible for the necessary materials and the tenant for labor.

(4) In making repairs or additions to old farmhouses or constructing new ones, the tenant should notify the landlord beforehand through the District or Township Office of the expenses and the construction plan in a written statement. At the end of the lease contract, the tenant might, with the support of vouchers, ask the landlord to pay back the expences for that part of the farmhouse which had not yet lost its utility.

Problem of water reservoirs and fish ponds. Reservoirs are used for the storage of water for the irrigation of paddy fields. Owing to rent reduction and consequently decreased income, some landlords would sell part of their reservoirs or stop the supply of water to the tenants. To cope with the situation thus presented, the Government worked out and promulgated three principles as follows:

(1) Any reservoir that had been originally used by the tenant should continue to be used by him and the landlord might not, under any pretext, refuse such use or divide the reservoir for sale.

(2) For any reservoir which had been used by the tenant unconditionally before rent reduction, the landlord might not ask for payment.

(3) All disputes arising out of failure to include the question

of reservoirs in the lease contracts should be settled according to the two above-mentioned principles.

In connection with fish ponds, it should be mentioned that there were many paddy fields in south Taiwan which were also used for raising fish.   The situation was as follows:

(1)   Some lands classified as paddy field were leased to tenants for planting rice during the first crop season and taken back by the landlords for raising fish during the second crop season of the year.

(2)   Some lands classified as fish pond were actually leased to tenants for planting rice during the first crop season and taken back by the landlords for raising fish during the second crop season of the year.

(3)   Some lands classified as fish pond were leased to tenants for raising fish all the year round.

With regard to these different kinds of farm land, disputes often arose over the amount of rent that should be paid owing to the various uses.   To settle such disputes, the Government prescribed the following rules:

(1)   For the first kind of fish-raising fields, a contract should be signed providing for the payment of rent during the paddy-raising season at one half of the standard harvest yield of the main crop of the general double-crop paddy fields of the same categories and grades.

(2)   For the second kind of fish-raising fields, permission should be given to change the land category, after which they should be treated according to the foregoing principle.

(3)   For the third kind of fish-raising fields, of which few were leased to tenants, lease contracts should be signed providing for the payment of rent either in kind or in cash according to the local practice.

Problem of tea plantations and orchards.   Tea plantations and orchards both belong to the category of dry land, but they are different from other kinds of dry land in that it takes several years after planting before tea leaves and fruit can be harvested.   In the case of tea trees, it is eight years after planting that they begin to have stable yields, which begin gradually to decline after the fifteenth year.   Therefore, the general rent reduction measures could not very well be applied to them.   As there are different kinds of orchards, each with special problems of its own, such questions mostly have been solved by following the provision of the original lease contracts on condition that new contracts be signed to replace the old ones.

Nine-tenths of the above-mentioned special problems arose because of deficiencies and inadequacies in the original laws and regulations.   But in view of the complex nature of worldly affairs, it would be impossible to provide adequately for every contingency or to put all things in legal straitjackets.   It would be preferable to take appropriate measures in the light of the circumstances of the time and place.

ACHIEVEMENTS OF RENT REDUCTION

INCREASE OF FARM PRODUCTION AND OF FARMERS' INCOME

With the implementation of rent reduction, tenancy rights were well protected and farm rents were strictly limited.   Moreover, as all increased production would go to the tenant, he was greatly encouraged to exert himself to the utmost to boost production.   In consequence, the quantity of foodstuffs produced at once showed a marked upswing.   The following chart* shows the production of brown rice after rent reduction and before the implementation of the Land-to-the-Tiller Program.

It will be seen from this chart that the production of rice, the staple food of the Chinese people, had increased 47 per cent in a period of four years.

* For detailed figures, see APPENDIX, Table 4, p. 309.

CHART 4

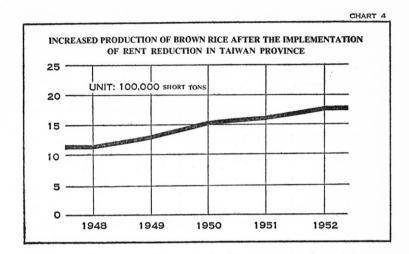

INCREASED PRODUCTION OF BROWN RICE AFTER THE IMPLEMENTATION OF RENT REDUCTION IN TAIWAN PROVINCE

UNIT: 100,000 SHORT TONS

According to investigations made by the Taiwan Provincial Land Bureau, one *chia* (2.3967 acres) of medium-grade paddy field produced 4,649 kg. (10,249 lbs.) of unhulled rice before rent reduction. But after the implementation of rent reduction the annual yield per *chia* of paddy field of the same grade increased to 4,860 kg. (10,715 lbs.) in 1949 and 5,530 kg. (12,192 lbs.) in 1952. Increased per unit yield coupled with a smaller amount of farm rent had the net effect of causing the tenant farmers' income to rise from year to year, as shown in the following chart.*

This chart shows that in the four-year period from 1949 to 1952 the tenant farmer's income had increased by 81 per cent. This was clear evidence of the beneficial effect of rent reduction.

BETTERMENT OF THE TENANT FARMERS' LIVELIHOOD

Besides devoting part of his increased income to boost production, the tenant farmer would, of course, use the other part

* For detailed figures, see APPENDIX, Table 5, **p. 309.**

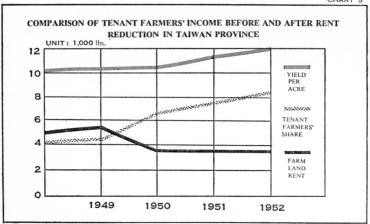

COMPARISON OF TENANT FARMERS' INCOME BEFORE AND AFTER RENT REDUCTION IN TAIWAN PROVINCE

,. Note: The yield per *chia* (2.3967 acres) in this Chart is based on the standard production of one *chia* of the ninth-grade paddy field in Taoyuan County.

to better the livelihood of his family. According to the *Findings of the Cabinet Rent Reduction Inspection Team,* which made an on-the-spot inspection from January 8 to February 15, 1951, "Everywhere we went, we saw newly built or newly repaired farmhouses. The women and children were better dressed. There is a general improvement in the food which people eat. Those whose main article of consumption has been sweet potatoes are now eating polished rice."

A concrete example was cited by the Inspection Team as follows:

"Out of a total farming population of about 200 families in Tahchiao Village, Changhua County, there are 140 tenant families which have better living conditions now, as may be seen from such facts as these: (a) seven families have built new houses; (b) 20 families have had their farmhouses newly repaired; (c) four families have purchased farm land; (d) 40 families have bought draft cattle; (e) 25 families have had marriage celebrations."

Rural prosperity after rent reduction could be seen everywhere in the villages. The farmers humorously called the cattle they bought as a result of rent reduction "37.5% cattle;" the houses they built as a result of rent reduction "37.5% house;" and even the brides they had married as a result of rent reduction "37.5% bride" — in commemoration of the reduced farm rent.

According to investigations, only one-fourth of the increased income was used by the tenant farmer to better the living conditions of his family and three quarters were used to boost production. This furnished another proof of the Chinese farmer's industriousness and frugality.

DECLINE IN THE VALUE OF FARM LAND

As the landlord was no longer interested in investing in land after the implementation of rent reduction, the value of land naturally declined. According to a comparative study made by the Chinese Research Institute of Land Economics, the average value of paddy fields in the various counties and municipalities of Taiwan dropped by 19.4 per cent from December, 1948, to December, 1949, and that of dry land by 42.3 per cent in the same period. The *Findings of the Cabinet Rent Reduction Inspection Team* pointed out that the average decline in the value of tenanted land in the various counties and municipalities after rent reduction was from one-third to one-half as compared with the period before rent reduction. For example, one *chia* (2.3967 acres) of high grade paddy field was worth 23,880 kg. (52,646 lbs.) of unhulled rice in 1948. It declined to 18,480 kg. (40,741 lbs.) in 1949 and still further to 10,920 kg. (24,075 lbs.) in 1950.

According to data collected by the Provincial Land Bureau, there was a steady decline in the value of tenanted land in the various counties and municipalities after rent reduction, as shown in the following chart.*

The value of land declined steadily after rent reduction, especially in 1951 and 1952. This was due to the impending im-

* For detailed figures, see APPENDIX, Table 6, p. 310.

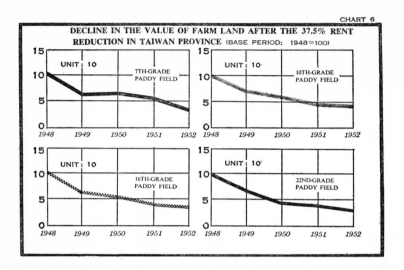

CHART 6

DECLINE IN THE VALUE OF FARM LAND AFTER THE 37.5% RENT REDUCTION IN TAIWAN PROVINCE (BASE PERIOD: 1948=100)

plementation of the Land-to-the-Tiller program. Landlords were unwilling to keep land in their own hands.

While the decline in the value of land made it easier for the tenant farmer to buy land, the landlord's anxiety to get rid of his land also provided a favorable environment for the eventual purchase of land by the Government and its resale to the incumbent tiller in the next stage, the Land-to-the-Tiller stage, of our land reform.

INCREASING NUMBER OF TENANT FARMERS BUYING LAND

With more income on hand and a simultaneous decline in land value, the tenant farmer, in his eagerness to satisfy his longing for land ownership, tried by every means to economize in order to buy land as soon as possible, though he knew well enough that the Government's Land-to-the-Tiller policy was in the works. On the other hand, the landlord was also eager to cut the price of his land so that he might dispose of it before it was compulsorily purchased by the Government for resale to the tenant, and might

in this way get paid for it in one lump sum.   The following chart*
shows the area of farm land bought by tenant farmers and the
number of tenant farmer families buying land for themselves.

CHART 7

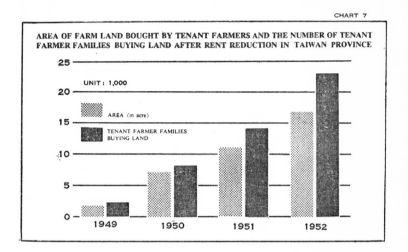

AREA OF FARM LAND BOUGHT BY TENANT FARMERS AND THE NUMBER OF TENANT
FARMER FAMILIES BUYING LAND AFTER RENT REDUCTION IN TAIWAN PROVINCE

UNIT : 1,000

AREA (in acre)

TENANT FARMER FAMILIES
BUYING LAND

PROMOTION OF RURAL STABILITY

Under the old tenancy system before the implementation of
rent reduction, the life of ease and happiness enjoyed by the landlord was built entirely on the miseries of the tenant.   This led to
irreconcilable opposition between the two and created internal
unrest in the rural districts and made them susceptible to external
propaganda.   This provided the Communist agitators with an
opportunity to infiltrate into the villages.   It was one of the main
reasons why the Chinese mainland fell into Communist hands.
On the eve of rent reduction in Taiwan, the situation on the
Chinese mainland was becoming critical and the villages on this
island were showing signs of unrest and instability.   It was feared
that the Communists might take advantage of the rapidly deteriorating condition to fish in troubled waters.   But with the
implementation of rent reduction, the livelihood of the broad

* For detailed figures, see APPENDIX, Table 7, p. 310.

masses of the farming population was immediately improved. The Chinese Communists were effectively deprived of propagandistic weapons by a new social order that had arisen in the rural areas.

CHAPTER 3

SALE OF PUBLIC
FARM LANDS

PUBLIC FARM LANDS
FROM LEASING TO SALE

ORIGIN OF PUBLIC FARM LANDS IN TAIWAN

PUBLIC farm lands in Taiwan were those which had belonged publicly to various levels of government and privately to individual Japanese under the Japanese administration. This was before the lands were taken over by the Chinese Government with the retrocession of Taiwan to China in 1945. According to statistics compiled by the Land Bureau of the Taiwan Provincial Government in June, 1952, at the time of the General Landownership Classification, there were 181,490 *chia* (434,981 acres) of such public lands, constituting a little more than 21 per cent of all farm lands on Taiwan. Of this area, dry land exceeded paddy fields by 10 per cent, the former being 55.5 per cent, while the latter was 45.5 per cent. Most of the public lands were in the southern part of the island, with 58.3 per cent of them in the seven counties and municipalities south of Yunlin, and 41.7 per cent in other counties and municipalities.

During the Japanese administration, the Japanese Government, in order to control the resources of Taiwan and bring about the immigration of Japanese nationals, had imposed strict restrictions on the purchase of public land, whether cultivated or uncultivated, by the Taiwanese, and had actively encouraged and facilitated Japanese nationals and Japanese organizations and enterprises to acquire ownership of land, both public and private. It is for this reason that the land possessed by the Japanese Government, Japanese nationals, and various organizations and enterprises under the Japanese administration amounted to more than 180,000 *chia* (430,000 acres). With the retrocession of Taiwan to China, all these lands were taken over by the Chinese Government and became public property. They were classified, according to the provisions of land laws and regulations, into the the following four kinds: state-owned, province-owned, county (*hsien*) or municipality (*shih*)-owned, and district (*hsiang*) or township (*chen*)-owned.

(1)   State-owned public land was made up of the following:
    (a)   Land owned by the Japanese Governor's Office;
    (b)   Land used by the Japanese for military purposes;
    (c)   Land owned by Japanese corporate bodies; and
    (d)   Private land owned by individual Japanese nationals.

(2)   Province-owned public land was made up of the following:
    (a)   Japanese settlement area;
    (b)   Alluvial land that had been reclaimed and made arable;
    (c)   Land owned by the former Taiwan Colonization and Settlement Corporation.

(3)   County or municipality-owned public lands were those that originally had belonged to counties or municipalities under the Japanese administration.

(4)   District or township-owned public lands were those that had belonged to districts or townships under the Japanese administration.

The areas of the four kinds of public land* mentioned above

* For detailed figures, see APPENDIX, Table 8, p. 310.

are as follows:

CHART 8

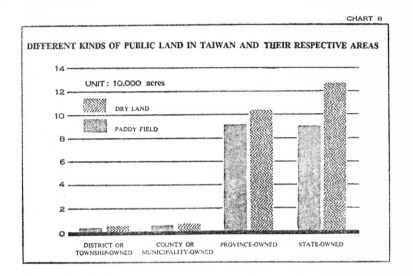

DIFFERENT KINDS OF PUBLIC LAND IN TAIWAN AND THEIR RESPECTIVE AREAS

UNIT: 10,000 acres

DRY LAND

PADDY FIELD

DISTRICT OR TOWNSHIP-OWNED   COUNTY OR MUNICIPALITY-OWNED   PROVINCE-OWNED   STATE-OWNED

Under the Japanese administration, these lands — with the exception of a small part which was not used for farming, as in the case of land for military use or cultivated by the corporate bodies themselves as in the case of the former Taiwan Sugar Corporation — were "farmed" by Japanese veterans, retired officials, the local gentry, and big industrial companies, which subleased them to tenant farmers for actual cultivation.   The annual rent which the Japanese Government received from the "farmers-general" was approximately 30 per cent of the total annual produce, but that which the tenants paid to these "farmers-general" amounted to as much as 55 per cent of production.

The difference represented income from exploitation on the part of the "farmers-general".   This added to the miseries of the tenants.   Even the land in the settlement area was seldom cultivated by the Japanese themselves, but frequently subleased to tenant farmers for exploitation.   After the retrocession of Taiwan to China, the Chinese Government began to effect reforms in the leasing of public lands.

LEASING OF PUBLIC FARM LANDS

After the retrocession, all public farm lands except those retained by public enterprises for their own use, were leased directly to farmers for cultivation, so that the deep-rooted abuses in land relations that had prevailed under the Japanese administration would be completely wiped out. For this purpose, the former Office of the High Commissioner of Taiwan Province promulgated in 1947 a set of Regulations Governing the Lease of Public Farm Lands in Taiwan Province, the essential points of which are as follows:

(1) Principle of lease: It was provided that all public farm lands should be leased to cooperative farms for them to cultivate, and that small pieces of lands unsuitable for cooperative use were to be leased to farmers who cultivated land themselves.

(2) Lessees: The public farm lands were to be leased to cooperative farms and individual farmers, the former with each farm as a lessee, and the latter according to the following order of priority: the incumbent tiller, farm hand, tenant farmer, and part-owner-farmer.

(3) Amount of land to be leased: In the case of individual farmers, the amount of public land to be leased to each family was, as a matter of principle, limited to from 15 to 45 *mow* (from 3.66 acres to 11 acres) of paddy fields, or from 30 to 75 *mow* (from 7.35 acres to 18.38 acres) of dry land; in the case of cooperative farms, the amount was, as a rule, to be the sum total of the lands that the individual farming families which were members of the farm would be entitled to lease if they were to be lessees in their individual capacity.

(4) Period of lease: The period of lease was limited to nine years in the case of cooperative farms and five years in that of individual farmers.

(5) Rental rate: It originally was provided that the maximum rental rate for public farm lands might not exceed eight per cent of the land value or one third of the annual yield of the main crop. The latter rate was subsequently reduced to one fourth of the

annual main crop yield, which was lower by 12.5 per cent than the 37.5 per cent rental rate fixed for private farm land.   In order to help cooperative farming, it was stipulated at the same time that out of the rent, 20 per cent would be earmarked for production improvements and public welfare.

(6)   Cooperative farms: A cooperative farm might be set up and lease land from the Government as a lessee where there were 300 *mow* (75.53 acres) or more of public farm land and ten or more farming families dwelling in the same place.

These lease regulations were to achieve a double purpose: to better the livelihood of the farmers by reducing the farm rent, and to improve methods of production by encouraging cooperative farming.   According to statistics furnished by the Land Bureau of Taiwan Province, 58.9 per cent of all public farm lands in Taiwan were leased in accordance with the provisions of these regulations.   The remaining 41.1 per cent were retained by the various public enterprises as owner-operated farms for the supply of raw materials and by government organs or vocational schools for agricultural demonstration and experimentation, and the growth of seedlings.   There were approximately 130,000 families of tenant farmers who leased public farm land for cultivation; this was about 22 per cent of the farming families in Taiwan in that year.

SALE OF PUBLIC FARM LANDS

The leasing of public farm land did not produce as good results as had been anticipated.   For one thing, the number of cooperative farms fell far short of the 293 that had been the target originally aimed at.   Up to 1950, the number of farms for which lease contracts had been signed and duly registered was no more than 120, and the farm land thus leased was only 5.9 per cent of all the lands to be leased, or only 6,331 *chia* (15,174 acres). Furthermore, there were many hindrances to the successful operation of the farms on a collective basis, such as lack of capital and equipment, the irregular configuration of land, and inability of the members to cooperate with one another.   In the case of public farm lands leased to individual farmers, owing to the low rental rate and keen competition for the lease, complete fairness could be hardly expected in the choosing of the lessees and in the parceling of the land.   It also often happened that some lessees subleased the public land or part of it to other farmers and that pieces of farm land lay uncared for and uncultivated.   In view of such a situation, the measures for leasing public land had to be reconsidered.   As a result, it was decided in 1948 that public lands should be sold to farmers.   But owing to the enforcement of the 37.5 per cent farm rent limitation program in 1949, the work of selling public lands was temporarily suspended.

With the successful operation of the farm rent reduction program in 1951, the Taiwan Provincial Government drew up, in the light of experience in previous sales of public land, another set of Regulations Governing the Sale of Public Farm Lands to Establish Owner-Farmers in Taiwan Province.   The new regulations provided for expanding the scope of the sale of public land to cover the whole province.   They also stipulated that all proceeds from the sale of state-owned land, and that part of the proceeds from the sale of province-owned land which exceeded the annual rent, should be earmarked as funds for the establishment of owner-farmers.   This event marked the beginning of a new stage of land reform in Taiwan.

AIMS IN THE SALE OF PUBLIC LAND

The ultimate objective of Dr. Sun Yat-sen's rural land reform was to realize the land-to-the-tiller ideal, as mentioned in Chapter 1.   The enforcement of the 37.5% farm rent limitation program was a step in reaching this ideal.   The Land-to-the-Tiller Act contains provisions for the compulsory purchase of cultivated land, according to which the Government may purchase cultivated land owned by the landlord in excess of the retention acreage for resale to the incumbent tiller.   Since even excess private cultivated land might be compulsorily purchased by the Government for resale to the incumbent tiller in implementing the land-to-the-tiller program, how could it be possible to make private landlords content if the Government continued to own a large amount of cultivated lands without offering them for sale and remained a landlord itself? In such case, the land-to-the-tiller program would be frustrated by the Government's own action.

Furthermore, Article 142 of the Constitution of the Republic of China stipulates: "National economy shall be based on the Principle of People's Livelihood, and shall seek to effect equalization of landownership and restriction of private capital in order to attain a well-balanced sufficiency in national wealth and people's livelihood." Article 143, Section 4, of the same document states: "In distribution and readjustment of land, the State shall, in principle, assist owner-farmers and persons who make use of land by themselves, and shall also regulate their appropriate areas of operation." Evidently these two provisions were included to carry out the teachings of Dr. Sun Yat-sen.

After the implementation of the farm rent reduction program had achieved its results, the Taiwan Provincial Government, acting in accordance with the teachings of Dr. Sun and with the provisions of the Constitution, took a further step to sell public lands to farmers.

The sale of public land was a device by which the Government offered to sell public farm land to farmers who were qualified to purchase such land according to relevant regulations and who made application for the purchase according to prescribed procedures. Farmers were permitted to acquire ownership after they had paid the land price in full. Having made clear the meaning of sale of public land, let us now take a look at the aims of the program.

PROMOTION OF OWNER-FARMERS

The sale of public farm land was to enable farmers who applied for the purchase of such land to terminate their tenant relations with the Government and become owner-farmers by acquiring the right of landownership. The substitution of farmer proprietorship for the State tenancy represented a great step toward realization of the provisions of Article 143, Section 4, of the Constitution.

REFORM OF THE LAND SYSTEM

The Government, by taking the initiative in sale of public farm lands, set an example for private landowners. This served as a harbinger for the compulsory purchase of private farm land for resale to farmers and thereby paved the way to realization of the land-to-the-tiller ideal. This would in turn help to reform the land system. Speaking of governing, Confucius said the essential point was "first to lead the people and then ask them to render services." The sale of public land was actually intended to lead the people.

INCREASE OF LAND USE

Since possession enhances pride and stimulates a desire for further gain, the owner-farmer could be expected to work his land with greater enthusiasm. Presumably he would spare no effort to develop the productivity of the land and increase the output. This would benefit not only the farmer and his family but the national economy as well.

With the implementation of the sale of public land in Taiwan, of the public land owned by the Taiwan Sugar Corporation only some 4,700 hectares (11,600 acres) were retained for such public uses as rural roads, waterways, windbreaks, special farms, and office sites. The remaining 34,400 hectares (85,000 acres) were sold to their incumbent cultivators in three installments. As the farmers who purchased the land were mostly its original tenants, there was actually no change in the relation between farmers and land, though land tenancy was replaced by landownership, and tenant farmers become owner-farmers. This is the most effective way to carry out the land policy advocated by Dr. Sun Yat-sen in his Principle of the People's Livelihood.

SALE OF PUBLIC LAND

ENACTMENT OF REGULATIONS

The sale of public farm land by the Taiwan Provincial Government was implemented in accordance with the Regulations Governing the Sale of Public Farm Lands to Establish Owner-Farmers in Taiwan Province, which was drafted by the Taiwan Provincial Government and passed by the Taiwan Provincial Assembly at its tenth general meeting. Having been approved by the Executive Yuan, the regulations came into effect in June, 1951. The essential provision of the regulations may be summed up under the following five points:

(1) Scope of the sale: The public lands to be offered for sale were, as a matter of principle, limited to farm lands, including for the most part paddy fields and dry land and some fish ponds and pastures. Farmhouses, their sites, water ponds, and ditches that formed inseparable parts of the farm land were sold along with the farm land to which they were attached. The total of public farm land leased at the time was 106,959 *chia* (256,351 acres). Of this only that part was retained which was necessary for water and soil conservation and for productive use by public enterprises. All the remainder was offered for sale to individual farmers.

(2) Purchasers of public lands: The public lands offered were to be sold chiefly to their incumbent tenant cultivators. But if the incumbent tenant cultivator of any given land did not want to buy, or if he was not qualified, the land might be sold to other applicants according to the following order of priority:

(a) Some other tenant cultivator of public land;

(b) farm hand;

(c) tenant farmer with insufficient land to till;

(d) part-owner-farmer with insufficient land to till;

(e) person who was originally an interested party to the land (i. e., the original reclaimer of the land) and who, having no land to cultivate, was in need of some for cultivation;

(f)   person who had newly become a farmer by changing his occupation.

(3)   Area of land to be purchased: The amount of public land which any one farming family might be permitted to purchase was to be determined by taking into consideration such factors as the types, categories and grades of the land to be sold, availability of the labor power of the farming family to be devoted to the cultivation of land and the minimum cost of living to maintain a family of six members.   The standard area of land to be purchased by a farming family was laid down as follows:

(a)   For paddy field: Of superior quality (1st to 8th grades): 0.5 *chia* (1.198 acres); of medium quality (9th to 18th grades): 1 *chia;* (2.397 acres); of inferior quality (19th to 26th grades): 2 *chia* (4.793 acres).

(b)   For dry land: Of superior quality (1st to 8th grades): 1 *chia;* of medium quality (9th to 18th grades): 2 *chia;* of inferior quality (19th to 26th grades): 4 *chia* (9.587 acres).

In practice, however, the amount of public land to be purchased by a farming family was to be determined in the light of the amount offered for sale in different places and the relation of a particular farming family to the land concerned.   If the purchaser was the original lessee of the public land offered for sale, he might be permitted to purchase as much of it as he had originally leased.

(4)   Appraisal of the land value: The sales price of public land purchased by the farmers was not, as a matter of principle, to exceed the prevailing market price.   It was to be paid in equal installments on an annual basis, and each installment was so determined as not to produce any adverse effects on the livelihood of the farming family or on the operation of the farm.   If some severe damage had been done to the farm land, or if it had been

washed away by floods, or if there had been a change in the quality of the soil, the payment might be postponed, or the purchase price reduced. Concrete provisions may be summed up as follows:

(a) The sales price was to be calculated in terms of farm products at 2.5 times the total annual yield of the main crop.

(b) The price was to be paid in ten annual installments without interest. The farmer might pay off the entire amount earlier, if he wished to do so.

(c) The annual payments were to be paid in two six-month installments to coincide with the harvest seasons. In places where there was only one harvest in a year, the yearly installment was to be paid in one transaction.

(d) Should there be any change in categories into which land was classified, the purchase price would be revised accordingly. If during the period in which the installment payments were to be made the land purchased lost a part or the whole of its usability, payments might be discontinued. The farmer might, after the restoration of the usability of the land, again apply for its purchase.

(e) The land price was to be paid in farm products, so that it would not be affected by fluctuations in the value of the currency.

(5) Protection and restriction: The farmer-purchasers became owner-farmers after the purchase. They would then be responsible for the payment of the land price and the land tax, and consequently their burden would be heavier than that of ordinary owner-farmers. Owing to their limited knowledge and their precarious economic position, the farmer-purchasers would be susceptible to outside influence and apt to lose their land. To protect the owner-cultivated land of the farmers and to safeguard the results of the sale of public lands, the Government continued to assist the farming families which purchased the land and to supervise the use of the land sold. Apart from extending produc-

tion loans to give the farmer-purchasers economic assistance through competent financial agencies, the regulations contain strict requirements that the purchaser himself should cultivate the land purchased and that he should not transfer it to another person without government approval, except in case of inheritance. If he offered the land for sale owing to his inability to undertake the cultivation, the Government could redeem it at the original purchase price and resell it to another farmer. If the purchaser died without leaving a lawful heir to undertake the cultivation, the Government could take back the land. If the purchaser did not cultivate the land himself or transferred it without approval, his purchase was annulled. Such provisions were intended to protect owner-farmers and to insure that farm lands belong to farmers.

INVESTIGATION AND SURVEY

Most of the public lands offered for sale were those that originally had been leased to tenants. Before the sale a thorough field investigation of the leased farm land was made for checking of the following:

(1) configuration, area, category and grade of each plot of land;

(2) land use and condition of utilization;

(3) name of the user, number of his family members, the available labor power, economic condition, and whether he had any land of his own or had leased any private farm land.

The field investigations were made with districts or townships as units. The Government sent out qualified workers who, armed with necessary cadastral maps and files in cooperation with representatives of the local assemblies, went to the countryside to make an on-the-spot check. The results were recorded forthwith in the maps and files. If during the investigation any discrepancies with the original maps and files were discovered owing to changes in such particulars as configuration, area or boundaries, or if it was found that the land had to be divided or amalgamated, a survey of the individual plots was to follow. If no survey had ever been effected, one was carried out. The number of plots of public land sold in all sales was about 300,000. Farming families purchasing such land totaled 150,000, and the number of land parcels surveyed was about one-fifth of the plots investigated. From this it can be imagined how laborious was the task.

APPLICATION AND SCREENING

When, after the completion of the field investigation, a tentative decision had been reached on the lands to be sold, the Government would, on basis of the data obtained through such investigation and survey, draw up a list of such lands for each district, township or urban district (*chu*) showing the plot number of each piece of land, its area, land category, land grade, condition of utilization and the name and address of its present user, and have it publicly announced for a period of 20 days, during which the qualified farmers might apply for the purchase and all other interested parties might examine it. Anyone who happened to have found any difference or dispute with regard to the land offered for sale might request a correction or raise an objection.

An applicant for purchase of public land had to fill out an application form and send it, together with all necessary documentary evidence such as a duplicate of his residence card and the original lease contract, to the local land bureau. This was done without charging the applicant any fee. Any cultivator who failed to file the application within the prescribed time limit forfeited his right of purchase, and the piece of land he had been cultivating was sold to another farmer.

Not until the applications had been screened and approved were the applicants permitted to purchase public land. The applications were first checked against the list of public lands offered for sale and against the original cadastral maps and files, and then submitted to the local Committee for Establishment of Owner-Farmers for screening according to law. The Committee was composed of representatives of responsible organs of the county or municipal government, local assemblies, farmers' association, farmers and land banks. When the applications had been screened, a list of qualified applicants were compiled and submitted to the Provincial Government for final approval. The approval of the Provincial Government was necessary because most of the public land offered for sale were either state-owned or province-owned.

When the applications had been approved by the Provincial Government, a list of farmer purchasers of public lands offered for sale was compiled for each district, township or urban district. This is the fundamental list[1] for the sale of public land.

PAYMENT OF LAND PRICE AND ISSUANCE OF OWNERSHIP CERTIFICATE

The Government notified the qualified farmer-purchasers in writing to pay the first semi-annual installment, which amounted to one-twentieth of the total price. The payment varied with different categories of land purchased. A farmer-purchaser who had bought paddy fields would pay in unhulled rice, and all rice payments were to be handed in to the local food warehouses. All dry land was to be paid for in cash by converting the installments, when due, into monetary terms according to the official rate for sweet potatoes at the time, and all cash payments were to be handed in to the local branch of the Land Bank of Taiwan. On the payment of the first installment, the Government issued a purchase certificate,[2] which would be exchanged for a landownership certificate after the entire purchase price was paid. The issuance of the landownership certificate would mark the completion of the procedure to acquire landownership.

INSPECTION AND CORRECTION

To establish owner-farmers, it was necessary that after the sale of public lands, close attention be paid to the farming families buying them and constant supervision be maintained over the way they used the lands, so that illegal practices might be averted.

(1) For a sample list, see APPENDIX, Figure 2, p. 316.
(2) For a sample certificate, see APPENDIX, Figure 3, p.317.

Periodic inspection was a necessary measure. The aim was two-fold: to expose such potential unlawful actions on the part of farmer-purchasers as transferring the lands purchased without approval or giving up cultivation by themselves; to keep an eye on all changes in farmer-purchasers and in the lands sold, and have such changes duly recorded so that the cadastral maps and files might be always complete and consistent with actual conditions.

RESULTS OF SUCCESSIVE SALES OF PUBLIC LAND

The sale of public land in Taiwan Province was carried out in stages. There were six sales from 1948 to 1958. Some public lands were stricken from the official list because of flood erosion, because some had become non-farm land, some were too poor in fertility, some lacked proper irrigation facilities and some could not, according to law, be owned by private individuals. Most of the land thus struck off was dry land on the seacoast or hillsides whose productivity was uncertain. As farmers were unwilling to purchase poor land, the authorities in charge of the sales program had to withhold it until improvements had been made.

In the six sales of public land, the number of families buying the 71,66 *chia* (171,763 acres) of land was 139,688. Value of the land was 271,155 metric tons (298,897 short tons) of rice for paddy fields and 657,959 metric tons (725,274 short tons) of sweet potatoes for dry land. With the successive sales, the area of land retained by public enterprises, government departments and schools for their own use or for continued lease to private cultivators also underwent changes. Of the 181,490 *chia* (434,981 acres) of public farm land, the 71,666 *chia* (171,763 acres) sold to farmers consituted a little more than 39.5 per cent. The remainder was to be sold gradually to carry out the policy of establishing owner-farmers and to realize the ultimate objective of the land-to-the-tiller program.

The kinds of public lands sold from 1948 to 1958 were for the most part, as follows: those offered for sale in 1948 and 1951, mainly the farm lands that had been administered by county and municipal governments and sold directly to individual cultivators; those offered for sale in 1952, farm lands that had been administered by different public enterprises; those offered for sale in 1953 were sold in two batches, the first batch having to do mainly with farm land that had been administered by county and municipal governments and leased to cooperative farms, while the second batch was land that had been administered by the Taiwan Sugar Corporation and leased to individual cultivators; and those offered for sale in 1958 had also been administered by the Taiwan Sugar Corporation. The results of the sales of public lands are shown in the following chart.*

CHART 9

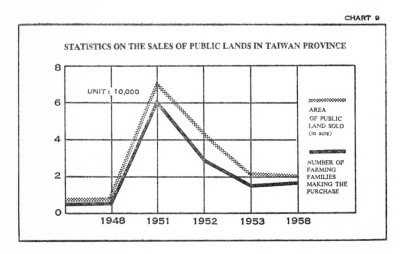

The number of plots of farm land sold, number of farming families making the purchases and the area of farm land sold are shown in the above chart. Each of the farming families had purchased 0.51 *chia* (1.222 acres) on the average. The average area purchased by each farming family is shown below:

* For detailed figures, see APPENDIX, Table 9, p. 311.

Year	Average Area Purchased by Each Farming Family
1948	0.45 *chia* (1.079 acres)
1951	0.48 *chia* (1.150 acres)
1952	0.60 *chia* (1.438 acres)
1953, first batch	0.47 *chia* (1.126 acres)
1953, second batch	0.59 *chia* (1.414 acres)
1958	0.49 *chia* (1.174 acres)

The area of public land purchased differed from individual to individual. According to a Taiwan Land Bureau statistical study of farming families that purchased public land under the sales programs of 1948, 1951 and 1952, about 66 per cent purchased less than 0.50 *chia* (1.198 acres) 20 per cent purchased from 0.50 to 1 *chia* (from 1.198 to 2.397 acres) and less than 14 per cent purchased more than 1 *chia*. From these statistics, it will be seen that most farming families purchased only a small amount of land. But a further analysis shows that the amounts of land the farming families purchased and the amounts they actually cultivated were not identical, the latter being much larger. According to statistics compiled by the Taiwan Land Bureau, the total of land which the farming families buying public land under the sales programs of 1948, 1951 and 1952 actually cultivated was 117,085 *chia* (280,620 acres). Of these, 50,622 *chia* (121,327 acres) were purchased from the Government, and the remaining 66,463 *chia* (159,293 acres) of other lands were either owned by the farming families or leased from others. By calculating on the basis of these figures, we find that the average amount of land cultivated by each of the farming families which had purchased public land was 1.18 *chia* (2.83 acres), 43 per cent of which was the public land purchased from the Government. This shows to what extent the farmers have been benefited by the public land sales program.

CHAPTER 4

THE LAND-TO-
THE-TILLER PROGRAM

FORMULATION OF THE POLICY

THE ultimate objective of rural land reform is to realize the "land-to-the-tiller" ideal. Following the reduction of farm rent to 37.5 per cent and the sale of public land, the Government made a final effort to implement the land-to-the-tiller program.

But the tenancy system has had a long history in the Chinese villages. It would have been virtually impossible to abolish such a deep-rooted system overnight and to enforce an all-out land-to-the-tiller program. As a result of study and discussion, the following three principles were adopted as the basis of the land-to-the-tiller policy.

TO HELP TENANT FARMERS ACQUIRE LANDOWNERSHIP WITHOUT INCREASING THEIR FINANCIAL BURDEN

Before the introduction of the rent reduction program, the tenant farmers had to pay high rents and were in desperate straits. With the limitation of farm rent, their lot was improved, but their economic position was still precarious. Any increase of their burden would have produced adverse effects on their livelihood and on the operation of their farms. This would have been tantamount to causing them loss before they could expect any benefit. Such was certainly not the intention of the land policy. So it was decided that in formulating measures to implement the land-to-the-tiller program, the first guiding principle should be to help tenant farmers acquire land without increasing their burdens.

TO PROTECT THE INTERESTS
OF THE LANDLORDS

The highest goal of government is to promote the interests and welfare of the people. A responsible official should be ashamed of himself even if just one man or one woman is not properly provided for. Consequently, while shaking off the shackles of the tenancy system for the farmers in order to improve their living conditions, the enforcement of the land-to-the-tiller program should also take into account the interests of landlords so as not to cause them to suffer too great a loss. The authorities were aware that landlords had acquired ownership of land by lawful means, and not through robbery or theft, and that the land therefore should not be subject to confiscation. By confiscating all the land of the people without compensation, the Communists have acted contrary to every principle of human nature. The measures we have adopted with respect to the land-lords are entirely different: we purchase their tenanted land, but pay them a reasonable price for it; we safeguard their livelihood by permitting them to retain a reasonable amount of land for themselves.

TO CONVERT LANDHOLDINGS INTO
INDUSTRIAL HOLDINGS

Having sold their tenanted land, the landlords no longer would be able to live on farm rents as they had in the past. To help solve their problems of livelihood for the future, they would require assistance and guidance. At the same time, if the money paid them by the Government were spent in uneconomic ways, financial conditions would be disturbed and serious social consequences could result.   To provide for the livelihood of the landlords and to make profitable use of the money paid to them for the land, the Government decided that the landlords should be encouraged to interest themselves in industrial development by converting their landholdings into industrial holdings.   Concrete measures taken in this connection were to transfer the state and province jointly owned Taiwan Cement Corporation and Taiwan Pulp and Paper Corporation, and the province-owned Taiwan Industrial and Mining Corporation and Taiwan Agricultural and Forestry Development Corporation to private ownership by offering the Government stock for sale to private investors.   Proceeds were used to pay for lands compulsorily purchased from landlords. Transfers of the four public corporations to private ownership have smoothed the way for private enterprise.

IMPLEMENTATION OF THE LAND-TO-THE-TILLER PROGRAM

GENERAL LANDOWNERSHIP CLASSIFICATION

The General Landownership Classification was a process whereby all lands owned by any one individual in the different places were singled out from the various local land registers and classified under his name.   The work was to investigate and register carefully the land categories, changes in land rights, conditions of land utilization and the distance between the land and the landlord's place of residence to show whether it was resident or non-resident owned.   In brief, the General Landownership Classification was an over-all rechecking of landownership.

The land-to-the-tiller program could not be initiated without a clear picture of landownership.   The General Landownership Classification was, therefore, a basic preparation for the implementation of the land-to-the-tiller program.

The General Landownership Classification began in January, 1951, with the technical assistance and financial support of the

Sino-American Joint Commission on Rural Reconstruction. The first two counties to do the work, which was completed in August of the same year, were Kaohsiung and Pintung. Immediately afterward, a special course was given to train more staff members. Similar programs of General Landownership Classification were initiated in other counties and municipalities in September 1951 and completed in February, 1952. Thereafter, changes in land rights were duly registered as they occurred. By the end of April, the statistics of General Landownership Classification for Taiwan Province as a whole were complete. The calculating of the land acreage under purchase and retention in the implementation of the land-to-the-tiller program was based on the "land-record cards" and "landownership cards" which were compiled during the period of landownership classification. The "land-record cards" identified the owner of the plot of land by giving first the plot and then the name of its owner, while the "landownership cards" reversed that order.

ENACTMENT OF THE
LAND-TO-THE-TILLER ACT

With the completion of the work of General Landownership Classification, the Taiwan Provincial Government began to draw up a set of draft Regulations Governing the Establishment of Owner-Farmers in Taiwan, consisting of 33 articles, which was the prototype of land-to-tiller legislation in Taiwan. This draft was transmitted in July, 1952, to the Taiwan Provincial Assembly for consideration along with two other draft Regulations, one Governing the Issuance of Land Bonds in Kind in Taiwan Province and another Governing the Disposal of Provincial Property. In order to save time, pending the consideration by the Provincial Assembly, whose comments were to be transmitted to the central Government for reference, the Provincial Government at the same time submitted the Regulations to the Cabinet for approval.

The Provincial Assembly was in favor of the land-to-the tiller policy. Upon receipt of the drafts transmitted by the Provincial Government, it handed them down to the different County and Municipal Assemblies for comment, and, at the same time, set up an *ad hoc* group to go over the matter thoroughly. After more than a month of careful study and discussion, it proposed amendments to the two drafts on the Establishment of Owner-Farmers and the Issuance of Land Bonds in Kind, and on August 29 sent them, as amended, to the Provincial Government for transmission to the central Government.

Upon receipt of the draft Regulations submitted by the Provincial Government, and of the amendments proposed by the Provincial Assembly, the Cabinet handed them down to competent ministries and experts on land administration for careful consideration. In examining the draft proposals, the Cabinet sought the opinions of foreign and Chinese experts, took notice of the Japanese postwar experiences in land reform and establishment of owner-farmers, carefully weighed the comments made by the Provincial Assembly and opinions expressed by the farmers' representatives of different counties and municipalities and Farm Tenancy Committees on all levels, and studied the cruel land struggle launched by the Communists on the Chinese mainland. After repeated studies and discussions, a final draft was decided upon.

In order to lend positive significance to the draft bill with a view to implementing Dr. Sun Yat-sen's teaching of equal land rights and assuring legislation that might be applicable to the whole country upon recovery of the mainland, the original title of the bill (Establishment of Owner-Farmers in Taiwan) was changed to Land-to-the-Tiller. Besides the substitution of title, there were other important changes. The Cabinet, at its meeting on November 12, 1952, approved the revised text of the draft bill, amended the draft Regulations Governing the Issuance of Land Bonds in Kind in Taiwan and drew up a set of draft Regulations Governing the Transfer of Government Enterprises to Private Ownership. All three draft documents were then submitted to the Legislative Yuan for its action.

The draft bill and regulations were presented before the meeting of the Legislative Yuan on December 2, 1952. After two sessions, during which many questions were asked and heated debate took place, the Legislative Yuan resolved to refer the Land-to-the-Tiller Bill to the Committees on Internal Affairs, Economic Affairs, Financial Affairs, and Civil, Criminal and Commercial Laws for examination. These four committees held 12 joint sessions and arrived at decisions on principles and main points of emphasis. Then they set up an *ad hoc* sub-committee composed of 25 legislators for further examination. This subcommittee met 14 times, day and night, drew up a report and submitted it to the four committees.

The four committees made a final examination, proposed amendments, and submitted a report to the Legislative Yuan. On January 20, 1953, the epoch-making bill was finally passed by the legislature.

The bill, as finally enacted under the title of the Land-to-the-Tiller Act, was divided into five chapters of 36 articles. In addition to the three principles mentioned in the preceeding section, other important features of the act were as follows:

(1) Abolition of the tenancy system by peaceful means: The highest principle of the act is to abolish land tenancy but by peaceful and gradual means. The first step taken for enforcement of the program was compulsory Government purchase of all tenant-cultivated land owned by the landlord in excess of the prescribed retention limit for resale to tiller or tillers. Next was purchase by tiller or tillers with loans granted by the Government.

(2) Purchase and resale through the Government: tenants were by no means on an equal footing with landlords. If the transfer of farm land to tenants were effected in a free transaction, irregularities would certainly occur, disputes arise, and the situation eventually would get out of control. Thus the act provides for transfer of landownership through the Government; i.e., the Government undertook to purchase the land from the landlord and resell it to tiller or tillers. During the process of purchase and resale, the landlord and the tenant had no direct contact with each other. In this way, ownership of the farm land was transferred in an atmosphere of harmony.

(3) Land reform through an orderly procedure: Taiwan is a bastion for counterattack and national recovery. Its land reform could not be carried out in a hurry and had to be realized gradually through orderly procedures. With this in view, the act provides for sale of land to the original tiller so that the tenure system might be gradually abolished. The procedure did not require the subdivision of the farm land, nor any change in its cultivation. The rational operation of land and its further readjustment were reserved for the future.

(4) Equal protection of other enterprises: Land reform has to do with the development of the rural economy and the improvement of farmers' living conditions, but it is equally true that the administration of the Government has to do with all other aspects of life and cannot pay exclusive attention to only one and neglect the others. Many educational and philanthropic undertaking and public and private enterprises depend upon farm land as a source of revenue or as the basis of their operations. Such lands should not be compulsorily purchased. The act therefore provides that land used for purposes of experimentation, research or agricultural extension, or land needed by educational and philanthropic institutions, and land required by public and private enterprises for the supply of raw materials, were to be exempted from compulsory purchase by the Government.

(5) Continued protection of owner-farmers: Tenant farmers who had just become owner-farmers after acquiring land under the land-to-the-tiller program might be short of funds, having just paid for their property. They might be easily deceived by tempting offers and end up as tenant farmers once again. The act therefore provides a production fund from which loans might be extended to the farmer-purchasers; they also were given encouragement and assistance to operate their farms with modern techniques on a cooperative basis. Negatively, restrictions provided that land acquired under the land-to-the-tiller program was not to be transferred before its purchase price was fully paid and that farmer-purchasers were not allowed to use the name of another person to purchase the land and lease it out after purchase.

ON-THE-SPOT RECHECKING

Of all the items of work involved in the procedure for the enforcement of the land-to-the-tiller program, rechecking was the most complicated. The accuracy of the results of rechecking had much to do with the success of the land-to-the-tiller policy. Although the data obtained in the General Landownership Classification might serve as important reference material, changes in land rights were so frequent, and the relations of man to land arising from failure to sign lease contracts, from subleases, fake ownei-cultivation, and false purchases and sales were so complicated, that it was necessary to undertake a comprehensive investigation. The items to be rechecked included whether the particulars of the land were correct, whether the conditions of its use and the amount of annual yields were normal, and whether the labor power of the families to undertake farming was adequate. Areas of the land to be exempted from compulsory purchase or to be retained by the landlords had to be identified, and immovable fixtures listed for compulsory purchase along with the farm land. The rechecking had also to find out whether the private farm lands concerned were owned by landlords or owner-farmers and whether they were cultivated by the owners themselves or by tenants. The results of such rechecking formed the essential part of the data on which were based all subsequent decisions about the compulsory purchase of the land, its resale to the cultivators, and the retention by the landlord and exemption of certain lands from compulsory purchase by the Government.

In carrying out rechecking, the staff was armed with different kinds of maps and forms. Altogether a total of 47,000 blueprint cadastral maps, 1,400,000 tenant farmer check sheets for tented land, 1,600,000 owner-farmer check sheets for owner-cultivated land and 1,860,000 landownership check sheets for owners of land were prepared. Beginning in all counties and municipalities simultaneously on March 16, 1953, the work of rechecking was made in "sections" (a "section" being a certain area of land for the purpose of cadastral management). Mobilized and trained for the task were 2,234 investigators for the province as a whole, and 30,369 assistants on the district (*hsiang*), township (*chen*), urban district (*chu*), village (*tsun*), and precinct (*li*) levels. They proceeded to the designated point at the appointed time, checked the land according to the cadastral maps and asked questions about items contained in the check sheets, making investigations plot by plot, and going from house to house. A total of 2,100,000 plots of private farm land were investigated, and 800,000 families of tenant farmers, farm hands and owner-farmers were visited. The work of rechecking was completed within one month.

PURCHASE AND RESALE OF FARM LAND

After the completion of rechecking, the compulsory purchase of farm land and its resale to the farmer-purchasers began on May 1, 1953. The county and municipal governments had checked the records, computed the areas of farm land to be compulsorily purchased by the Government from the landlords and those to be retained by them, and compiled the lists of farm lands to be compulsorily purchased [1] and the lists of farm lands to be resold to farmer purchasers. [2] After the lists had been considered and confirmed by the farm tenancy committees at different levels, and approved by county and municipal governments, the compulsory purchase and resale of farm land were publicly announced. The period of the public announcement was 30 days. The method used was for the district, township, or urban district offices in whose jurisdiction the lands were located to announce the lists and place them in their respective offices for examination by the public. During the period of public announcement widespread publicity was organized in the different districts, townships, urban districts or precincts, and landlords and prospective purchasers were notified to examine the lists. Upon discovering any discrepancies, the interested party might file a request for correction. After the expiration of the period of public announcement, areas of the farm land to be compulsorily purchased by

(1)   For a sample of the List, see APPENDIX, Figure 4, p. 318.
(2)   For a sample of List, see APPENDIX, Figure 5, p. 319.

the Government and those to be resold to farmer-purchasers became definitive.

When the land earmarked for purchase and resale became definitive, the different county and municipal governments notified landlords and required them to surrender their title deeds and collect the compensation. Tenant farmers were notified to purchase the land and pay the first installment. At the same time, they would register changes in land rights and transfers of land, issue landownership certificates,* and make necessary changes in the lease contracts. The whole work of the land-to-the-tiller program was brought to a successful conclusion by the end of December, 1953. Altogether a total of 143,568 *chia* (344,092 acres) of farm land had been compulsorily purchased by the Government and resold to farmer-purchasers, not including 14,045 *chia* (33,662 acres) of farm land which tenant farmers had purchased directly from landlords, and the total number of farming families which had purchased farm land resold by the Government was 194,823. The detailed statistics are shown on the next page.

COMPENSATION FOR LANDLORDS AND COLLECTION OF THE LAND PRICE

(1) Compensation for Landlords: According to the provisions of the Land-to-the-Tiller Act, compensation to landlords was paid 70 per cent with land bonds in kind and 30 per cent with government enterprise stock shares (avoidance of cash was to avert inflation which would have caused heavy loss to the landlords, as happened during the Japanese land reform). Land bonds are of two kinds according to different categories of land: rice bonds and sweet potato bonds. Compensation for paddy fields was paid with rice bonds, and that for dry land with sweet potato bonds. The methods of paying rice bonds differed with different kinds of paddy fields: double-crop, single-crop, "weather-depending," three-year rotation and specially irrigated. As the main crop on double-crop paddy fields was rice, and the purchase

* For a sample of landownership certificate, see APPENDIX, Figure 6, p. 320.

Table 1

**AREA OF FARM LAND PURCHASED FROM LANDLORDS AND
RESOLD TO FARMERS AND THE NUMBER OF
FARMING FAMILIES BENEFITED UNDER
THE LAND-TO-THE-TILLER PROGRAM,
TAIWAN PROVINCE**

County or Municipality	Area of Farm Land Purchased from Landlords & Resold to Farmers (acre)			Number of Farming Families Making the Purchase	Number of Landlord Families Affected
	Total	Paddy Field	Dry Land		
Taipei County	30,204	27,788	2,416	14,084	9,193
Ilan County	18,344	16,499	1,845	9,171	5,363
Taoyuan County	56,138	52,023	4,115	16,883	9,527
Hsinchu County	33,323	23,430	9,793	13,626	7,779
Miaoli County	21,065	16,317	4,748	10,912	6,609
Taichung County	27,651	26,230	1,421	16,871	12,266
Changhua County	22,637	20,245	2,392	20,233	10,727
Nantou County	8,290	6,991	1,299	6,128	3,237
Yunlin County	22,255	18,816	3,439	14,269	5,662
Chiayi County	19,536	16,732	2,804	13,036	6,935
Tainan County	28,418	20,983	7,435	18,724	8,340
Kaohsiung County	12,542	9,477	3,065	10,449	4,024
Pingtung County	23,610	19,557	4,053	16,362	5,517
Taitung County	2,765	1,512	1,253	1,464	327
Hualien County	3,235	2,318	917	1,658	642
Penghu County	599	--	599	1,830	925
Taipei Municipality	506	494	12	333	2,577
Keelung Municipality	497	463	34	262	398
Taichung Municipality	6,172	5,834	338	4,037	2,979
Tainan Municipality	714	287	427	856	1,084
Kaohsiung Municipality	2,450	2,313	137	1,724	1,111
Yangmingshan Admin.	3,241	2,977	264	1,910	825
GRAND TOTAL	344,092	291,286	52,806	194,823	106,049

price was expressed entirely in terms of rice, rice bonds used to pay for such paddy fields would be paid in rice. As the main crop on all other kinds of paddy fields was usually rice and sweet potatoes, and included even sugar cane in case of three-year rotation fields, and the purchase price was not directly expressed in terms of rice but converted into rice, rice bonds used as compensation for these paddy fields were as follows: those for single-crop fields and "weather-depending" fields were to be paid 50 per cent in rice and 50 per cent in cash by converting the rice into cash at the current market price; those for rotation fields, including specially irrigated fields, were to be paid in cash by converting the rice into cash at the current market price. There thus were four methods of paying rice bonds. Rice bonds were mostly paid in rice with the exception of the small part that was paid in cash by converting the rice into cash. Sweet potato bonds were paid in cash by converting the sweet potatoes into cash. The conversion of vice or sweet potatoes into cash was made at the current market price of the locality. The two kinds of bonds[1] were to be paid in equal installments spread over a period of ten years, and bore an interest of four per cent per annum. The 30 per cent compensation in government enterprise stock shares[2] to landlords was paid with stocks of the four corporations transferred to private ownership: Cement Corporation, Pulp and Paper Corporation, Industrial and Mining Corporation, and Agricultural and Forestry Development Corporation.

The payment of compensation began when the areas of farm land to be purchased by the Government and resold to farmer-purchasers had become definitive. The land bonds in kind were the first to be issued and paid to the landlords. As for that part of the compensation to be paid with industrial stocks, a temporary certificate was issued in the first instance, which could be used later in exchange for regular stocks. This was due to the extremely

(1) For samples of the bonds, see APPENDIX, Figures 7-8, pp. 321-324.

(2) For samples of the stock shares, see APPENDIX, Figures 9-12, pp. 325-328.

complicated processes involved in the re-evaluation of the capital values, the allocation of the shares, and the transfer of the public enterprises to private ownership. With the exception of a few landlords whose land had not been sold because of land disputes or other special causes, the work of compensation to landlords was completed in 1954 when all payments had been effected.

(2) Collection of the Land Price: Proceeds from the sale of the Government purchased land were the chief source of revenue to pay compensation for lands compulsorily purchased from landlords. From this it will be readily seen that the success or failure of the land-to-the-tiller program hinged on how the resale price was to be collected from the farmer-purchasers. According to the Land-to-the-Tiller Act, the price of farm land offered by the Government for resale was calculated on the same basis as that of farm land compulsorily purchased from landlords, namely, two and half times the amount of the annual main crop yield. Land-ownership certificates were to be issued only after the payment of the first installment.

The entire price was to be paid in equal annual installments over a period of ten years, and each annual amount was to be collected in equal semi-annual amounts to be closely coordinated with the harvest seasons. Thus the entire purchase price was to be paid off in 20 installments spread over a period of ten years. Collection of the first semi-annual installment payment began in July, 1953. It went smoothly. In view of the enthusiastic response of farmer-purchasers and the good results of subsequent installment payments, there is no doubt that completion of the landownership transfer will be peaceful and harmonious.

PRESERVATION AND EXTENSION OF ACHIEVEMENTS OF THE LAND-TO-THE-TILLER PROGRAM

It is a common saying that "a good beginning is half done." But it is also an indisputable fact that "if it is difficult to initiate an undertaking, it is still more so to keep it going." The compulsory purchase of farm land and its resale to tillers have proceeded smoothly, and the whole work is near completion. Yet the farmer-purchasers, who were either tenant farmers or farm hands in the past, and who for generation after generation had been guided solely by the wishes of landlords, and whose economic position was still feeble, could be easily persuaded to give up the land they have just purchased from the Government, or make a change in its use, or commit other acts in violation of the law or regulations. This is regrettable not only because of harm to the future interests of farming families, but because it would destroy results of the land-to-the-tiller program. In order to forestall such an unfortunate turn of events and to preserve the achievements of the program, the Government adopted the following measures:

(1) General rechecking of farming families: An annual general rechecking of the farming families which purchased farm land from the Government has been carried out since 1954. The recheck has been in accordance with rules drawn up and promulgated by the Taiwan Provincial Government, which directs and supervises the lower echelon personnel in work with districts, townships, or urban districts. The methods used include visits, inquiries, investigation and correction of irregularities summarized as follows:

(a) *House-to-house visits* are to indicate the significance and advantages of the farm land reform, explain laws, regulations and rules and answer questions.

(b) *Inquiries* are made into post-reform improvements in the farmers' living conditions, progress in land reform and agricultural operations, and changes in rural life and farm economy, as well as special difficulties that might have arisen.

(c) *Investigation* ascertains whether there has been any change in the use of the land purchased, or its transfer or lease, or any other irregularity.

(d) *Correction of irregularities* deals with cases in which farmer-purchasers have violated the law.

The annual rechecking has produced good effects. In preventing and handling unlawful cases, it is especially effective for preserving the achievements of the reform.

(2) Precautionary measures in connection with advance payment of land price: It is true that the Land-to-the-Tiller Act contains provisions encouraging the farmer-purchasers to pay their land price in advance. The aim originally was to enable prosperous tillers to pay in fewer than ten yearly installments. However, such an advantage may bring a disadvantage in its wake. Most farmer-purchasers are poor and might be tempted by deceptive offers of immediate gain to pay off the purchase price in advance and to transfer the land to another person or use it for purposes other than farming. Others might transfer the land to another person, or change its use, and, having done so, fraudulently ask for government permission by making use of the advance payment clause to evade their legal obligations. Such acts are contrary to the original intention of the Government to help establish owner-farmers, and in contravention of the law. The Taiwan Provincial Government therefore formulated, in August, 1955, a set of Measures Encouraging Advance Payment of the Purchase Price of Farm Land Resold by the Government in the Implementation of the Land-to-the-Tiller Program. Express provisions are included to prevent irregularities and handle any cases that might arise.

(3) Extending of government loans to farmers: To free the farmers of usurious debts, loans in exchange for rice or loans for production purposes were already available. To strengthen the granting of such loans and to protect and help owner-farmers, the Government has authorized the Land Bank of Taiwan to extend the following loans:

(a) To farmers for the purchase of the landlord's retained land as provided in Article 12 of the Land-to-the-Tiller Act.

(b) To farmers for the improvement of land use and increase of farm production as provided in Article 23 of the same act.

(c) To farmer-purchasers from the purchase of public farm land as provided by the Regulations Governing the Sale of Public Farm Lands to Establish Owner-Farmers in Taiwan Province.

(d) To farmers for the repair and construction of irrigation facilities and for reclamation of waste land as provided by the same regulations.

With such financial assistance, farm families have found they do not need to transfer the land they purchased, nor change its use in violation of the law.

The sources for loan funds are as follows:

(a) Thirty per cent of the proceeds (in government enterprise stock shares) from the resale of private farm land that had been compulsorily purchased from landlords by the Government in the implementation of the land-to-the-tiller program;

(b) Part of the proceeds from the sale of public farm land;

(c) Special sums earmarked by the Government.

The sources of funds are sufficient and reliable. There is no reason to fear that they will not meet the needs of the farmers.

With adoption of these measures, the achievements of the land-to-the-tiller program have, with only a few exceptions, been preserved and gradually extended.

RESULTS OF THE LAND-TO-THE-TILLER PROGRAM

Although the land-to-the-tiller program was implemented only a few years ago, the results are clearly visible to all. Following are some of the most important accomplishments:

REALIZATION OF THE ALL-FARM-LAND-OWNED-BY-FARMERS IDEAL

Since the implementation of the 37.5% farm rent limitation program in 1949, the income of the tenant farmers who availed themselves of this opportunity to buy land from their landlords and the area of farm land have increased from year to year. From 1949 through 1956, a total of 77,965 tenant families bought, from their own resources, as much as 41,383 *chia* (99,184 acres) of farm land.

As a result of the sale of public land from 1948 to 1958, 139,688 additional tenant families have become owner-farmers by purchasing 71,666 *chia* (171,763 acres).

With the completion of the land-to-the-tiller program, the Government compulsorily purchased 143,567 *chia* (344,090 acres) of private farm land from landlords and resold it to 194,823 tenant families.

As a result of these successive land reforms, 71 per cent of the 360,736 *chia* (864,583 acres) of public and private leased farm land throughout the province has been transferred to private ownership of the tenant farmers. The ratio of the number of owner-farmers to farming families and that of the area of owner-cultivated land to farm land have been increasing rapidly, and the ideal of all farm land owned by farmers is being realized. The following two charts* give a broad picture of the situation:

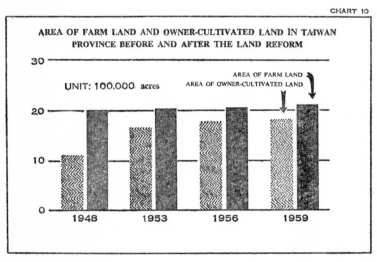

CHART 10

AREA OF FARM LAND AND OWNER-CULTIVATED LAND IN TAIWAN PROVINCE BEFORE AND AFTER THE LAND REFORM

UNIT: 100,000. acres

AREA OF FARM LAND
AREA OF OWNER-CULTIVATED LAND

1948   1953   1956   1959

INCREASE OF AGRICULTURAL PRODUCTION AND IMPROVEMENT OF FARMERS' LIVING CONDITIONS

The factors contributing to the increase of agricultural pro-

* For detailed figures, see APPENDIX, Table 10-11, p. 312.

CHART 11

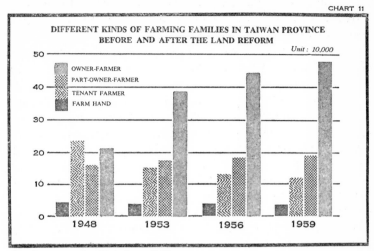

DIFFERENT KINDS OF FARMING FAMILIES IN TAIWAN PROVINCE
BEFORE AND AFTER THE LAND REFORM

Unit : 10,000

OWNER-FARMER
PART-OWNER-FARMER
TENANT FARMER
FARM HAND

1948   1953   1956   1959

duction may be listed as follows:

(1) Psychological factor: With the enforcement of the 37.5% farm rent limitation program, tenant rights were protected. But, psychologically, the tenant farmers might still have some fears that on the expiration of the lease contract, the landlords might take back the land. After tenant farmers had acquired ownership of the farm land following the land-to-the-tiller program, all such fears were removed. Stimulated by the constant interest in his land as a landowner, the farmer put all his energy into farming. Agricultural production has, therefore, shown a considerable increase.

(2) Improvement of farm land use: When tenant farmers were cultivating land that belonged to landlords, they frequently hesitated to make agricultural investment of a permanent nature. Now that they have land of their own, and that all fruits of the investment are to be enjoyed by themselves exclusively, it is only natural that long-term projects for agricultural improvement should be undertaken. As investment keeps on increasing, the volume of production also goes up. The attached table (*see on P. 85*) gives a general idea of the improvement in farm land utilization.

(3) Increase of Farm Implements and Agricultural Equip-

ment: Following the implementation of the land-to-the-tiller program, farm implements and agricultural equipment also have been on the increase as revealed in Table 3 on P. 86.

These are some of the factors that contributed to the increase of agricultural production. As the volume of production increases, so do the incomes of the farmers.

In 1952, before the implementation of the land-to-the-tiller program, the annual harvest on medium-grade paddy fields was 5,530 kg. (12,912 lbs.) of unhulled rice per *chia* (2.3967 acres). The yield increased to 7,258 kg. (1,001 lbs.) in 1959 after the implementation of the land-to-the-tiller program. Deducting from this the annual installment payments and interest, the cost of fertilizer, and land taxes in kind, the farmer has a net gain of 4,542 kg. (10,013 lbs.) of unhulled rice per *chia*. That is to say, the net income of the farmer-purchaser in 1959 had increased by more than 50 per cent as compared with 1952. It is believed that income will keep on increasing as shown in the following chart.*

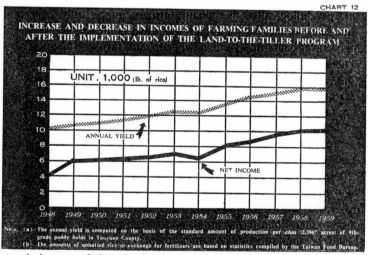

CHART 12

INCREASE AND DECREASE IN INCOMES OF FARMING FAMILIES BEFORE AND AFTER THE IMPLEMENTATION OF THE LAND-TO-THE-TILLER PROGRAM

Note. (a) The annual yield is computed on the basis of the standard amount of production per *chia* (2.3967 acres) of 9th-grade paddy fields in Taoyuan County.
(b) The amounts of unhulled rice in exchange for fertilizers are based on statistics compiled by the Taiwan Food Bureau.

It is natural that the increased income of the farmer not only encourages him to greater production, but also enables him to

* For detailed figures, see APPENDIX, Table 12, p. 313.

TABLE 2

FACILITIES EMPLOYED TO IMPROVE FARM LAND USE BEFORE AND AFTER THE IMPLEMENTATION OF THE LAND-TO-THE-TILLER PROGRAM IN TAIWAN PROVINCE

Item	Total		July 1949 to June 1953		July 1953 to June 1950		July 1957 to June 1960	
	Quantity	Annual Average	Quantity	Annual Average	Quantity	Annual Average	Quantity	Annual Average
Storage of Compost (S.T.)	634,271,741	57,661,067	193,520,898	48,130,225	249,733,320	62,433,330	191,017,523	63,672,508
Water Pumps Bought	4,709	428	311	78	2,484	621	1,914	638
Wells Sunk	10,650	968	1,124	281	4,343	1,086	5,183	1,727
Windbreaks Planted (in ft.)	2,836,050	257,823	434,608	108,652	1,107,710	276,928	1,293,732	431,244

Note: The figures in this table are based on statistical materials of an investigation made of 284,590 farming families purchasing public and private farm land throughout the province.

TABLE 3

INCREASE OF FARM IMPLEMENTS, DRAFT CATTLE, AND AGRICULTURAL EQUIPMENT BEFORE AND AFTER THE IMPLEMENTATION OF THE LAND-TO-THE-TILLER PROGRAM IN TAIWAN PROVINCE

Item	Total		July 1949 to June 1953		July 1953 to June 1957		July 1957 to June 1960	
	Quantity	Annual Average	Quantity	Annual Average	Quantity	Annual Average	Quantity	Annual Average
Farm Implements:								
a. Threshers	80,014	7,274	16,139	4,035	30,616	7,654	33,259	11,086
b. Winnows	36,327	3,302	6,709	1,677	11,605	2,901	18,013	6,004
c. Deep-furrow Plows	225,479	20,498	54,999	13,750	87,232	21,808	83,248	27,749
d. Ox Carts	24,101	2,191	675	169	10,071	2,518	13,354	4,451
e. Sprayers	27,759	2,524	1,565	391	4,327	1,082	21,867	7,289
f. Handcarts	17,423	1,584	1,532	383	9,007	2,252	6,884	2,295
Draft Cattle	246,949	22,450	73,551	18,388	152,564	38,141	120,834	40,278
Agricultural Equipment Repaired or Constructed:								
a. Drying Grounds (sq. ft.)	74,752,481	679,568	12,804,445	3,201,111	19,525,853	4,881,463	42,422,183	14,140,728
b. Compost Houses (sq. ft.)	22,469,538	2,042,685	2,668,299	667,075	11,047,976	2,761,994	8,753,263	2,917,754
c. Animal Shelters (sq. ft.)	12,798,322	1,163,484	2,173,047	543,262	5,999,134	1,499,784	4,626,141	1,542,047

Notes: (a) The implementation of the land-to-the-tiller program in Taiwan Province began in July 1953.
(b) The figures in this table are based on the statistical materials of an investigation made of 284,590 farming families purchasing public and private farm land throughout the province.

improve his living conditions.   This can be seen from payments for food, clothing, dwellings, travel, education and entertainment, and from the number of children attending school.   Before land reform, most farmers in Taiwan Province had non-staple cereals as their main articles of consumption, and lacked subsidiary food. Undernourishment was fairly common.   With the implementation of the land-to-the-tiller program, however, food production has increased and opportunities for part-time rural employment have multiplied.   Average farmers are eating polished rice as their main article of consumption, and subsidiary food has been very much improved. Undernourishment is rare. The attached chart* and table (*see next page*) show the improvements made in clothing, dwellings travel, education and entertainment.

CHART 13

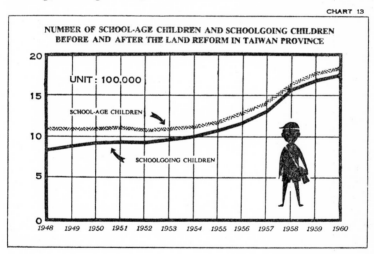

NUMBER OF SCHOOL-AGE CHILDREN AND SCHOOLGOING CHILDREN BEFORE AND AFTER THE LAND REFORM IN TAIWAN PROVINCE

UNIT: 100,000

SCHOOL-AGE CHILDREN

SCHOOLGOING CHILDREN

ELEVATION OF THE FARMERS' SOCIAL STATUS

For thousand of years the Chinese farmer, groaning under the oppressions of corrupt officials, village bosses, the wicked gentry, and landlords, had almost no social status.   The plight of

* For detailed figures, see APPENDIX, Table 3, p. 308.

IMPROVEMENT OF FARMERS' LIVING CONDITIONS BEFORE AND AFTER THE IMPLEMENTATION OF THE LAND-TO-THE-TILLER PROGRAM IN TAIWAN PROVINCE   TABLE 4

Item	Total		July 1949 to June 1953		July 1953 to June 1957		July 1957 to June 1960	
	Quantity	Annual Average	Quantity	Annual Average	Quantity	Annual Average	Quantity	Annual Average
Clothing:								
a. New Clothes (piece)	24,828,810	10,438,983	31,274,896	7,818,724	48,259,004	12,064,751	35,324,910	11,774,970
b. Sewing Machines Bought	93,730	8,521	9,934	2,484	30,256	7,564	53,540	17,847
Housing:								
a. Houses Newly Built (square feet)	11,881,410	1,080,128	1,497,821	374,455	4,556,573	1,139,143	5,827,016	1,942,339
b. Houses Newly Repaired (square feet)	31,104,160	2,827,651	5,825,875	1,456,469	13,289,342	3,322,336	11,988,943	3,996,316
Bicycles Bought	212,251	19,296	43,178	10,795	86,173	21,543	82,900	27,633
New Furniture:								
a. Tables	168,780	15,344	24,418	6,105	57,336	14,334	87,026	29,008
b. Chairs & Stools	546,046	49,641	73,092	18,273	172,232	43,058	300,722	100,241
c. Cupboards & Wardrobes	136,379	12,398	19,478	4,870	47,090	11,773	69,811	23,270
d. Beddings & Mosquito Nets	171,361	15,578	12,036	3,009	28,815	7,204	130,510	43,503
e. Electric Lamps Newly Installed	440,369	40,034	17,385	4,346	96,168	24,042	326,816	108,939
f. Radio Sets	32,186	2,926	602	151	11,44	1,103	27,173	9,058
Marriages	217,839	19,804	42,660	10,665	98,835	24,709	76,344	25,448

Note: New clothes figure for the period from July 1957, to June 1960, is smaller than that for the period from July 1953, to June 1957, because materials used were of a better quality.

farmers on Taiwan under the Japanese administration was even more pitiable than that of those on the mainland.   After retrocession of the island to China, the Chinese Government, in selecting public servants and administering public affairs, not only has done away with discrimination, but in introducing local self-government, has encouraged able native-born leaders to come to the fore.   But owing to force of habit, few farmers participated. The whole picture changed with the enforcement of land reform.

The main cause is the improvement of economic conditions. Not until the betterment of their livelihood did farmers have time and energy to take part in activities for the improvement of their social position.   This proves once more that an individual has to have enough to eat before he devotes himself to the finer things of life.

Furthermore, during the period of land reform, the farmers were required by law to attend various kinds of meetings.   These served as a sort of social education, whereby the farmers' self-consciousness and self-respect were awakened.

Since enforcement of land reform, the number of holders of public office coming from farm families has been on the increase, as shown in the following chart:*

CHART 14

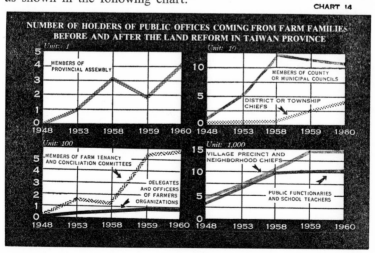

* For detailed figures, see APPENDIX, Table 14, p. 314.

This chart provides evidence that the social status of the farmers has been elevated and will continue to rise.

PREVENTION OF COMMUNIST PENETRATION AND STRENGTHENING OF POLITICAL APPEAL

The Communists took over the Chinese mainland by forcing the farmers to take part in rebellion conducted under the guise of "agrarian reform." Having realized their designs on the mainland, they set afoot a similar scheme to penetrate Southeast Asia with "land reform" as a bait. Like China, Southeast Asia is a densely populated agricultural area swarming with poor farmers. But as most farmers in Taiwan have acquired land and a higher standard of living, the Communist scheme for penetration of this island has been frustrated. Since the Communists took over, people of the mainland have gone through such successive ordeals as "land reform," "agricultural collectivization" and the "people's communes." The people know now that the Communists will say all the nice words and do all the evil things in the world. Land reform in Taiwan has been highly successful, the ideal of land-to-the-tiller has become a fact, and, with the improved conditions of farmers, an era of social progress has set in. In contrast to the situation on the mainland, people on this island are living in a veritable paradise. Little wonder that the people of the mainland should pin their hopes on us and look forward to an early counteroffensive mounted from Taiwan to shake off their shackles and deliver them. Such has been the political appeal of the land-to-the-tiller program as implemented in Taiwan.

Apart from this, the sale of the four corporations and their transfer to private ownership, which transformed a large amount of private capital into industrial investment, have helped in the industrial reconstruction of Taiwan. In the past, the indifference to public affairs on the part of the farmers busily toiling in the fields all the year round was an obstacle to the successful working of a constitutional government. Now, with the introduction of farm land reform, they are called upon more and more to take

New farm houses sprang up
everywhere after land reform

Courtyard scene shows prosperity of typical Taiwan farm

Rich soil produces two to three crops of rice annually

Land reform has raised harvest yield and has helped food supply keep up with extremely high birth rate

Concrete drying ground helps speed rice to market

Despite big families. rural life is abundant, happy

After drying. rice is stored in these beehive-type bins

part in public meetings and exercise their civil rights. This has been of immense help in the satisfactory working of a democratic and constitutional government. Additionally, the vast quantity of rice in the hands of the Government, paid by the farmer-purchasers as the land price following the implementation of the land-to-the-tiller program, has been extremely useful in stabilizing food prices and has contributed in no small measure to a stable social and economic order. In short, the implementation of the land-to-the-tiller program has not only helped the development of the agricultural and industrial economy, but also has made important contributions to the political, social, and cultural life of the people.

CHAPTER 5

DEVELOPMENT AND UTILIZATION OF FARM LAND

DEVELOPMENT OF FARM LAND

MENTION was made in Chapter I of four traditional land problems of China: distribution, taxation, cadastration and utilization. In Taiwan, these problems were created by scarcity of arable land, population pressure, maladjustments in land distribution and worsening of the tenancy situation.

A series of land reforms beginning in 1949 sought solutions for the problems. From the actions set forth in Chapters II, III and IV, it could be concluded that:

1. With the implementation of the farm rent reduction program, difficulties of land taxation and tenure had ceased to exist.

2. The problem of cadastration had been solved after completion of the General Landownership Classification program.

3. Maladjustments in land distribution had been materially reduced as a result of the implementation of the public land sales and the land-to-the-tiller programs.

4. Scarcity of arable land and population pressure could not be solved by such measures.

5. Rent reduction and the land-to-the-tiller program had heightened the interest of farmers in their land and increased production, but land utilization remained far short of the maximum.

The problem of population pressure is not within the scope of this book and will not be discussed. However, every possible effort should be made to minimize the serious situation posed by scarcity of arable land. Development of arable land will be considered now and utilization in the next section.

Nearly all of Taiwan barren lands have been brought under cultivation and it is consequently difficult to increase the arable area. There are only two ways to do it: by leveling mountains or reclaiming coastal lands. During the Sino-Japanese War, the author was in charge of provincial administration in Hupeh Province for several years and became familiar with disputes arising out of conflicting claims to river channel lands of Hunan and Hupeh provinces. These were delicate cases which, if not properly handled, could lead to much trouble. To reclaim land on the seacoast is far better.

Careful planning can afford bright prospects for such reclamation in Taiwan. From Hsinchu County in the north to Kaohsiung County in the south, tidal lands of more than 60,000 hectares (148,000 acres) have accumulated on the west coast and can be reclaimed. Emptying into the sea along this stretch of coast are 13 rivers. Because of rapid currents and soft banks on the upper reaches of the rivers, large amounts of sediment are brought down to the sea after torrential rains. Take the Chushui Hsi (Creek), for instance. Fifty million cubic meters (100,006,400 cubic ft.) of soil, equivalent to 2,500 hectares (6,178 acres) with a depth of two meters (6.56 ft.), are washed down annually. The accumulating soil at the mouths of the rivers moves from north to south, washed by waves of the northeast monsoon, and forms a shoal. This grows in height and with the passing of years, the area between the shoal and the coastline becomes new land.

There is no complete record available as to the annual increase in area of tidal land. Some Taichung County areas have shown an annual increase of about 26 meters (85.3 ft.) for the last 17 years and the coastline of Yunlin County has grown about 20 meters (66 ft.) a year for 50 years. These figures tally with survey estimates made on a basis of old landmarks. It can be presumed that the annual increase ranges from 20 to 30 meters (from 66 ft. to 99 ft.).

About 30 per cent of the new land is used for dam sites, construction of windbreaks, drainage, roads, and houses. The remaining part, estimated at about 44,000 hectares (108,727 acres), can be reclaimed and used as farm land. If one and a half hectares (3.7 acres) were allotted to a family, the 44,000 hectares would be sufficient for 30,000 families. Figuring six persons to a family, 180,000 persons could be supported, thus relieving food and population pressures.

In 1956, the Taiwan Provincial Government drew up and promulgated a set of "Measures for the Development of Tidal Lands in Taiwan Province." Lacking full conformity with the spirit of the land-to-the-tiller policy, they were not adequate. The Cabinet then set up a committee to study problems of policy and technique. After its report Cabinet adopted the following as guiding principles:

1. Uniform planning: Development of tidal lands must be studied in conjunction with regulation of waterways, management of salt fields, and construction of fishing ports, windbreaks, and national defense works. Projects should be permanent. The requirement is for utilization of shoals already in existence and the development of new ones. An overall plan is required. In March, 1961, the Cabinet established a Tidal Land Development Planning Commission and invited experts and scholars to help draw up a uniform plan for systematic development.

2. Separate implementation: Once a uniform plan is laid down, it is to be implemented in different areas separately in accordance with the following procedure:

(a) The funds may be raised by the Central or Provincial Government. With the completion of projects, lands are to be distributed to farmers and fishermen in accordance with the land-to-the-tiller principle.

(b) Funds for development of new tidal lands may be raised either by the Vocational Assistance Commission for Retired Servicemen for resettlement of former armed forces personnel or by the Taiwan Sugar Corporation for increased sugar production. However, the land should be sold to owner-farmers at an appropriate time in accordance with the regulations governing sale of public farm lands.

(c) Chinese and foreign land reclamation organizations approved by the Government may invest in development of tidal lands. However, once construction is completed, the land should be distributed to farmers and fishermen in accordance with the land-to-the-tiller principle. Profit from capital invested is legitimate but may not include the right of landownership.

3. Sale of tidal land and management: When construction work—such as dams for flood control, windbreaks, drainage, roads, and salt fields—have been completed, the land should be sold to owner-farmers or independent fishermen according to the following order of priority:

(a) Farmers and fishermen who use tidal lands and need more land as a means of livelihood (including fishermen who are engaged in oyster culture).

(b) Farmers, fishermen, and salt workers of the district, township, county or municipality who need land.

(c) Persons who need land and have farming experience and ability.

The purchaser of tidal land acquires ownership and should pay the prescribed price by installments and the land tax. He cannot transfer title to another person before he has paid in full.

Competent government authorities should regularly give guidance for the maintenance and management of construction, improvements, and farm management until farmers can take care of themselves and carry out cooperative operations and mechanized farming to increase their income and attain maximum utilization of land.

4. Period of development of tidal land: Tidal lands available for development are estimated at 44,000 hectares (108,727 acres). The average amount of money needed for development of one hectare (2.47 acres) is estimated to be NT$70,000 and the total about NT$3,080 million. The period for the completion of the development is 15 years. Thus, the fund required each year is over NT$200 million. The funds may be raised in the following ways:

(a) The central and local governments may budget funds annually, if their financial resources permit.

(b) Investment from the Land Bank of Taiwan.

(c) Joint or individual investments by public or private banks, or by public or private enterprises, with approval of the Government.

(d) Issuance of bonds by the Government.

(e) U.S. aid or International Development Fund loans.

These measures already have been put into practice. By the end of November, 1960, development of the Hsinchu tidal experimental area was completed. It was a project of the Vocational Assistance Commission for Retired Servicemen, which began work in 1957. Though the area covers only some 80 hectares (197.6 acres), the test proves it is possible to turn barren coastline into fertile land.

Development of marginal areas is also an effective measure for expanding arable land.

In Taiwan two-thirds of the land is mountainous. As estimated by experts, mountain land totals 2,510,000 hectares (6,202,361 acres), of which about 1,300,000 (3,212,328 acres) are uplands with an elevation of 1,000 meters (3,280 ft.) or less. Of such uplands, more than 500,000 hectares (1,235,530 acres) can be used for agriculture or animal husbandry.

The Taiwan Provincial Government set up a Mountain Agricultural Resources Development Bureau in April, 1961, to develop marginal lands. It is estimated that 300,000 hectares (741,318 acres) can be used as pasture. Grass planted in one hectare (2.47 acres) would be sufficient for feeding three head of cattle and 300,000 hectares would, therefore, feed 900,000 head. If both cattle and sheep were raised, it would be still better. As a matter of fact, the problem of limited arable land is actually one of insufficient food supply. In its broad sense, food is not confined to rice and cereals but includes everything that can be eaten. The rapid development of animal husbandry in Taiwan will be of immense help in solving the scarcity of land.

In addition to the 300,000 hectares (741,318 acres) of marginal land for animal husbandry, there are 200,000 hectares (494,212 acres) which may be utilized for the planting of cereals, fruits, vegetables and herbs for medicinal use. Cereals are the main source of cattle feed. They can, of course, also be used as human food. The increased production of cattle feed will reduce the cost of meat to consumers. This is also one of the ways to better the livelihood of the people. So far as the production of fruits, vegetables and herbs for medicinal use is concerned, the cost is higher than for food production. In recent years, agriculturally advanced countries have ignored this and produced specialized farm products. If nutrition is used as the criterion for food production, then agricultural produce can be divided into three classes: that which lays emphasis on starch is low grade, that which lays equal emphasis on both starch and protein is medium grade, and that which lays emphasis on vitamins is high grade. Japan is developing her agriculture along this line. If an effort is made to use marginal lands for the development of both animal husbandry and vegetable and fruit production, it will contribute to expansion of arable land, raise the quality of produce and provide better nutrition for the people.

Development of marginal and tidal lands holds out a bright prospect for the solution of the problem of limited arable land. It is theoretically sound and practically feasible. If we work hard, success is ensured.

FULL UTILIZATION OF FARM LAND

Need for increased food production in Taiwan is urgent and cannot await the slow process of developing marginal and tidal lands. Besides, there is a limit to land development which cannot be reconciled with the unlimited increase in population. Thus every effort should be made to increase the per unit production on existing farm lands. This is what we call full utilization.

For the full utilization of farm lands, Taiwan has taken many measures which may be summed up as follows:

WATER CONSERVATION

Water and land are equally important in agricultural production. That is why we always speak, in Chinese, of "farm land and water facilities" in one breath.

There are four principal goals for water conservation projects: flood control, irrigation, power generation and water supply. They are all closely related to the development of agriculture. But with the exception of irrigation, by far the most important is flood control.

Taiwan is a mountainous island. Its Central Range extends from north to south with 95 peaks over 3,000 meters (9,843 ft.) high. When mountain torrents rush down from the slopes, it is like "pouring water from the housetop," as the Chinese saying goes. The great damage to life and property caused by mountain floods can be easily imagined. This is why water conservation measures are more urgently needed on Taiwan than in any province of the mainland. In the event of heavy rainfall, Taiwan runs the danger of being flooded. In the event of drought, rivers dry up.

Taiwan has always set much store by flood control. But as its effect on agriculture is negative, it will not be discussed further.

Irrigation projects began when the first settlers from the mainland came to Taiwan. Much was done during the Manchu Dynasty. When the Japanese occupied the island, no effort was

Before land consolidation, farms are carved up like this

Multipurpose dams provide irrigation, flood control, power

Canal carries irrigation water, provides adjacent roadway

Old-style pumps (*above*) have given way to
locally produced mechanical pumps (*below*)

spared to promote irrigation projects in an effort to carry out Japanese policy of "making Taiwan an agricultural region." The important engineering works completed during the period included the Liukung, Tsaokung, Peinan and Chianan Creeks.

According to an investigation made in 1960, Taiwan had 877,740 hectares (2,168,948 acres) of farm land, of which only 335,161 hectares (828,203 acres) were well-irrigated and double-crop paddy fields. The other 542,579 hectares (1,340,745 acres) were either poorly irrigated one-crop paddy fields or dry land. In other words, if the irrigation system could be improved, more than 540,000 hectares (1,334,372 acres) of one-crop paddy fields and dry land could be turned into two-crop paddy. The result would be a sharp rise in food production.

In recent years, water conservation projects in Taiwan have been following two main directions. One is the construction of engineering works with multiple purposes. The Akungtien, Tapu, Shihmen and Tachien reservoirs combine such features as flood control, irrigation, power generation and water supply. They are as economical as they are intelligent and are generally regarded as the most progressive projects for water conservation. Take for example, the Shihmen Reservoir, construction of which will be completed soon. It will irrigate more than 21,000 hectares (51,-892 acres) and improve an area totaling more than 75,000 hectares (185,330 acres). The other approach to conservation is through the digging of deep wells. The Taiwan Sugar Corporation began to dig such wells in 1950 to irrigate sugar cane fields and has been quite successful. The Taiwan Provincial Government drew up a five-year project calling for the digging of 1,600 wells. When completed, it will supply irrigation water to 78,000 hectares (192,743 acres) of paddy fields and improve the irrigation system for more than 170,000 hectares (420,080 acres) of paddy. Crop output will increase by 246,000 metric tons (271,168 short tons).

In four or five years, irrigation facilities will be available throughout the province. By then, there will be no fields entirely dependent upon rainfall and the people will no longer look exclusively to Heaven for bread and butter. Human efforts will have triumphed over the forces of nature.

LAND REPLOTTING AND CONSOLIDATION

China is a country of small-scale farming. Farm plots are fragmentary and irregular. This is the situation in all provinces of the mainland, and even more so in Taiwan. Of 22 counties and municipalities (including the Yangmingshan Administration) in Taiwan, only ten have an average area of between one and two *chia* (between 2.3967 and 4.7934 acres) of farm land for each family. In the other 12, the average area of farm land per family is under one *chia* (2.3967 acres). Big farms are almost non-existent, and most are so small that they are unsuitable for large-scale cultivation. Much space has to be set aside as paths at the expense of arable land, thereby causing difficulty in management and cultivation and wasting time, labor and money. This state of affairs is obviously contrary to the principle of economy. The Joint Commission for Rural Rehabilitation made a survey of 16 districts and townships in 1952 and found that an owner-farmer had an average of 1.1 hectares (2.718 acres) of land fragmented into 14 tiny plots, and that a tenant-farmer had less than one hectare of land divided into nine tiny pieces. Though the survey was made by the sampling method, it is illustrative of the fragmentary nature of farm lands in China as a whole.

To assure economical and rational utilization of land and to remedy the fragmentation of agricultural holdings, a program for the replotting and consolidation of farm lands has been proposed. It is aimed at drawing up new boundary lines by scientific methods so that the fragmentary plots will take on an entirely new shape and so that their cultivation will be economical and convenient. However, in cutting up certain pieces of land and combining them with other pieces, or in exchanging one piece for another, there must be strict fairness and impartiality. This is a very difficult task and must be carefully planned before it is carried out.

Taiwan has effected several small-scale programs of land consolidation with fairly good results. That in the Tachia area,

Farmland consolidation will reduce wasted acreage

Consolidated paddies are more accessible to irrigation

Tractors and power-tillers are widely utilized

Tainan County, and that in the rehabilitated areas affected by the flood of August 7, 1959, are examples. These programs have achieved the following generally recognized results:

(1)   Proportionally, there is an increase in the planting by seven per cent.

(2)   By doubling the size of farm plots, 88 per cent of landowners have their lands concentrated in one place and 11 per cent have their lands concentrated in two places.

(3)   The area of farm land adjacent to paths and roads has increased from 19 to 95 per cent.

(4)   Lands directly irrigated have increased from 18 to 96 per cent. In fact the whole area is under an irrigation system. Lands coming under direct drainage have increased from 17 to 98 per cent.

(5)   There is an estimated increase of 34 per cent in agricultural output.

Such are the benefits of the land consolidation program that if it can be carried out on a large scale, it will be tantamount to increasing arable lands by a third.

Land consolidation differs somewhat from place to place according to the points of emphasis. Generally speaking, it includes the following features:

(1)   To change the shape of farm plots, to reduce their number, to economize in use of land on the sides of farm plots, and to reclaim land occupied by unused ditches and paths.

(2)   To consolidate the scattered landholdings of one and the same owner and do away with fragmentation of farm plots so as to expand the area of farm land and facilitate cultivation and management.

(3)   To readjust water supply and drainage and promote efficiency of irrigation.

(4)   To level lands by filling and to improve the soil through the application of chemical and organic fertilizers.

(5)   To improve the road system in such a way as to facilitate

communications and the transportation of agricultural products and fertilizers.

(6) To prescribe shapes for farm plots and standard areas of unit farms so as to facilitate work and the use of machinery.

(7) To design farm houses and the layout of farms so as to economize in the use of land for roads.

The effort involved is tremendous and these tasks cannot be accomplished within a short period. The Taiwan Provincial Government has made a preliminary survey of the lands to be replotted and consolidated. A recheck is now under way for the 300,000 hectares (741,318 acres) earmarked for consolidation. It is estimated that the expense for the whole program will be more than NT$880,000,000 and ten years will be required. Funds for administrative expenses, large-scale water conservation projects and road networks will come from the Government. Those for improvement of the land and for agricultural development will be provided by the farmers. Those for construction of small-scale irrigation and drainage projects will be shared by Government and farmers. Funds from farmers will be their own or loans from land banks.

MECHANIZED FARMING

In his lectures on the Principle of People's Livelihood, Dr. Sun Yat-sen said: "For thousands of years, China has farmed entirely with man power and has never used machinery. If we should introduce farming machinery, we could at least double China's agricultural production and we could reduce the cost of production to one tenth or one hundredth of what it is now. If China with human labor can support four hundred millions, she should with machines produce enough for eight hundred millions." In his letter to Li Hung-chang, he said: "How can labor be saved without the use of machines? How can work be done with dispatch without mechanical appliances? That is why agricultural implements are so important." The advantages of mechanized farming are many and Dr. Sun Yat-sen mentioned them several decades ago. It is a pity that even now farming in our country remains largely in the stage of human labor.

According to an investigation presuming draft animals as the chief motive force in farming, Taiwan still needs more than 100,000 head of draft cattle. Let us assume that one small power tiller can take the place of three head of draft cattle. Then the whole province requires from thirty to forty thousand power tillers. Experiments made in recent years show that one power tiller can cultivate 2.5 *chia* (5.9918 acres) of paddy fields each crop season and increase the annual rice output by 2,700 kg. (5,953 lbs.). On the basis of this figure, 30,000 power tillers would raise rice production by 80,000 metric tons (88,184 short tons) a year. If mechanized farming is applied to all the lands in Taiwan, the total increase in rice output would be immense.

When Dr. Sun Yat-sen said that mechanized farming would double the results of production, he was referring to the use of machines for land reclamation, irrigation and other farm work. So far as unit production is concerned, with conditions the same in other respects, the difference between mechanized farming and farming by man or man and animal cannot be as great as that. However, in terms of cost, the difference between the two is tremendous. Mechanized farming saves both labor and time, and these are money. If this method of farming can be promoted, the following results can be obtained:

(1) With greatly increased income, farmers can devote part of it to improvements. They may also invest in industry or business, or spend more in purchases which will help boost trade and industry.

(2) Farmers will have more time to spare for non-farming activities or recreation, thereby bringing about social progress and raising the cultural level.

(3) The agricultural population will be reduced and the manpower thus released can be channeled into other enterprises.

Promotion of mechanized farming in Taiwan, will also accelerate the process of industrialization through the increased purchasing power of farmers and decrease of the agricultural population. Taiwan already has 3,600 power tillers. The industry engaged in the production of agricultural machinery is expanding. The time when mechanized farming becomes general is not far distant.

SCIENTIFIC FARMING

In his lectures on the Principle of People's Livelihood, Dr. Sun Yat-sen, in pointing out the important relations between science and farming, had this to say: "To apply fertilizers to the land, we must study science and manufacture fertilizers by chemical methods." The characteristic feature of modern civilization is science. Measures for water conservation, mechanized farming, and land consolidation cannot be carried out without science. However, the greatest and most obvious contributions to agriculture by science are these three:

(1) Use of chemical fertilizers: The cultivation of land requires fertilizer. This has been known for thousands of years. But the use of chemical fertilizer for the purpose is something new. Fertilizers used in China have been principally manure, compost, green manure, and human feces and urine, which are called natural fertilizers. The contents of natural fertilizers are rather limited and cannot meet the needs of agricultural production. Compared with chemical fertilizers, they are far less efficient. It is generally estimated that the application of a suitable amount of chemical fertilizers can raise production at least by 20 per cent and under especially favorable conditions, by 40 per cent.

The amount of chemical fertilizers needed in Taiwan annually is estimated at more than 700,000 metric tons (771,617 short tons), only two-fifths of which is produced locally. The shortage is made good partly by compost and green manure but chiefly by imported fertilizers, amounting to more than 300,000 metric tons (330,693 short tons) valued at US$20 million. Taiwan for years has had an unfavorable balance of trade which has been made up by U.S. aid, and fertilizer is a major contributor to this weakness in the international balance of payments.

The Second Four-Year Economic Reconstruction Plan, which

began in 1960, envisages progress toward self-sufficiency in fertilizers. When sufficiency is attained, there should be an increase in food production.

Fertilizer supply also is closely connected with the food policy of the province. In the past ten years or so, the rise of commodity prices has been slight, and this must be chiefly attributed to stability in the price of rice. A stable rice price indicates that food policy has been largely correct. The basic feature of that policy is the barter of fertilizers for rice at fixed ratios.

When the plan to barter fertilizers for rice was proposed, it won very little support and U.S. aid agencies were strongly opposed. However, the author stood by this proposal and did everything he could to carry it out. The proposal was finally accepted. The author's reasons were threefold:

(a)   Free sale and purchase of fertilizers would force farmers to accept usurious loans and expose them to exploitation. Also, it would be difficult to obtain fertilizers at precisely the time when they were most needed.

(b)   Purchase of fertilizers by farmers and purchase of foodstuffs by the Government to be stored for emergency use inevitably would increase the issuance and circulation of currency, thus causing inflation.

(c)   It would be best for farmers to keep only enough food for their own needs and to concentrate all surplus rice in the hands of the Government. This would make certain the rice was stored properly and cut down on storage loss. With huge quantities of rice in the hands of the Government, there would be no danger of food shortage for the armed forces or the people. In this way the historic dilemma between the harmful effects of cheap rice and those of expensive rice, as reflected in the ancient Chinese saying, "Cheap rice is detrimental to the farmer and dear rice to the people," could be eliminated and the whole economy stabilized.

(2)   Pest control: Disease and insects are the most formidable enemies of farm crops. In the past they were considered natural calamities over which farmers had little control.

From the scientific point of view, however, such losses are a result of human failure. Disease and pests can be brought under effective control.

Taiwan has made progress in pest control and losses have declined. However, pests still destroyed 13 per cent of crop production in 1960 for a loss of more than NT$1,500 million. If additional efforts were made, we could have what amounted to a 13 per cent increase in agricultural production.

The work of controlling pests is being carried out on two fronts. New kinds of insecticide are being researched, manufactured, and supplied to farmers as needed. Meanwhile, personnel are being trained and organized for pest prevention and control. The estimated number of 40 million field rats in the province consume about 200,000 metric tons (220,462 short tons) of foodstuffs annually. Elimination of rats would increase human food resources by the same amount.

(3) Variety improvement: All farm crops of today have evolved from wild plants through a gradual process of selection and variation. Based on this fact, variety improvement has become one of the most important objectives of agricultural scientists.

The variety improvement movement in China can be traced to the beginning of the Chinese Republic. The first improved crop was seedless cotton. The result was highly satisfactory, with an increase of 187.5 kg. per hectare (167.3 lbs. per acre).

Variety improvement is intricate scientific work and calls for long years of research and experiment. But once an experiment is successful, it will bring boundless benefits to all.

The Taiwan Provincial Agricultural Experiment Station has achieved important results in the improvement of rice varieties, among which "Chia Nung No. 242" is most noteworthy. It produces 11,000 kg. per hectare (9,814 lbs. per acre) in two crops a year, or 2,000 kg. (4,409.24 lbs.) more than ordinary rice varieties. Furthermore, it is immune to rice blast. If this new variety were cultivated throughout the province, production could be increased by 20 per cent. Total Taiwan production in 1960 was more than 1,900,000 metric tons (2,094,389 short tons), and 20 per cent of that would be 380,000 metric tons (418,878 short tons). Total farm land in the same year was more than 870,000 hectares (2,149,822 acres). Calculated on the basis of two metric tons of rice production per hectare (0.8922 short tons of rice production per acre), the increased output resulting from the new variety would be equal to a gain of 190,000 hectares (469,501.4 acres) in arable land.

The double problem of limited area and dense population can be solved only by full utilization of land. Of the many methods for such utilization, variety improvement offers the best hope. Though population pressure may never cease, neither can there be an end to variety improvement. If the introduction of "Chia Nung No. 242" today has helped increase rice production by one-fifth, who can say that another new variety may not boost output by 50 per cent? Only science can solve problems which have seemed to be insoluble.

PROMOTION OF SELF-GOVERNING
SPIRIT AMONG FARMERS

Everybody strives for "self-interest," which is a sin only when it is promoted at the expense of others. The interests of farmers are identical. With the elimination of exploitation by landlords, there is no reason why farmers should not cooperate with one another closely. For these reasons, self-governing bodies organized by farmers themselves and devoted to the promotion of their own interests will be more efficient than government bureaucracies. This is why Rent Reduction Committees and Farm Tenancy Committees were set up at the time of land reform. Additionally, farmers' and irrigation associations have contributed much to land utilization and efficient production.

There were farmers' associations in the days of the Japanese occupation, but they were used by the Japanese authorities for purposes of control. With the retrocession of Taiwan to the Republic of China, they became organizations of the local gentry and landlords. Following their reorganization in 1949, it was provided that responsible officers should be elected by the farmers themselves, and that one-third of the members of boards of directors and supervisors and also of delegates to the members' representative congress must be tenant farmers. The associations went through another reorganization in 1952 and the new regulations contained the following points:

(1)   Members of a farmers' association are limited to those engaged in land cultivation, with more than one-half of total income earned from farming, or who are carrying on agricultural improvements.

(2)   Those who cannot meet these qualifications may be listed as honorary members.

(3)   Members of the association have the right of election and the right of being elected, while honorary members have no right of election or of being elected to any office except that of supervisor. The number of supervisors elected from among honorary members may not exceed one-third of all supervisors.

(4)   More than two-thirds of the delegates to the members' representative congress must be owner-farmers, tenant farmers and farm hands.

(5)   Members of the boards of directors and supervisors have general authority and the executive secretary has executive power. Authority and executive power are thus vested in different hands. It is the principal function of the farmers' association to guide members in increasing production. It takes charge of rice and wheat storage and processing, distribution of fertilizers and cattle feed, increased production of self-supporting fertilizer, pest control, improvement of agricultural implements, promotion of agricultural by-products, breeding demonstrations, and improvement of livestock. It also acts as the district and township treasury, takes over the functions of a cooperative bank, and extends loans and accepts deposits. Thus all matters relating to rural economy, production and finance are centered in the farmers' association.

Farmers' associations are organized on three levels: one on the provincial level, 22 on the county and municipal level and 317 on the district and township level. At the base, they are composed of about 5,000 small agricultural units. Organized

Hogs are raised for export as well as local sale (*right*). Livestock population is growing; milk is in demand (*below*)

Farmers' association provide knowhow for increased productio

Cooperative credit ends high-interest evil of moneylenders

by villages and districts, these units are responsible for promoting fellowship, giving technical guidance and offering direct services. Most foreign visitors have been deeply impressed by the farmers' associations. In September, 1958, a Vietnamese agricultural group came to Taiwan and praised their organization and activities highly. After return to Vietnam, the group encouraged Vietnamese farmers to organize associations in the Chinese pattern.

Irrigation associations also date to the period of Japanese administration. Of both official and private character, they had given rise to many abuses and had been a disappointment to the people. It was not until the promulgation by the Cabinet of a set of "Measures for Improving Irrigation Associations in Taiwan Province" in September, 1955, that the Provincial Government took steps to reorganize the associations. The important points of reform included the following:

(1) Defining the nature of an irrigation association:
    (a) As a local self-governing body.
    (b) As a public juristic person.

(2) Readjustment of areas: Under the original setup, there were many small units, each of which had a small area under its jurisdiction. Authority was not unified. By way of improvement, the areas were reorganized on the basis of the three principles:
    (a) If the original area covered more than one county or municipality, an irrigation association would be organized according to the original area whenever possible.
    (b) If feasible, only one irrigation association would be organized in an area irrigated by one water system.
    (c) In principle, only one small-scale irrigation associa-ed in each county or municipality.

(3) Strengthening organization: To democratize the irriga-tion associations, both owners and users of farm land were qualifi-ed for membership.

The internal organization of the association was based on a system under which authority and executive power were vested in separate hands. The Members' Representative Congress composed mainly of farmers was the organ of supreme authority. Over two-thirds of the delegates to the congress had to be actual tillers of land.

(4) Systematization:

(a) Strengthening the system of guidance and supervision.

(b) Fixing standards for membership dues so as to be fair and reasonable to all.

(c) Division of engineering responsibilities.

(d) Setting up personnel and accounting systems.

The reform was completed by the end of 1956. Since then the work of the irrigation associations has made remarkable progress. Following is a summary of the results obtained:

(1) Development of a democratic and self-governing spirit: Of the 1,426 delegates elected in the province, 1,121 are tillers of land. Of the 240 members of Advisory Committee elected in the province, 137 are tillers of land. Thus the associations have become self-governing bodies in fact as well as name.

(2) Readjustment of water sources: By making full use of water sources and reducing the number of disputes arising out of water distribution, farm lands that formerly suffered from shortages are now well irrigated. Incidents involving disruptions of water supply have been reduced by 80 or 90 per cent. In Hukow which became part of the Taoyuan Irrigation Association, the area of paddy fields has been increased from 2,900 hectares (7,166 acres) to more than 4,700 hectares (11,614 acres) with resulting gain of more than 13,000,000 kg. (28,660,000 lbs.) in rice production.

(3) Extension of the rotational irrigation system: The rotational irrigation system has the advantage of economizing water in the irrigation of a larger area. According to estimates for a four-year rotational irrigation project, with the application of rotational irrigation to about 116,700 hectares (288,373 acres) of land, the water saved each year would be sufficient to convert 10,000 hectares (24,710.6 acres) of dry land into two-crop paddy fields, as well as supplying water to another 10,000 hectares of irrigated land which had suffered from shortage of water. This should lead to additional production of 60,000 metric tons

(66,138.6 short tons) of unhulled rice every year.

(4) Other measures for land improvement: Besides undertaking such tasks as irrigation and drainage, the irrigation associations devote themselves to forestation, construction of windbreaks, building of dams for flood control, and soil conservation.

CHAPTER 6

COMPARISON OF TAIWAN LAND REFORM WITH COMMUNIST 'LAND REFORM'

HISTORICAL CHANGES IN CHINESE COMMUNIST 'LAND REFORM'

BEING dedicated to Soviet Russian Communism, the Chinese Communists base their "land reform" on the views of Karl Marx and his successors. Marx regarded the private ownership of land as the foundation of capitalism and as the principal cause for the decline of the village economy. As private landowner-ship stimulated the growth of class consciousness and obstructed the development of agriculture, he wanted to abolish it and nationalize all land. The "Communist Manifesto" calls for the adoption of the following measures: (1) "Abolition of property in land and application of all rents of land to public purposes." (2) "The bringing into cultivation of waste lands, and the improve-ment of the soil generally in accordance with a common plan." (3) "Establishment of industrial armies, especially for agriculture." (4) "Combination of agriculture with manufacturing industries;

gradual abolition of the distinction between town and country by a more equable distribution of the population over the country." Marx and Engels regarded confiscation as a means to the nationalization of land which would deal a merciless blow to the landlords and win the support of the rural proletariat. Lenin also addressed himself to the task of securing the support of agricultural laborers. As Stalin has pointed out in his "Foundations of Leninism": " . . . indifference towards so important a question as the peasant question . . . is the reverse side of the repudiation of the dictatorship of the proletariat, it is an unmistakable sign of downright betrayal of Marxism." He thinks of the peasant question as "the question of the ally of the proletariat in its struggle for power."

It is clear that the Communists set much store by the power of peasants and that the peasant problem is only an incidental one in the dictatorship of the proletariat. They work night and day to stir up a "peasants' armed rebellion." They make use of the peasant problem to fan up class hatred to facilitate their own capture of political power. The Chinese Communists are heirs to this Marxist-Leninist legacy. Their "land reform" is merely a means for the seizure of political power.

LAND REFORM AND AGRICULTURAL
COLLECTIVIZATION IN THE EARLY FIFTIES

Before they overran the mainland, the Chinese Communists had publicly announced in the period from 1928 to 1947 a series of measures entitled "Land Program," "Land Law," "Land Law of the Chinese Soviet Republic," and "General Outline of the Land Law." Following their occupation of the mainland, they promulgated the "Land Reform Law" in 1950. The documents were drawn up to meet their needs and in the light of the objective situation. They may be different in form, but the purpose has always remained the same: to mobilize the peasants to serve as Communist tools to achieve the double objective of capturing political power for the Communists and then of consolidating their rule.

From the time of the Nanchang Uprising in 1927, the Chinese Communists have used "land reform" to induce the peasants to take part in armed rebellion.   Following the victorious conclusion of the War of Resistance against Japan, they used land reform and land redistribution to induce the peasants to join the rebellion against the Chinese Government.   Having gained full control over the mainland in 1949, they carried out nationwide land reform beginning in June, 1950.   As a result of liquidations and struggles, 1,200,000 of our brethren were slaughtered and more than 20 million were either driven from their homes or sent to concentration camps in the name of "reform through labor."

Beginning in February, 1952, the Chinese Communists undertook to carry out their so-called agricultural collectivization.   This first took the form of labor mutual-aid teams and then of primary production cooperatives, which the peasants were called upon to join by offering their land as shares so that all lands might come under unified management.   The next step was the creation of higher production cooperatives in which the most important capital for production (i.e., land), instead of being privately owned by the members, was transformed into capital owned by the cooperatives as a whole.   Following the transformation of private landownership into cooperative ownership, part of the harvest would be set aside as reserves and part as a welfare fund.   The remainder would be distributed to the peasant members in kind or in cash as reward for their labor.   Up to the end of June, 1957, there were 750,000 agricultural production cooperatives with 117 million farm families, or 96.8 per cent of all the farm families in the country.

In forcing the broad masses of the farming population to join cooperatives, the Communists resorted to deception, intimidation, and inducements which were employed in combination to strengthen one another; but of these three methods, intimidation was their principal weapon.

The basic purpose of agricultural collectivization was, negatively, to bring about the gradual extinction of private property and the economy of private enterprise so as to prevent the revival of capitalism; and, positively, to realize socialism in agriculture and thus to pave the way for the establishment of a Communist economy based on total slavery. Besides, there were two other urgent and realistic reasons for it:

(1) To strengthen totalitarian rule: The inhuman system which the Communists set up would inevitably give rise to strong opposition, especially to resistance by people in the rural areas. To forestall such resistance, it was necessary for the Communists to tighten their control in the villages. "Agricultural collectivization" was aimed at placing the 500 million unorganized people of the rural population under a rigid organization and merging over 100 million independent farms into more than 700,000 cooperatives from which the labor, production, and life of farmers could not be separated. Under such circumstances, the agricultural cooperative was at once the basic unit of the rural economy and the basic center of rural administration. In this basic unit, in which the party organization played an active part, every movement of the farmer was closely watched. This contributed immensely to the consolidation of totalitarian rule.

(2) To step up preparations for war: Aggressive expansionism is one of the basic characteristics of Communism. In preparing for war, "agricultural collectivization" has an important task to perform. First, it accumulates capital for heavy industry and national defense, extracting it from farmers. Secondly, it lays the foundation for mobilization. In wartime, manpower includes both armed personnel and laborers. Manpower and food supply needs are so large that it would be difficult to meet them if rural areas were poorly organized. Following agricultural collectivization, 500 million farmers and their output come under control of the cooperatives. No evasion is possible. Agricultural collectivization may seem to be economic in nature but also has political and military significance.

Farm products and by-products produced in a cooperative are subject to exploitation in the form of taxes and compulsory sales at prices fixed by the Communist authorities. Also to be deducted are costs of production, reserves and welfare. Only what is left can be apportioned to members as a reward for labor. For toil day in and day out the year round, farmers can receive only a third of the total income. The agricultural tax and the differential prices fixed for purchase account for another third. The remaining third includes the cost of production, free labor service, welfare funds, preferential treatment for dependents of military personnel and so on. Farmers have never suffered so much and been exploited to such an extent since the beginning of agriculture in China.

SETTING UP PEOPLE'S COMMUNES

After establishment of cooperatives, the Communists went a step further to introduce the so-called "people's commune" system in April, 1958. At first they merged the cooperatives devoted to production, supply and marketing, credit, handicrafts and transportation. This was followed by amalgamation of the Village People's Committee with the agricultural cooperative, thus carrying out the so-called "integration of village and cooperative system." Members of the commune were organized into production corps, production companies, and production gangs and were required to work and receive training at one and the same time. This is what the Communists call "collectivization of production," "militarization of labor," and "organization of the people like an army." Under such tyrannical rule, the life of the people became still more intolerable.

The people's communes first were set up in Honan on a trial basis. Liaoning was the next province. By July, 1958, communes were operating in all provinces of the mainland. On August 29 of the same year, the Central Committee of the Chinese Communist Party passed a "Resolution on the Establishment of People's Communes in Rural Areas." This marked the high water mark of the commune system.

According to statistics compiled by the Chinese Communist

Department of Rural Works, by the end of September, 1958, there were 23,397 communes established in rural areas throughout the mainland with 90.4 per cent of all farming families participating in them. Each commune had an average of 4,797 families. Statistics of ten provinces showed that among 5,538 communes, 3,343 had fewer than 5,000 families each, 1,628 had from 5,000 to 10,000 families each, 516 had from 10,000 to 20,000 families each, and 51 had over 20,000 families each. According to the statistics of 13 provinces, 94 communes were established in counties with one commune each or in counties with joint communes.

The *People's Daily* reported on November 10, 1958, that up to October 20 of that year, the mainland had 26,578 communes with 127 million farming families as members. The first stage of the commune system had been completed in a campaign a hundred times more cruel and inhuman than agricultural collectivization.

Basing his thinking on Lenin's theory of the "withering of the state," Mao Tse-tung regards the commune system as the form of organization best suited to hastening of socialist construction and the phase of Communism. The development from agricultural cooperative to the people's communes, said Mao, "is a natural tendency of the historical process in China." As a matter of fact, the idea is the same as that of the Paris Commune of 1871 and the so-called "advanced stage of Communism" which was tried unsuccessfully in Soviet Russia. It was also the same as the "syndicate" and "commune" of the Bolsheviks. The Chinese Communists have introduced it on the mainland in utter disregard of its disastrous effects on the people.

The characteristics of the commune and the purposes of its implementation may be summarized as follows:

CHARACTERISTICS OF THE PEOPLE'S COMMUNE:

(a) Integration of village and the commune: According to the principle announced by the Chinese Communists for the establishment of the commune, it was to be an organization formed through the integration of the agricultural production co-operative and the Village People's Committee. What once had been an economic productive unit was now turned into a basic unit with multiple purposes including trade, agriculture, commerce, education, and military affairs. All productive materials and labor were placed at the disposal of the commune. Such matters as industry, agriculture, forestry, animal husbandry, side jobs, public health, and communications were put under the unified management of the commune so as to facilitate overall control by the Communists.

(b) Confiscation of private property: During the stage of agricultural cooperatives, farmers were allowed to keep a portion of their land for themselves to be used for raising domestic animals and poultry. They thus could obtain subsidiary food and extra income. Also retained by farmers as private property were houses and fruit and other trees. But with the introduction of the people's commune system, the land which farmers had retained was confiscated and even their houses, trees, animals and fowls became public property.

(c) Collective living: Public mess halls and nurseries were established and sewing teams organized all over the country. Farmers no longer had to cook their own meals, children could now be sent to nurseries, and clothes were made by the sewing teams. All aspects of the farmers' life were now collectivized.

(d) Farmers treated like workers: Wage and food ration systems were applied to the farmers. Wages were classified into different grades on the basis of the complexity or simplicity of work, of the physical strength or weakness of the individual worker, of the high or low quality of his skill, and of his attitude toward his work. Food rations were supplied in accordance with criteria fixed by the Communists. Foodstuffs produced by the farmers were confiscated.

(e) Organization of the people like an army: All able-bodied farmers, men and women, were required to join the so-called "labor army of workers, peasants, and soldiers" which was established throughout the country. They were organized according to age into reserve workers to be sent by rotation to mines, communication enterprises, or the sites of large-scale reservoirs operated by government units above the county level. According to a report of August, 1958, there was in Shansi province a labor army of workers, peasants, and soldiers more than 3,660,000 strong, ranging in age from 15 to 55. All able-bodied men from 16 to 40 had to join the militia to engage in productive work in time of peace and were subject to army draft in wartime.

PURPOSES IN THE ESTABLISHMENT OF THE PEOPLE'S COMMUNES:

(a) To enslave and exercise tighter control over the people: With the integration of village and commune into one, the administrative unit and productive unit became identical. In this way, the village chief was concurrently the commune chief; the secretary of the "village party committee" was concurrently secretary of the "commune party committee"; the "village people's delegates conference" became identical with the "commune representatives"; and the "village people's committee" identical with the "commune management committee." Agricultural production was placed under the direct control and disposal of the state. The fruits of production and the whole of the labor force came into the hands of the Communists. Farmers were reduced to the status of slavery.

(b) To exploit the labor of the peasants: From the winter of 1957 to the spring of 1958, the Communists mobilized 100 million farmers to take part in the construction of large-scale water conservation works. Again from the winter of 1958 to the spring of 1959, the amount of work done in water conservation construction doubled that of the previous year. As the male labor force on the mainland was about 100 million strong, the only way to have additional labor to exploit was to set up communes so that the female half of the rural population could also be mobilized for production. This was another instance of the cruelty with which the Communists exploited labor.

(c) Disruption of the family system: Following establishment of public mess halls, nurseries, and sewing teams, families of farmers fell apart. During the stage of agricultural collectivization, farmers were deprived of what they had produced, but farm families still constituted the basic units of production and distribution. So long as farm families remained, their interests were opposed to those of the cooperative. In the view of the Communists, the system of agricultural collectivization could never be strengthened as long as the conception of "family" had a strong hold on the minds of the farmers. So they tried by every means to break up the family organization, to cut off all family relationships so as to transform every individual into an isolated entity, a higher type of animal knowing only labor.

(d) To make everybody a soldier: All able-bodied men and retired military personnel in the communes were organized into militia. They were given regular military training and required to take up such duties as were assigned to them. This was the so-called "organization of the people like an army" and was a means to make everybody a soldier. According to Communist reports, the mainland people from 16 to 30 years of age were organized into field armies. Women from 16 to 50 were organized into field armies or local armies. Those below 15 years of age and above 50 were organized into a militia supply service. Being trained on the spot and supplied on the spot, all people thus were made into soldiers. This shows the essentially bellicose nature of Chinese Communism.

There was another reason for establishment of communes. Some party members and cadres had over the years become a new class of rich farmers in rural areas and had taken the place of the landlords of old. The strongest opposition against "agricultural collectivization" in rural areas had come from these party members and cadres. Establishment of the communes was the only effective measure to eradicate this new class.

From August, 1958, the Communists began to confiscate all private houses in cities and towns under the guise of "leasing by the state." All handicraft cooperatives were forced to become state-operated factories. In this way the traditional social organization based on individual operation which had existed for thousands of years was completely wiped out and a slave society was established under absolute control of the Communist Party.

COMMUNIST REACTION TO
THE COMMUNE SYSTEM

Establishment of the communes was in reality the final step in building up the Chinese Communist war economy. The Soviet Union had tried a similar system, had failed, and was forced back to the so-called "collective farms." But less than two years after the establishment of collective farms on the mainland and at a time when popular discontent with collectivization was mounting, the Chinese Communists decided to introduce the hateful commune system in utter disregard for changes in the five hundred million people on the mainland. It would certainly lead to the early downfall of the puppet Peiping regime.

The *People's Daily* of Peiping, in a series of articles from September 3 to 5, 1958, had this to say:

"While in the process of being established, the people's commune system did not proceed at all smoothly and aroused deep misgivings and misunderstandings. Many people, when they heard of the commune, sold out all pigs, sheep and fowl they had raised and abandoned themselves to feasting. In discussing the establishment of the communes in some places, comparatively rich peasants expressed dissatisfaction with such an innovation. For example, an old middle peasant by the name of Tsui Chao-fu said: 'What is a commune? It's just another form of exploitation.' "

The *Hopei Daily News* reported on November 15, 1958:

"At the present moment, over 80 per cent of the industrial and commercial circles are opposed to the commune system. Once the name of the commune is mentioned, they conjure up all sorts of things in their minds. Instead of rejoicing over the bright future of Communism, they first think of their own gains or losses or their own personal interests. They are fearful for one reason or another. Their minds are full of contradictory thoughts."

Again, the *People's Daily* confessed on November 19, 1958:

"The people's communes in various places, because of the opposition of farmers to the 'ration system' and 'unified distribution,' were in a state of great confusion and the organization of the communes was loose and shaky." The paper cited the Tung Feng Commune at Yangkiang County, Kwangtung province, as an example and said:

"Not a few farmers in this commune, and even basic level Communist cadres, are opposed to the ration system and maintain that its implementation has resulted in a general diminution of their income.

"Some farmers in Changho County, Hunan province, in their opposition to the commune system, carried out passive sabotage. Wu Liang-cheng and others of Kao Tang Commune went so far as to say: 'After all, everything is gone. Just eat and get some pay, and muddle through. Why should we work hard?' "

Realizing the seriousness of the situation posed by the people's opposition to the commune system, the Communists called a conference at Chengchow in the early part of November, 1958, during which "remedial measures" for the implementation of the commune system were discussed. At the end of the same month, the 6th Plenary Session of the 8th Central Committee of the Chinese Communist Party passed a "resolution on certain problems concerning the people's communes" and decided to "reorganize the communes." The "Central Political Bureau" of the Chinese Communist Party again convened an enlarged meeting at the end of February, 1959. In this so-called second Chengchow Conference, measures for reorganizing the communes

were laid down in detail.   The 8th Plenary Session of the 8th
Central Committee of the Chinese Communist Party, held at
Lushan in August of the same year, again brought up the com-
mune system for discussion.   Within a period of one year, the
Communists called five important conferences to discuss and
revamp the commune system.   This was a measure of the unfavor-
able and serious reaction against the commune system among the
Chinese people.

CRISIS FACING THE CHINESE REDS FOLLOWING THE ESTABLISHMENT OF THE COMMUNES

(1)   Conflict between freedom and slavery: It is human
to love freedom and to have hope.   Freedom is the fountainhead
of all progress and hope is the mainspring of all human endeavor.
With the establishment of the communes, the people were reduced
to the status of serfs or slave laborers with no freedom to speak
of.   When the fruits of their toil were taken away from them,
they no longer had any hope.   Under conditions wherein there
was neither freedom nor hope, the communes became big prisons
whose inmates had to do hard labor.   Having lost all interest in
life, how could the people have any enthusiasm for production or
advancement?   The commune system is basically a kind of collective slavery.   Being contrary to man's desire for freedom, it can
never succeed.   This is indeed the greatest danger posed by the
commune system.

(2)   Decline of agricultural production: For the expansion
of agricultural production, the Chinese Communists had made
certain improvements in water conservation, land reclamation,
adjustment of arable lands, and farm planning.   But whatever
improvements they had made were offset by the establishment of
communes and changes in productive relations.   The year 1955
witnessed a bumper harvest on the mainland.   Yet production
per *mou* (0.1644 acre) was still 7.6 kg. (16.72 lbs.) less than
the pre-war years.   Production per unit of labor was still less.

The chief method upon which the Communists rely for increased production is to intensify the exploitation of both labor

and land.

The exploitation of labor has been discussed. The exploitation of land is achieved by continuously expanding the area of farms on which more than one crop is raised in a year. The average index of the area where more than one crop is raised in a year was 137.1 in 1955. But the supply of chemical fertilizers in 1962 will still be less than 21 catties (27.72 lbs.) of fertilizer for each *mou* (0.1644 acre) of land under cultivation. The natural result is loss of soil fertility. Take 1955, which was a bumper year, and pre-war years for purposes of comparison. With the sole exception of soya beans, total food production in pre-war years (with only 70 per cent of normal production) was about 82.04 per cent of that in 1955. But the pre-war area of lands under cultivation was 78.85 per cent of that in 1955. As to manpower, pre-war agricultural population was 70 per cent of the 1955 agricultural population, and the rate of labor utilization in the pre-war years was at least 30 per cent lower than in 1955. It is obvious that agricultural production on the mainland has been steadily declining.

The Communists force the people to work and look upon the farmers as beasts of burden. The farmers have the function of an animal and not of human beings in the Communist view. A drop in agricultural production on the Communist-dominated mainland therefore cannot be avoided.

(3) Deterioration of the living conditions of farmers: While agricultural production has been on the decline, population has been increasing. With steadily heavier burdens, the farmers face deteriorating living conditions. The mainland is suffering from an acute shortage of staple foodstuffs. The actual shortage after the autumn harvest of 1955 and before the autumn harvest of 1956, as measured by the pre-war standard of consumption, was about 42 million metric tons (46,297,020 short tons) of medium-grade rice. If measured by the post-war standard of food consumption in 1947, a year in which the people's livelihood was low after eight long years of war, there was still a shortage of 24 million metric tons (26,455,440 short tons) of medium-grade rice. In the past few years, the mainland has suffered from

catastrophic natural calamities in the form of floods and droughts, so that the life of the farmers must have deteriorated still further.

The crisis created by the people's communes cannot be overcome. Though the Communists called a series of conferences and made concessions to the farmers, they merely lowered objectives for the communes, and agreed to a longer time to attain these objectives. The basic plan for the communes remains unchanged. This is another way of saying that the contradiction between freedom and slavery can never be reconciled.

DIFFERENCES BETWEEN LAND REFORM IN TAIWAN AND THE COMMUNIST "LAND REFORM"

From the foregoing, it is clear that the land reform in Taiwan and that of the Chinese Communists are entirely different. By way of comparison, the following summary notes the differences with respect to their purposes, the methods used, and results achieved.

PURPOSE OF REFORM

(1)   In Taiwan:

(a)   In order to realize the ideal "of the people" as embodied in the Three Principles of the People, the ownership of farm lands has been gradually turned over to the farmers themselves.

(b)   In order to realize the ideal of "by the people" as embodied in the Three Principles of the People, such tasks as the distribution, utilization, and management of farm land are turned over, as far as feasible, to the farmers in accordance with the spirit of self-government.

(c)   In order to realize the ideal of "for the people" as embodied in the Three Principles of the People, all the income derived from farm production, except part of it to be used for payment of taxes according to law, goes to the farmers.

(2) On the Chinese mainland:

(a) In the name of land nationalization, all land has become the property of the Communist Party.

(b) In the name of production through "cooperation" and "collectivization," the Peiping regime takes over all fruits of production.

(c) In the name of liberating the oppressed farmers, all farmers on the mainland have been turned into productive tools of the Peiping regime.

(d) In the name of "making all people into soldiers," mainland farmers have become tools of war for the Peiping regime.

METHODS OF REFORM

(1) In Taiwan:

(a) Concerning land reform:

1. Implementation of the 37.5% farm rent limitation program.

2. Implementation of sale of public lands.

3. Implementation of the Land-to-the-Tiller Program.

a. Purchase of excess farm land from landlords and payment of compensation to them.

b. Retention by the landlords of a part of their tenanted land in accordance with law.

c. Resale by the government of compulsorily purchased land to its incumbent cultivator.

d. Payment of the purchase price by the farmer-purchaser either in kind or with land bonds by installments spread over a period of ten years.

e. Prior right of purchase of landlords' land by incumbent cultivator and right of asking the Land Bank for loan in making such purchase.

(b) Concerning development and utilization of land:

    1. Development of new tidal lands.
    2. Development of marginal lands.
    3. Promotion of water conservation projects.
    4. Land replotting and consolidation.
    5. Promotion of mechanized farming.
    6. Scientific farming.
    7. Promotion of the farmers' capacity for self-government.

(2) On the Chinese mainland:

(a) Methods used in the earlier stage:

    1. Farmers were forced to engage in struggle and the liquidation of landlords, to create a reign of terror, to divide the lands of landlords, to destroy the families of landlords, and even to demand their heads.

    2. There was unceasing checking and rechecking of the people and their lands in an effort to intensify the class struggle so that poor peasants were raised to the status of middle peasants, middle peasants to the status of rich peasants, and rich peasants to the status of landlords. The end result was that all genuine farmers became objects of liquidation and struggle and ran the risk of having their families broken up and even losing their own lives.

(b) Methods used in the middle stage:

    1. Agricultural collectivization was practiced to force farmers to join collective farms and deprive them of their landownership.

    2. In the name of the "leadership of the Party and Government," full control was exercised over both the cooperatives and the farmers.

    3. In the name of subordinating "individual interest" to "collective interests" and "collective interests" to the "interests of the state," agricultural cooperatives were turned

into tools for the exploitation and enslavement of farmers by the Communists.

(c) Methods used at present:

    1. To carry out the "people's commune" system in order to deprive the people of all their possessions and turn them into "worker ants of an ant colony."

    2. To practice "collective living," "to make all activities partake of the nature of a combat," and "to organize the people like an army" so that the Peiping regime may drive and enslave the people under its domination to do what it wants them to do and turn them into tools of war.

RESULTS ACHIEVED

(1) In Taiwan:

    (a) Production has increased and the rural areas are thriving. Nurtured by agriculture, industry has flourished. Stimulated by industry's need for farm products, agriculture has been making steady progress.

    (b) With the amelioration of their living conditions, farmers have gained a better understanding of the importance to themselves of politics and culture, thereby laying the foundations for a democratic life and self-government and raising the general cultural level of the people.

    (c) Industrial and agricultural development has led to social stability and progress, thereby laying a solid foundation for a counterattack against the Communist-controlled mainland and for national recovery.

(2) On the Chinese mainland:

    (a) Under the rule of Communist tyranny, the people have had nothing for themselves except their physical existence and have lost interest in life.

(b) The so-called "land reform" carried out by the Chinese Communists is really a changing of the farmer's status. Farmers have been transformed into serfs. How can serfs be expected to take any interest in production? That is why agricultural production of the mainland has been on the decline. Besides, natural disasters flow one after another in rapid succession and famine has become a universal phenomenon and more and more serious.

(c) The Communist Party has become a new class with special privileges, and exploits the people for the furtherance of its own interests. To carry out its plans to exploit the people, it has to resort to such ruthless measures as repression, persecution, and mass massacre. Groaning under the weight of this tyrannical rule, the people on the mainland have come to a point at which they are ready to die together with their oppressors.

To summarize briefly, the goal of land reform in Taiwan is to promote the welfare of the people through changes in the land system and increase of land productivity. On the other hand, the so-called "land reform" of the Chinese Communists has as its chief goal the seizure of political power and the consolidation of their rule. "Land reform" has been used as a cloak to cover up their deception, persecution, massacre, and other acts of violence committed by baiting the people with land and entrapping them thereby. No contrast can be sharper than that between the land reform in Taiwan and the so-called "land reform" of the Chinese Communists.

APPENDIX

I. Relevant Laws and Regulations

Explanatory notes:

1. There are many laws and regulations bearing on land reform in Taiwan. These have been collected by other compilers. As it is impossible to be exhaustive, only the more important ones are given in this appendix.

2. As the main objective of land reform is to realize Dr. Sun Yat-sen's land-to-the-tiller ideal, most of the documents in this appendix have to do with that aspect of the land reform program.

3. This appendix has been compiled mainly as a work of reference for other countries that may be interested in land reform. China's experience and practical reforms conceivably could have value in such cases, provided that adaptations are made to suit local conditions.

The Land Law

(Promulgated by the National Government, June 30, 1930; enforced,
March 1, 1936; amended, April 29, 1946)

Part I. General Principles

Chapter I. Definitions and Application

Article 1: The term "land" referred to in this Law shall denote dry land, bodies of water, and natural sources of wealth.

Article 2: Land is hereby classified according to its use into the following types:

Type I. Land used for construction, such as land for dwelling houses, government offices, public buildings, schools, factories, warehouses, parks, amusement centers, clubs, ancestral halls, temples, churches, city walls and battlements, barracks, fortresses, jetties, wharves, air bases, cemeteries, etc.

Type II. Land used for direct production, such as agricultural land, forest land, fisheries, pastures, hunting grounds, lands with mineral deposits, salt fields, sources of water, ponds, etc.

Type III. Land used for communication and water conservancy, such as highways and roads, canals and ditches, waterways, lakes, harbors, bays, coasts, embankments, dikes, etc.

Type IV. Other lands such as deserts, snowy mountains, etc.

Each of the preceding types of land may be subdivided into categories.

Article 3: In the absence of any provision to the contrary, the land offices shall be responsible for the execution of this Law.

Article 4: The term "public land" referred to in this Law shall denote land owned by the State, the Province, the Municipality *(Shih),* the County *(Hsien),* the District *(Hsiang),* or the Township *(Chen).*

Article 5: "Improvement on land" referred to in this Law shall be divided into two different kinds: constructional improvements and agricultural improvements.

Constructional improvements shall denote buildings or construction works affixed to land; agricultural improvements shall denote farm crops and other plants grown on land as well as improvement in irrigation and drainage and in soil.

Article 6: The term "owner-cultivation" referred to in this Law shall mean cultivation done by the landowner himself. Cultivation directly managed by the land-owner for the maintenance of his family shall be regarded as owner-cultivation.

Article 7: The term "land bonds" referred to in this Law shall mean bonds issued by the Land Bank according to Law.

Article 8: The term "absentee landlords" referred to in this Law shall mean landowners of any of the following descriptions:

(1) Landowners who, together with members of their families, have been living for three full years without intermission away from the Municipality or County wherein the land is situated.

(2) Co-owners of land under joint ownership who have all been living for one full year without intermission away from the Municipality or County wherein the land is situated.

(3) Business organizations owning land which have suspended business for one full year without intermission in the Municipality or County wherein the land is situated.

The provisions of the preceding paragraph shall not apply in cases of landowners who have to live away from the Municipality or County wherein the land is situated, to perform military service, to attend school, to carry out public functions, or to escape calamities or commotions.

Article 9: A law governing the application of this Law shall be separately enacted.

Chapter II.   Land Rights

Article 10: All land lying within the territorial limits of the Republic of China shall belong to the Chinese people as a whole. Any part of the land whereof the ownership is lawfully acquired by an individual Chinese shall be private land.

Any land whereof private ownership is extinguished shall be owned by the State.

Article 11: The kinds of rights to be created over land other than ownership shall conform to the provisions of the Civil Code.*

Article 12: Wherever private land becomes part of a lake or navigable waterway by the operation of natural forces, the ownership thereof shall be deemed to have been extinguished.

When any land referred to in the preceding paragraph reverts to its original condition and its original owner produces evidence to substantiate his original ownership, his ownership thereof shall be restored.

Article 13: Where riparian land along lakes or waterways naturally accretes owing to the change of current, the owners of lands adjoining such accretions shall have the preferential right to acquire the ownership thereof, or to use them and enjoy incomes therefrom in accordance with law.

Chapter III. Restrictions on Land Rights

Article 14: Lands of the following descriptions shall not be privately owned:

(1) Lands lying within certain limits of the seacoast.

---

*According to the provisions of Articles 832, 842, 851, 860 and 911 of the Chinese Civil Code, the following five kinds of rights over land other than ownership may be created: superficies, **yungtien,** servitude, mortgage, and **dien.**

By **yungtien** is meant the right permanently to use another person's land for the purpose of cultivation or pasturing by paying a rent therefor (Article 842); the **yungtien**-holder may transfer his right to another person (Article 843), but he may not sublease the land to another person (Article 845).

By **dien** is meant the right to take possession of another person's immovable property and to use it and to enjoy incomes therefrom by paying a price for it (Article 911). The **dien**-holder may transfer the right of **dien** to another person (Article 917) or lease the property to another person under **dien** (Article 915). If the **dien**-obligor fails to redeem it at the original price within two years after the expiration of the contractual period of **dien,** the **dien**-holder shall acquire the ownership of the property under **dien** (Article 923).

(2) Lakes of natural formation that are needed for public use and riparian lands lying within certain limits of the shores thereof.

(3) Navigable waterways and riparian lands lying within certain limits of the banks thereof.

(4) Waterways and lakes within the territorial limits of cities and townships, and riparian lands lying within certain limits of the banks thereof.

(5) Public thoroughfares.

(6) Lands with mineral springs.

(7) Lands where waterfalls pass over.

(8) Sources of water for public use.

(9) Scenic spots and historic remains.

(10) Other lands whereof private ownership is prohibited by law.

Any land referred to in the preceding paragraph whereof private ownership has been acquired may be compulsorily purchased by the Government according to law.

Article 15: Minerals attached to any land shall not become private property, even if private ownership of the said land has been duly acquired.

The minerals referred to in the preceding paragraph shall be limited to those which are specified in the Mining Industry Law.

Article 16: The National Government may prohibit the transfer of ownership, the creation of encumbrance over, or the lease of any private land, if such transfer, encumbrance, or lease is considered to be inconsistent with national policies.

Article 17: Lands of the following descriptions shall not be transferred or leased to aliens, nor may encumbrance on them be created in favor of aliens:

(1) Agricultural lands.

(2) Forest lands.

(3) Fisheries.

(4) Pastures.

(5) Hunting grounds.

(6) Salt fields.

(7) Lands with mineral deposit.

(8) Sources of water.

(9) Lands lying within fortified and military areas and lands adjacent to the national frontiers.

Article 18: Only those aliens may acquire or create rights over land in the Republic of China who are nationals of States that have diplomatic relations with the Republic of China and permit, according either to treaty or to their municipal laws, Chinese nationals to enjoy the same rights in their respective countries.

Article 19: Aliens may lease or purchase land for any one of the following purposes, but the area and location of such land shall be subject to restrictions imposed according to law by the competent Municipal or County Government:

(1) Residences.

(2) Shops and factories.

(3) Churches.

(4) Hospitals.

(5) Schools for the children of aliens.

(6) Diplomatic and consular buildings and office buildings of organizations for the promotion of public welfare.

(7) Cemeteries.

Article 20: In leasing or purchasing land for any one of the purposes specified in the preceding Article, aliens shall submit jointly with the original landowner a written request to the competent Municipal or County Government for approval.

If any change in the purpose, for which the land referred to in the preceding paragraph is used, is to be made according to the provisions of the serveral sections of the preceding Article, or if any transfer of the said land is to be effected, a written request shall be submitted to the competent Municipal or County Government for approval.

All requests duly approved by the Municipal or County Government according to the provisions of the preceding two Articles shall be immediately reported to the Executive Yuan through the regular channels of official communication.

Article 21: Aliens who have, pursuant to relevant laws and ordinances, obtained special permission from the National Government to engage in industrial enterprises may lease or purchase land according to their actual requirements.

The area and location of the land referred to in the preceding paragraph shall be subject to the approval of the competent authorities of the central Government in charge of such enterprises.

Article 22: In leasing or purchasing land according to the provisions of the preceding Article, aliens shall present the permit issued by the competent authorities of the central Government to the local Municipal or County Government for examination, and request its assistance in effecting the lease or purchase; and the results thereof shall be reported by the Municipal or County Government to the Executive Yuan through the regular channels of official communication.

Article 23: Any land leased or purchased by aliens for the use of a specially permitted enterprise shall not be used for any purpose other than the one officially approved, unless the nature of the enterprise itself is allowed to change by special official permission. The said land shall be taken back by the Government at the original price, if the said enterprise suspends business for whatever cause.

Article 24: Aliens who have leased or purchased land and have the lease or purchase duly registered shall enjoy rights and be liable for obligations according to laws and ordinances.

Chapter IV. Public Land

Article 25: All public lands under the jurisdiction of the Provincial, Municipal, or County Government shall not be disposed of, or encumbered, or leased for a period longer than ten years without the consent of the local assembly and the approval of the Executive Yuan.

Article 26: Whenever any governmental organization of whatever level requires the use of public land, it shall consult with the competent Municipal or County Government and shall submit, through the regular channels of official communication, a written request therefor to the Executive Yuan for approval and allocation.

Article 27: Provincial, Municipal and County Governments shall include in their respective budgets all incomes from public lands under their jurisdiction.

Chapter V. Readjustment of Land Rights

Article 28: Provincial Governments or Municipal Governments under the direct jurisdiction of the Executive Yuan may, in the light of local conditions and with due regard to the different categories and the nature of land, prescribe limits on the maximum area of private land which individuals or corporate bodies may own respectively.

The limits on the maximum area of private land prescribed according to the provisions of the preceding paragraph shall be subject to the approval of the Central Land Administration.

Article 29: Wherever limits are prescribed on the area of private land according to the provisions of the preceding Article, the competent County or Municipal Government shall formulate measures requiring that all lands in excess of the prescribed limits shall be set apart and sold within a definite period of time.

All private lands in excess of the prescribed limits that are not set apart and sold according to the provisions of the preceding paragraph may be compulsorily purchased by the competent County or Municipal Government according to the provisions of this Law.

Compensation for the lands compulsorily purchased according to the provisions of the preceding paragraph may, in the light of actual conditions, be paid partly with land bonds.

Article 30: The ownership of private farm land shall be transferred only to such transferees as can cultivate the land themselves after the transfer is effected.

Article 31: The County or Municipal Land Offices may, in the light of local economic conditions and with due regard to the nature of land and the use to which it is put, prescribe minimum units for the different categories of land lying within their jurisdiction and prohibit any subdivision of such units.

The minimum units prescribed according to the provisions of the preceding paragraph shall be subject to the approval of the competent superior authorities.

Article 32: Provincial Governments or Municipal Governments under the direct jurisdiction of the Executive Yuan may set maximum limits to the amount of debts which may be contracted by any owner-cultivator on account of his farm land, and such limits shall be reported to the Central Land Administration for record.

Article 33: Any tenant who has cultivated any leased land continuously for eight full years may request the competent County or Municipal Government to purchase it for him at its statutory value, if the said land is under either of the following conditions:

(1) If the owner of the said land is an absentee landlord.

(2) If the owner of the said land is not an owner-cultivator.

But land owned by old and infirm, orphaned, widowed, or physically disabled persons, or by educational or philanthropic institutions or organizations for the promotion of public welfare, that depend upon incomes from such lands for their support, shall be exempt from being so purchased.

Article 34: Governments of all levels may, upon approval by the Executive Yuan, make compulsory purchase of land for the creation of owner-cultivated farms according to the following order of precedence, and pay for the value of the land with land bonds:

(1) Private uncultivated land.

(2) Land owned by absentee landlords.

(3) That part of the land under tenancy which exceeds the maximum

limits prescribed according to the provisions of Article 28 of this Law.

Article 35: The creation of owner-cultivated farms shall be regulated by separate law.

Part II. Cadastration

Chapter I. General Provisions

Article 36: Unless cadastration has been already completed according to law, it shall be carried out according to the provisions of this Law.

The procedure of cadastration shall be: cadastral survey and land registration.

Article 37: Land registration shall mean the registration of the ownership of, and other rights over, land and constructional improvements thereon.

Article 38: Cadastral survey shall be undertaken before land registration. In localities where cadastral survey has been already completed according to law, the general registration of land shall be immediately undertaken according to the provisions of this Law.

"The general registration of land" referred to in the preceding paragraph shall mean the registration, within a definite period of time, of all lands in a given Municipality or County.

Article 39: Land registration shall be carried out by the competent Municipal or County Land Office, but the general registration of land may, if necessary, be carried out by a land registry set up *ad hoc* in a County or Municipality by the competent Provincial Land Administration.

Article 40: Cadastration shall be carried out with each Municipality or County as an independent unit. Each Municipality or County shall be divided into districts; each district into sections; and each section shall comprise a number of plots, to each of which a serial number shall be given.

Article 41: Lands pertaining to Types III and IV according to the classification of Article 2 of this Law shall be given no serial numbers and be exempted from registration.

Article 42: The general registration of land may be carried out by districts to be known as "registration districts."

The registration districts referred to in the preceding paragraph shall not be smaller than an urban district in the case of Municipalities, or a District or Township in the case of Counties.

Article 43: Registrations duly made according to this Law shall have conclusive validity.

Chapter II. Cadastral Survey

Article 44: Cadastral survey shall be carried out according to the following steps:

(1) Triangulation.

(2) Surveying of supplementary control points.

(3) Surveying of individual plots.

(4) Computation of area.

(5) Map drawing.

Article 45: Where cadastral survey is to be carried out by the competent Provincial, Municipal or County Government, the projects thereof shall be submitted to the Central Land Administration for approval.

Article 46: If cadastral survey is to be effected by aerophotography, it shall be planned and carried out by the Central Land Administration.

Article 47: Rules governing cadastral survey shall be formulated by the Central Land Administration.

Chapter III. General Registration of Land

Article 48: The general registration of land shall be carried out according to the following steps:

(1) Cadastral investigation.

(2) Proclamation of registration districts and of the period of application for registration.

(3) Filing of applications and documents.

(4) Critical examination of applications and public announcement of the results thereof.

(5) Entry on the register, issuance of certificates, and compilation of registration books.

Article 49: The period of application for registration in any registration district shall not be shorter than two months.

Article 50: The cadastral map of a registration district shall be exposed to public view before the general registration of land begins.

Article 51: Application for the general registration of land shall be made by the landowner by filing a written application together with documents of evidence during the period of application for registration. In case rights over land other than ownership are to be registered, the application shall be made jointly by the obligee and the obligor.

The application referred to in the preceding paragraph may be made by an agent, provided that he is given the power of attorney.

Article 52: The registration of public land shall be effected by the competent Municipal or County Land Office at the request of the authority which is entrusted with the care of the said land or which is using it; and under the "Owners" column a note shall be inserted to indicate whether the land is owned by the State, the Province, the Municipality, the County, the District or the Township.

Article 53: Any public land which is neither entrusted to the care of, nor used by any public authority, or any public land which has come to light as a result of cadastration, shall be directly registered by the competent Municipal or County Land Office; and under the "Owners" column a note shall be inserted to indicate that the said land is owned by the State.

Article 54: Any person who has peaceably and continuously taken possession of any land and may, according to the provisions of Articles 769 and 770 of the Civil Code*, apply to be registered as its owner shall, during the period of application for registration, file an application for the

---

*Article 769 of the Chinese Civil Code provides:

"Any one who has, with the intent of acquiring ownership thereof, taken possession
(Continued on next page)

registration of the ownership of the said land on the testimony of those persons who own the adjacent lands.

Article 55: All applications and requests for registration that are found upon examination and testimony to be correct and proper shall be publicly announced by the competent Municipal or County Land Office. The same rule shall apply to those lands that are to be directly registered according to the provisions of Article 53.

In case additional documents of evidence are required in respect of the applications and requests for registration referred to in the preceding paragraph, the competent Municipal or County Land Office shall prescribe a time limit for the presentation of such documents.

Article 56: Where an application for registration is dismissed on account of flaws found therein upon examination according to the provisions of the preceding Article, the applicant may bring an action before the competent judicial authorities for the confirmation of his rights. If his rights are duly confirmed by a judicial decision, he may again apply for registration on the strength thereof.

Article 57: Any land of which no person has applied for registration during the period of application, or any land of which the applicant for registration has failed to present the required additional documents of evidence within the prescribed time limit, shall be regarded as ownerless land and publicly announced as such by the competent Municipal or County Land Office. If, on the expiration of the period of public announcement, no objection has been raised thereto, such land shall be registered as land owned by the State.

Article 58: The period of the public announcements made according to the provisions of Articles 55 and 57 shall not be shorter than two months.

Article 59: During the period of public announcement referred to in the preceding Article, any person with interests in such land may raise

---

of another person's unregistered immovable property peaceably and continuously for a period of twenty years may request that he be registered as the owner thereof."

Article 770 of the same Code provides:

"Any one who has, with the intent of acquiring ownership thereof, taken possession of another person's unregistered immovable property peaceably and continuously for a period of ten years and whose possession has been **bona fide** and faultless from its very beginning, may request that he be registered as the owner thereof."

objections thereto by submitting a written statement together with documents of evidence to the competent Municipal or County Land Office.

Any dispute over land rights arising out of the objections raised according to the provisions of the preceding paragraph shall be submitted to the competent Municipal or County Land Office for conciliation. Any party who refuses to abide by the terms of the conciliation shall, within 15 days on receipt of the notice of the said terms, bring the case before the judicial authorities for settlement. If he fails to bring the case before the judicial authorities within the said time limit, the terms of the conciliation shall be carried out accordingly.

Article 60: Any person who has lawfully taken possession of any land but has failed to apply for its registration during the period of application for registration and has raised no objections during the period of public announcement shall forfeit his right of possession.

Article 61: The judicial authorities in localities where the general registration of land is being carried on shall set up special courts to handle cases involving land rights and to hear and decide on them with all dispatch.

Article 62: Any land right of which application for registration has been duly made and to which no objection has been raised during the period of public announcement, or which has been established through conciliation or confirmed by judicial decision, shall be definitively registered, and a certificate of landownership or of other right over land shall be issued to the obligee.

The certificate of landownership referred to in the preceding paragraph shall be issued with a plot map attached thereto.

Article 63: The area of the land that is to be definitively registered according to the provisions of the preceding Article shall be that which is obtained by an actual survey of the land made within the boundaries indicated by documentary evidences.

In case the boundaries indicated by documentary evidences referred to in the preceding paragraph are not clearly defined or show discrepancies, the area obtained by an actual survey of the land shall be registered, if it does not exceed the area indicated in the documents by 10 per cent*. But if the area obtained by an actual survey exceeds that indicated in the documents by more than 20 per cent, the excess area shall be regarded as land owned by the State; but the original occupant shall have preferential right to purchase it and apply for registration thereof.

Article 64: For each registration district a general register of all lands duly registered shall be compiled and permanently kept in the files of the Municipal or County Government.

The form of the general register shall be prescribed by the Central Land Administration.

Article 65: In applying for the general registration of land, the obligee shall pay a registration fee at the rate of 0.2 per cent of the declared value of the land, or 0.2 per cent of the value of any right over it other than ownership, as the case may be.

Article 66: If the original obligee of any land in respect of which public announcement has been made according to the provisions of Article 57 raises due objection thereto and submits documentary evidence to apply for the registration of the said land during the period of public announcement, such application, if found to be correct and proper, shall be publicly announced, and the registration of the said land shall be effected according to the required procedure, but the applicant shall pay a 50% extra charge in addition to the regular registration fee.

Article 67: For each certificate of landownership or of any other right over land issued, a fee shall be charged according to the following provisions:

(1) One (silver) dollar shall be charged, if the declared value of land or the value of any right over land other than ownership is below 1,000 (silver) dollars.

(2) Two (silver) dollars shall be charged, if the declared value of land or the value of any right over land other than ownership is 1,000 (silver) dollars or more but below 5,000 (silver) dollars.

(3) Five (silver) dollars shall be charged, if the declared value of land or the value of any right over land other than ownership is 5,000 (silver) dollars or more but below 10,000 (silver) dollars.

---

*The phrase "by 10 per cent" is a correct translation of the Chinese text; but it is apparent from the context that the phrase should read "by 20 per cent."

(4) Ten (silver) dollars shall be charged, if the declared value of land or the value of any right over land other than ownership is 10,000 (silver) dollars or more but below 100,000 (silver) dollars.

(5) Twenty (silver) dollars shall be charged, if the declared value of land or the value of any right over land other than ownership is 100,000 (silver) dollars or more.

Article 68: Where damage is sustained through error, omission, or fraud in registration, the competent Land Office shall be liable to pay compensation therefor, unless the Land Office can prove that the person injured is responsible for the cause of such damage.

The compensation for damage referred to in the preceding paragraph shall not exceed the value prevailing at the time when damage was sustained.

Article 69: If any error or omission in registration is discovered by the registration officer or an interested party after registration has been completed, no rectification shall be made until the said error or omission has been reported in writing to the competent superior authorities and they, after due investigation, have approved of the rectification.

Article 70: Ten per cent of the registration fees received by the Land Office shall be earmarked as a Registration Fund to be used for the specific purpose of paying the compensations provided by Article 68.

Compensation for damage borne by the Land Office shall be paid back by the registration officer, if the said damage is a result of his gross negligence. All sums thus paid back shall be turned over to the Registration Fund.

Article 71: If any claim for compensation is rejected by the competent Land Office, the person injured may bring the case before the judicial‚ authorities for adjudication.

Chapter IV.   Registration of Changes in Land Rights

Article 72: After the general registration of land, any change in land rights such as transfer, subdivision, consolidation, augmentation, diminution, or extinction, shall be duly registered.

Article 73: Application for the registration of any change in land rights shall be made by the landowner; but application for the registration of any change in rights over land other than ownership shall be made jointly by the obligee and the obligor.

The application referred to in the preceding paragraph shall be made within one month after any change in a land right has been effected. In case the application is made after the expiration of the said period, or is made on instructions from the authorities who have found out that no application has yet been filed since the expiration of the said period, a fine no more than the registration fee payable may be imposed on the applicant.

Article 74: Application for the registration of any change in a land right shall be filed together with the original certificate of landownership and the attached plot map, or with the original certificate of any other right over land, as the case may require.

Article 75: Where an application for the registration of a change in a land right has been examined and found to be correct and proper by the competent Municipal or County Land Office, the said change shall be immediately entered in the general register, a certificate of landownership or of any other right over land, as the case may require, shall be issued to the applicant, and the original certificate of landownership or of other right over land shall be either nullified or duly annotated, as the case may require.

A plot map shall be attached to the certificate of landownership issued according to the provisions of the preceding paragraph.

Article 76: In applying for the registration of any change in a land right, the obligee shall pay a registration fee at the rate 0.1 per cent of the declared value of the land or 0.1 per cent of the value of any right over it other than ownership, as the case may be. But no registration fee shall be charged for the registration of the extinction of a land right or of a change in land right as a result of land replotting.

Article 77: For each certificate of landownership or of any other right over land issued in the registration of a change in land right, a fee shall be charged according to the provisions of Article 67.

Article 78: For each of the following registrations the applicant shall pay one (silver) dollar as registration fee:

(1) Registration of rectification.

(2) Registration of deletion.

(3) Registration of change in name.

(4) Registration of change in domicile.

In case the "registration of rectification" referred to in Section (1) of the preceding paragraph is necessitated by causes for which the registration officer must be held responsible, the applicant shall be exempt from paying the registration fee.

Article 79: Requests for the replacement of certificates of landowner-ship or of other rights over land that are either damaged or entirely destroy-ed or lost shall be made according to the following provisions:

(1) Any one making a request for the replacement of a certificate that is damaged shall submit the original damaged certificate for examination.

(2) Any one making a request for the replacement of a certificate that is entirely destroyed or lost shall fully explain the causes of its destruction or loss and shall furnish a written guarantee from his neighbors or a business firm vouching that he is the original rightful obligee, and a replacement may be issued to him after his request has been publicly announced for one full month by the competent Land Office.

Part III. Land Use

Chapter I. General Provisions

Article 80: By land use shall be meant the utilization of land through the application of labor and capital.

Article 81: The Municipal or County Land Office may, in consulta-tion with other government authorities concerned, classify the lands under its jurisdiction into different categories for specific uses with reference to national economic policies and due consideration of local needs and the possible uses for which the nature of the lands is suitable.

Article 82: Any land which is classified for a specific use shall not be put to some other use, unless such other use is approved by the com-petent Municipal or County Land Office.

Article 83: Any land which is classified for a specific use may continue to be utilized for its original purpose pending the time when such specific use begins.

Article 84: The classification of lands into different categories for specific uses or any subsequent changes therein shall be made by the competent Municipal or County Land Office and announced by the Municipal or County Government.

Article 85: After the classification of lands into different categories for specific uses has been announced, the superior Land Administration may issue instructions to make changes therein, if, in its judgment, some more important interests are to be served thereby or some more important uses justify such changes.

Article 86: In respect of agricultural lands under its jurisdiction, the Municipal or County Land Office may, in consultation with the competent agriculture and forestry authorities, prescribe the size of collective farms to be operated according to the methods of collective farming.

Regulations governing collective farms shall be separately prescribed by law.

Article 87: Any land which is classified for constructional use but is not so used according to law shall be regarded as vacant land.

Any land on which the value of constructional improvements is less than 20 per cent of its declared value shall be regarded as vacant land.

Article 88: Any land which is classified for agricultural use or for other purposes of direct production but is not so used according to law shall be regarded as uncultivated land. But this provision shall not apply to lands lying fallow as necessitated by agricultural production.

Article 89: In respect of private vacant lands and uncultivated lands under its jurisdiction, the Municipal or County Land Office may mark off areas and prescribe a time limit within which such lands shall be duly used according to law.

If the private uncultivated lands referred to in the preceding paragraph are not duly used according to law after the expiration of the prescribed time limit, the competent Municipal or County Government may purchase them at their declared values.

Chapter II. Restrictions on Land Use

Article 90: In cities and municipalities, lands to be used for roads, diches, sewers, and other public purposes shall be delimited in advance according to the City Planning Law.

Article 91: All the land in cities and municipalities may, according to the City Planning Law, be demarcated into one area wherein the use of land is subject to restrictions and another area wherein the use of land is free.

Article 92: The Government may, according to law, compulsorily purchase all the lands or part of them in a newly created city for the purpose of replanning and replotting in accordance with the City Planning Law, and resell the replotted plots individually and severally at the purchase price originally paid plus an additional charge to cover the expenses required for replanning.

The lands subject to compulsory purchase according to the provisions of the preceding paragraph may be so purchased at different times and offered for development area by area. The lands in areas not yet offered for development may be reserved for compulsory purchase, and any use thereof which obstructs the execution of the city planning project shall be prohibited.

Article 93: Lands which have been announced to be used as roads or for other public purposes according to the city planning project may be reserved for compulsory purchase, and any construction thereon shall be prohibited except structures of a temporary nature.

Chapter III. Lease of Houses and Building Sites

Article 94: In cities and municipalities, an appropriate number of reserve houses shall be built by the Government and leased to citizens for residence.

The rental of the houses referred to in the preceding paragraph shall not exceed an amount equivalent to an annual interest of 8 per cent on the total value of the land and the buildings thereon.

Article 95: In order to relieve housing shortage, the Municipal or County Government may, with the approval of the Executive Yuan, reduce or remit both the land tax and the improvements tax on those lands whereon new houses are built and fix a time limit for such reduction or remission.

Article 96: In cities and municipalities, necessary restrictions on the number of rooms to be occupied by each citizen for his own dwelling may, with due regard to local conditions, be prescribed by the Municipal or County Government; but such restrictions shall be subject to the approval of the local assembly.

Article 97: In cities and municipalities, house rentals shall not exceed an amount equivalent to an annual interest of 10 per cent on the total declared value of the land and buildings thereon.

If any house rental already agreed upon exceeds the amount prescribed in the preceding paragraph, the competent Municipal or County Government may compulsorily reduce it to the limit prescribed in the preceding paragraph.

Article 98: Where cash deposit is paid as security for the lease of a house, the interest on such cash deposit shall be deemed as part of the house rental.

The rate of interest referred to in the preceding paragraph shall be the same as that by which the house rental is computed.

Article 99: The cash deposit referred to in the preceding Article shall not exceed the total amount of two months' house rental.

If he cash deposit already paid exceeds the limit prescribed in the preceding paragraph, the lessee may use the excess deposit to counterbalance the house rental.

Article 100: The lessor shall not take back his house unless one of the following conditions obtains:

(1) The lessor takes the house for his own residence or for reconstruction.

(2) The lessee subleases the house in violation of Paragraph one, Article 443 of the Civil Code*.

---

*Article 443 of the Chinese Civil Code provides:

"The lessee shall not, except with the consent of the lessor, sublease to another person the thing leased; but if the thing leased is a house, the lessee may, unless there

(Continued on next page)

(3) The cumulative amount of house rental which the lessee has failed to pay exceeds the equivalent of two months' rental, after the entire cash deposit has been used to counterbalance the amount in arrears.

(4) The lessee puts the house to illegal use in violation of laws or ordinances.

(5) The lessee violates the terms of the lease contract.

(6) The lessee causes damage to the house or the fixtures and fails to pay due compensation.

Article 101: Any dispute arising out of the lease of a house may be submitted to the competent Municipal or County Land Office for conciliation. Any party to the dispute who refuses to abide by the terms of conciliation may bring the case before the judicial authorities for adjudication.

Article 102: Where a building site is leased for house construction, the lessor and the lessee shall, within two months after the contract is concluded, apply to the competent Municipal or County Government for the registration of the right of superficies over the said site.

Article 103: The lessor shall not take back the site leased for house construction unless one of the following conditions obtains:

(1) The period of the contract has expired.

(2) The lessee puts the site to illegal use in violation of laws or ordinances.

(3) The lessee subleases the site to another person.

(4) The cumulative amount of the rental which the lessee has failed to pay exceeds the equivalent of two years' rental, after the entire cash deposit has been used to counterbalance the amount in arrears.

(5) The lessee violates the terms of the contract.

is a provision in the agreement to the contrary, sublease a part thereof to another person.

   "If the lessee subleases to another person the thing leased in violation of the provisions of the preceding paragraph, the lessor may terminate the contract."

Article 104: When the building site is offered for sale, the lessee shall have preferential right to purchase it on the same terms as are offered to any other person, and when the house on the leased site is offered for sale, the owner of the site shall have preferential right to purchase it on the same terms as are offered to any other person.

The preferential right referred to in the preceding parapraph shall be deemed to have been waived, if the said lessee or owner does not express his intention to make the purchase within ten days upon receipt of the sales notification.

Article 105: The provisions of Articles 97, 99, and 101 shall, *mutatis mutandis,* apply to the lease of building sites for house construction.

Chapter IV.   Lease of Farm Land

Article 106: By lease of farm land shall be meant the use of another person's agricultural land for the purpose of cultivation by oneself by paying a rent therefor.

The term "cultivation" referred to in the preceding paragraph shall include fishing and pasturing.

Article 107: When the lessor offers his farm land for sale or *dien,* the lessee shall have preferential right to purchase it or accept the *dien* on the same terms as are offered to any other person.

The provisions of Paragraph two of Article 104 shall, *mutatis mutandis,* apply to the purchase or *dien* referred to in the preceding paragraph.

Article 108: The lessee shall not, even with the consent of the lessor, sublease the whole or part of the leased farm land to another person.

Article 109: Any farm lease contract for a definite period shall, unless the lessor takes back the land for his own cultivation on the expiration of the contractual period, be deemed to have been renewed for an indefinite period, if the lessee continues to cultivate the said land.

Article 110: Farm rent shall not exceed 8 per cent of the value of the land. If any contractual or customary rent exceeds 8 per cent of the value of the land, it shall be reduced to 8 per cent; if it is less than 8 per cent, it shall remain unchanged.

"The value of the land" referred to in the preceding paragraph shall mean the statutory value of the land, or, in localities where the value of land has not been assessed according to law, the average value of the land for the last three years.

Article 111: The lessee of a farm land may, according to custom, pay the rent with farm crops in lieu of cash.

Article 112: The lessor of a farm land shall not collect farm rent in advance. But if cash deposit is payable according to local custom as security for the lease of a farm land, the amount of such deposit shall not exceed one-fourth of the annual rent.

The interest on the cash deposit referred to in the preceding paragraph shall be deemed as part of the farm rent, and its rate shall be determined by the general rate of interest prevailing in the locality.

Article 113: If the lessee is unable to pay the rent in full when due, but pays only a fraction thereof, the lessor shall not refuse to accept such payment, nor shall the lessee presume that the acceptance of such payment indicates the lessor's consent to a reduction of rent.

Article 114: Any farm lease contract for an indefinite period may be terminated only under any one of the following conditions:

(1) Where the lessee dies without leaving an heir.

(2) Where the lessee waives his right of cultivation.

(3) Where the lessor takes back the farm land for his own cultivation.

(4) Where the farm land is to be put to some other specific use in accordance with law.

(5) Where the lessee violates the provisions of Article 432 and Paragraph two of Article 462 of the Civil Code.*

(6) Where the lessee violates the provisions of Article 108.

---

*Article 432 of the Chinese Civil Code provides:

"The lessee shall keep and preserve the thing leased with the solicitude of a good administrator. If the thing leased has productivity, he shall also preserve its

(Continued on next page)

(7)   Where the cumulative amount of the rent the lessee has failed to pay is equivalent to the total of two years' rent.

Article 115:   If the lessee intends to waive his right of cultivation, he shall declare his intention to the lessor three months in advance. Noncultivation for one full year by the lessee for any cause other than *force majeure* shall be considered as a waiver of the right of cultivation.

Article 116:   Where a farm lease contract is to be terminated according to the provisions of Sections (3) or (5) of Article 114, the lessor shall notify the lessee of the intended termination one year in advance.

Article 117:   Where the farm land taken back by the lessor for his own cultivation is again offered for lease, the original lessee shall have preferential right to accept the lease. Where the said land is again offered for lease within a year from the date when it was taken back by the lessor, the original lessee may acquire the lease on identical terms as those agreed upon in the original lese contract.

Article 118:   The lessor shall not exercise the right of retention provided for in Article 445 of the Civil Code* over such farm implements, livestock, fertilizers, and farm products of the lessee as are necessary for cultivation.

---

productivity.

"If the lessee acts contrary to the provisions of the preceding paragraph and thereby causes loss or damage to the thing leased, he shall be liable to pay compensation therefor. But he shall not be held responsible for any damage or change caused to the thing leased through its use, or through the enjoyment of the incomes accruing therefrom, in such ways as are agreed upon or as are in consonance with the inherent nature of the thing itself."

Parapraphs one and two of Article 462 of the Chinese Civil Code read:

"Where agricultural implements, livestock, or other accessories are leased together with the farm land, an inventory of the same showing their respective values shall be made in duplicates and signed by both parties at the time when the lease contract is signed. Each party shall keep one copy of the said duplicates.

"If any accessory mentioned in the inventory be destroyed or lost owing to circumstances for which the lessee must be held responsible, he shall be liable to make it good."

*Article 445 of the Chinese Civil Code provides:

"For the settlement of claims arising out of the lease contract, the lessor of an immovable property shall have the right of retention over the movables which belong to the lessee and are fixed to the said immovable property. But this provision shall not apply to movables that are not subject to attachment."

Article 119: By special improvements on farm land shall be meant improvements resulting from the increased application of labor and capital which, besides preserving the original qualities and utility of the land, increases its productivity or facilitates its cultivation.

The lessee may freely make the special improvements referred to in the preceding paragraph, but he shall notify the lessor of the amount of the outlay incurred thereon.

Article 120: When any farm land is returned to the lessor on the termination of the lease contract according to the provisions of Section (2), (3), (5) or (6) of Article 114, the lessee may claim from the lessor repayment of the outlay incurred on the special improvements referred to in Paragraph two of the preceding Article, but such repayment shall be limited to the cost of that part of the special improvements which has not lost its utility.

The provisions of the preceding paragraph shall apply *mutatis mutandis,* when the right of perpetual lease *(yungtien)* is revoked according to the provisions of Articles 845 and 846 of the Civil Code.[1]

Article 121: The lessor of any farm land who supplies the lessee with draft animals, seeds, fertilizers, and other implements of production may, besides conforming to the provisions of Articles 462 and 463 of the Civil Code[2], charge a reasonable fee therefor in addition to the farm rent, if such fee is stipulated in the lease contract; but such fee shall not exceed an amount equivalent to an annual interest of 10 per cent on the value of the things supplied.

---

(1) Article 845 of the Chinese Civil Code provides:

"The **yungtien**-holder shall not lease the land to another person.

"If the **yungtien**-holder acts contrary to the provisions of the preceding paragraph, the landowner may revoke the **yungtien**."

Article 846 of the Chinese Civil Code provides:

"If the rent which the **yungtien**-holder has failed to pay amounts to the equivalent of two years' total rent, the landowner may, unless there is a different local custom, revoke the **yungtien**."

(2) The relevant paragraph of Article 462 of the Chinese Civil Code reads:

"Where agricultural implements, livestock, or other accessories are leased together with the farm land, an inventory of the same showing their respective values shall be made in duplicates and signed by both parties at the time when the lease contract is

(Continued on next page)

Article 122: Any dispute arising out of the lease of a farm land between the lessor and the lessee may be submitted to the competent Municipal or County Land Office for conciliation. Any party to the dispute who refuses to abide by the terms of conciliation may bring the case before the judicial authorities for adjudication.

Article 123: In case of any crop failure, the competent Municipal or County Government may, in the light of actual crop conditions in the current year, make decisions on the reduction or remission of farm rent in the affected localities, but such decisions shall be subject to the approval of the local assembly of people's representatives.

Article 124: The provisions of Article 107 or 113 inclusive and of Article 121 shall, *mutatis mutandis,* apply to lands subject to perpetual lease *(yungtien).*

Chapter V. Use of Uncultivated Land

Article 125: The competent Municipal or County Land Office shall complete within a definite period of time the survey of public uncultivated lands under its jurisdiction and formulate a program for the use of such lands.

Article 126: On public uncultivated lands suitable for cultivation, except those reserved by the government for its own use, the competent Municipal or County Land Office shall, in conjunction with the competent agriculture and forestry authorities, delimit reclamation areas, prescribe reclamation units and fix a definite period of time in which to call for settlers.

Article 127: Where private uncultivated lands are purchased by the competent Municipal or County Government according to the provision of Article 89, they shall be open to settlement after irrigation works and soil improvement have been completed.

Article 128: Settlers on public uncultivated lands shall be limited to

---

signed. Each party shall keep one copy of the said duplicates."

Article 463 of the Chinese Civil Code provides:

"The lessee of a farm land shall, at the termination of the lease, hand back to the lessor all the accessories he has received from him as listed in the inventory. Any accessory which the lessee cannot hand back to the lessor shall be compensated for at the value specified in the inventory, minus the normal depreciation caused by its use."

citizens of the Republic of China.

Article 129: Settlers on public uncultivated land shall be of the following two types:

(1)   Farming families cultivating land themselves.

(2)   Agricultural production cooperatives.

The agricultural production cooperatives referred to in the preceding paragraph shall be limited to those that have been duly registered according to law and whose component members cultivate land themselves.

Article 130: Public uncultivated land to be applied for by a settler shall be limited, in the case of a farming family, to a single reclamation unit, and in the case of an agricultural production cooperative, to such a number of reclamation units as do not exceed the number of its component farming family members who cultivate land themselves.

Article 131: Any settler shall commence reclamation work within a year from the date when he receives the certificate of reclamation, and the time limit in terms of years for the completion of the reclamation work shall be fixed by the competent agriculture and forestry authorities. If any settler fails to commence reclamation work within the prescribed period, the certificate of reclamation issued to him shall be revoked.

Article 132: If any settler fails to complete the reclamation work within the prescribed time limit, the certificate of reclamation issued to him shall be revoked; but if such failure is due to *force majeure,* he may request the competent agriculture and forestry authorities for an extension of the time limit.

Article 133: Any settler shall, from the date when the reclamation work is completed, acquire gratis the right of cultivation over the reclaimed land, and shall, in accordance with law, apply to the competent Municipal or County Land Office for the registration of the said right. If he has continued to cultivate such land for ten full years, he shall acquire the ownership thereof gratis.

The right of cultivation referred to in the preceding paragraph shall not be transferred, but this provision shall not apply to inheritance by or donation to legitimate heirs.

The reclaimed land referred to in the first paragraph may be exempted from the land tax for a period of two to eight years at the discretion of the competent Municipal or County Government.

Article 134: Where the reclamation of public uncultivated lands can not be done by farming families or agricultural production cooperatives, a government reclamation office may be established to carry out the reclamation work thereon.

Chapter VI. Land Replotting

Article 135: The Municipal or County Land Office may, with the the approval of its superior authorities, mark out replotting areas in the territorial limits under its jurisdiction and carry out land replotting and demarcate anew the plots of land in such areas in any one of the following cases:

(1) Where a city planning project is to be implemented.

(2) Where the plots are so small or so narrow in size as to be unsuitable for purposes of construction.

(3) Where farm lands are so ill distributed as to be unsuitable for farming or unfavorable to drainage and irrigation.

(4) Where scattered small plots are to be exchanged or consolidated to form standard farms.

(5) Where collective farms are to be set up the introduction of mechanical farming.

Article 136: The replotted plots of land shall be redistributed to their original owners in proportion to the area or value of the original plots, but if, owing to practical difficulties, they cannot be redistributed in exact proportion to the area or value of the original plots, due compensation therefor shall be paid instead.

Article 137: Where plots of land are so small or narrow in size that their area is smaller than the minimum unit prescribed in Article 31, such plots may be abolished as independent units or consolidated by replotting.

Article 138: In areas subject to replotting, parks, roads, embankments, dikes, ditches, sewers, and other lands used for public purposes may be put to a different use or abolished, or new ones be set up, by replotting.

Article 139: After the replotting of land, the landowners who have sustained loss thereby shall be compensated by those who have gained thereby. The compensation for the value of lands used as roads or for other public purposes shall be paid by the Government.

Article 140: If, within thirty days from the date when any project of land replotting is announced, objections to the project are raised by more than half of the interested landowners who own among themselves over half of the total area of the lands to be replotted, excluding public lands, the competent Municipal or County Land Office shall immediately report the case to its superior authorities for instructions.

Article 141: The land replotting provided for in Article 135 may be initiated by a joint request of more than half of the landowners who own among themselves over half of the total area of the lands to be replotted, excluding public lands, and be carried out upon approval by the competent Municipal or County Land Office.

Article 142: In newly created cities the replotting of land shall be carried out before the land is offered for development area by area.*

Part IV.   Land Tax

Chapter I.   General Provisions

Article 143: Land and improvements thereon shall be taxed according to the provisions of this Law, unless otherwise exempted from taxation by law.

Article 144: Land tax shall be of two kinds: the land value tax and the land value increment tax.

Article 145: The value of land and that of improvements thereon shall be separately assessed.

Article 146: Land tax shall be a local tax.

Article 147: No tax or surtax under whatever name shall be imposed on land and improvements thereon except in accordance with the provisions of this Law.   But to meet the expenses required for the construction of roads, embankments, dikes, ditches, sewers, or other engineer-

---

*Compare Article 92.

ing works on ground or in water for the improvement of land, a "construction benefit charge"* may be levied according to law.

Chapter II. Value of Land and of Improvements Thereon

Article 148: The value of land declared by its owner according to this Law shall be the statutory value of such land.

Article 149: The declaration of the value of land shall be carried out by the Municipal or County Land Office according to the following procedure:

(1) Investigation and assessment of the standard values of lands.

(2) Declaration of the values of lands by their owners.

(3) Compilation of land value rolls.

Article 150: To serve as the basis for the assessment of the standard land value, an investigation by sampling shall be made of the market values or income values of land prevailing during the last two years. The number of plots of land to be investigated by sampling may vary with the number of categories of land involved and with the greater or lesser differences in the values of the plots under investigation.

Article 151: On the basis of the results obtained from the investigation made according to the provisions of the preceding Article, different grades of land values shall be fixed by grouping together plots of land whose values approximate to one another and whose location is mutually adjacent or which belong to the same category; and under each of these grades the average or the median of the market values or income values of those plots of land which are investigated by sampling shall be taken as the average land value of that grade.

Article 152: The average land value of each land value grade shall be publicly announced as the standard land value of that grade by the competent Municipal or County Government upon the request of the competent Municipal or County Land Office.

Article 153: The public announcement of the standard land values shall be made district by district, before the general registration of land

---

*The term "construction benefit charge" is a literal translation of the Chinese text. It is generally known in the United States as "special assessment."

begins.

Article 154: If any landowner considers the standard land value to be incorrectly assessed, he may, with the concurrence of the majority of the owners of lands of the same land value grade in the same district, raise objections thereto with the competent Municipal or County Government within thirty days after the announcement of the said standard land value.

On receiving the objections raised according to the provisions of the preceding paragraph, the Municipal or County Government shall immediately refer them to the Committee on Standard Land Values for consideration.

Article 155: Rules governing the organization of the Committee on Standard Land Values shall be formulated by the Central Land Administration.

The Committee referred to in the preceding paragraph shall include members representing the local assembly.

Article 156: On applying for the registration of landownership, the landowner shall simultaneously declare the value of his land, which may not be more than 20 per cent either above or below the standard land value.

Article 157: If any landowner considers the standard land value to be too high and declines to declare the value of his land according to the provisions of the preceding Article, he may request the competent Municipal or County Government to purchase his land at the said standard land value.

Article 158: If, on applying for the registration of landownership, any landowner fails to declare the value of his land simultaneously, the standard land value shall be taken as the statutory value of his land.

Article 159: When the declaration of land values is completed in any Municipality or County, land value rolls and general registers of landowners shall be compiled and transmitted to the competent financial authorities of the Municipality or County.

Article 160: The value of land may be re-assessed after the lapse of five full years since its declaration, or after the lapse of one full year since its declaration if the land value fluctuates by more than 50 per cent either above or below the standard land value; and the provisions of Articles 150 to 152 inclusive and of Articles 154 to 156 inclusive shall apply in such re-assessment.

Article 161: The value of constructional improvements shall be assessed by the competent Municipal or County Land Office at the time when the value of land is assessed.

Article 162: The value of constructional improvements shall be assessed on the basis of the expenses required for the construction, at the time of assessment, of the same improvements, minus the depreciation caused by the lapse of time.

Article 163: In the re-assessment of the value of the original constructional improvements, additional improvements made thereto shall be considered as part of the original improvements, but repairs made for the maintenance of the original improvements in a sound condition shall not be regarded as additional improvements.

Article 164: The assessed values of improvements shall be submitted by the Municipal or County Land Office to the Committee on Standard Land Values for confirmation. The values confirmed by the said Committee shall be reported to the competent Municipal or County Government to be publicly announced as the statutory values of such improvements, and the owners of such improvements shall be individually notified in writing of the respective statutory values by the Municipal or County Land Office.

Article 165: If any recipient of the notification made according to the preceding Article takes exception to the value confirmed, he may, within thirty days after the receipt of such notification, request the Committee on Standard Land Values to make a re-assessment.

Article 166: The value of constructional improvements may be reassessed when the value of land is re-assessed.

Chapter III.   Land Value Tax

Article 167: The land value tax shall be levied once every year on the basis of the statutory land value. Payment thereof may, if necessary, be made in two installments.

Article 168: The land value tax shall be levied according to a progressive scale on the basis of the statutory land value.

Article 169:   The basic rate of the land value tax shall be 1.5 per cent of the statutory land value.

Article 170:   Where the total value of all the lands owned by any landowner does not exceed the initial point of land value subject to progressive rates, the land value tax on his lands shall be levied according to the basic rate prescribed in the preceding Article.   Where the total value of all the lands owned by any landowner exceeds the initial point of land value subject to progressive rates, the land value tax on that part of the total value of his lands which exceeds the said initial point shall be levied according to the following progressive rates:

(1)   Where the total land value exceeds the said initial point by no more than 500 per cent, a rate of 0.2 per cent in addition to the basic rate shall be levied on that part of the total land value which exceeds the initial point.

(2)   Where the total land value exceeds the said initial point by no more than 1,000 per cent, another rate of 0.3 per cent in addition to the rates prescribed in the preceding section shall be levied on that part of the total land value which exceeds the initial point by more than 500 per cent.

(3)   Where the total land value exceeds the said initial point by no more than 1,500 per cent, a still another rate of 0.5 per cent in addition to the rates prescribed in the preceding section shall be levied on that part of the total land value which exceeds the initial point by more than 1,000 per cent.   Thereafter , another rate of 0.5 per cent in addition to all the preceding rates shall be levied on every additional 500 per cent increase in the total land value, until the total cumulative rate has reached the maximum limit of 5 per cent.

Article 171:   The initial point of land value subject to progressive rates referred to in the preceding Article shall be fixed by the Provincial Government or the Municipal Government under the direct jurisdiction of the Executive Yuan, with due consideration of the area of land necessary for the owner's dwelling or cultivation and in the light of land values and local economic conditions; and the initial point of land value so fixed shall be submitted to the Executive Yuan for approval.

Article 172:   The land value tax shall be levied on the landowner.   In the case of any land subject to *dien,* the said tax shall be paid by the *dien*-holder.

The land value tax on any land belonging to an absentee landlord may be paid by the lessee on his behalf, and such payment shall be deducted from the land rent payable by the lessee for the current year.

Article 173: Where a private vacant land is not duly used after the expiration of the time limit within which it is required to be duly used, a vacant land tax shall be imposed on the said land in addition to the land value tax, until it is duly used according to law.

The vacant land tax referred to in the preceding paragraph shall not be less than three times, or more than ten times, the land value tax leviable on the said land.

Article 174: Where a private uncultivated land is not duly used after the expiration of the time limit within which it is required to be duly used, an uncultivated land tax shall be imposed on the said land in addition to the land value tax, until it is duly used according to law.

The uncultivated land tax referred to in the preceding paragraph shall not be less than the amount of, or more than three times, the land value tax leviable on the said land.

Article 175: The land value tax leviable on lands owned by absentee landlords shall be double the amount of the regular land value tax leviable thereon.

Chapter IV.   Land Value Increment Tax

Article 176: The land value increment tax shall be levied on the basis of the net increment of the value of land, when the ownership thereof is transferred, or after the lapse of ten full years though the ownership thereof has not been transferred.

The period of ten full years referred to in the preceding paragraph shall begin from the date when the value of land is assessed for the first time according to law.

Article 177: In areas where the construction works referred to in Article 147 are executed, the land value increment tax shall be levied after the lapse of five full years since the completion of such works.

Article 178: The gross increment of the value of land shall be determined according to the following provisions:

(1) Where any land which has undergone no transfer since the assessment of its value is transferred by a sale without the right of redemption, the amount by which its present sales price exceeds its value originally assessed shall be taken as the gross increment of the value of such land.

(2) Where any land which has undergone no transfer since the assessment of its value is transferred through inheritance or donation, the amount by which its value assessed at the time of the transfer exceeds its value originally assessed shall be taken as the gross increment of the value of such land.

(3) Where any land which has undergone transfers since the assessment of its value is transferred again, the amount by which its value at the present transfer exceeds its value at the penultimate transfer shall be taken as the gross increment of the value of such land.

Article 179: "The value of land originally assessed" and "the value of land at the penultimate transfer" referred to in the preceding Article shall be called the original value of land.

In case a violent fluctuation of commodity prices occurs, the original value of land mentioned in the preceding paragraph shall be adjusted according to the local price index by the Municipal or County financial authorities and with he concurrence of the local assembly.

Article 180: The gross increment of the value of any land minus the amount of tax remission shall be the net increment of the value of such land.

Article 181: The land value increment tax shall be levied at the following rates:

(1) Where the net increment of the value of any land is no more than 100 per cent of the original value of such land, the rate shall be 20 per cent of the net increment.

(2) Where the net increment of the value of any land is no more than 200 per cent of the original value of such land, the rate shall be 40 per cent of that part of the net increment which exceeds the original value by more than 100 per cent, aside from the rate prescribed in the preceding section.

(3) Where the net increment of the value of any land is no more than 300 per cent of the original value of such land, the rate shall be 60 per cent of that part of the net increment which exceeds the original value by more than 200 per cent, aside from the rates prescribed in the preceding section.

(4) Where the net increment of the value of any land is over 300 per cent of the original value of such land, the rate shall be 80 per cent of that part of the net increment which exceeds the original value by more than 300 per cent, aside from the rates prescribed in the preceding section.

Article 182: Where the ownership of any land is transferred by a sale without the right of redemption, the land value increment tax shall be levied on the seller. Where the ownership of any land is transferred through inheritance or donation, the said tax shall be levied on the heir or donee, as the case may be.

Article 183: Where any land has undergone no transfer after the lapse of ten full years since the assessment of its value, or after the lapse of five full years since the completion of the construction works which have been carried on in the area where the said land is located, the land value increment tax shall be levied on the landowner.

If the land referred to in the preceding paragraph is subject to *dien,* the land value increment tax shall be levied on the *dien*-holder, but the *dien*-obligor shall refund the payment thereof without interest to the *dien*-holder when the *dien*-obligor redeems the land.

Article 184: In computing the net increment of the land value, the capital expenses incurred by the landowner for the improvement of his land and the "construction benefit charge" paid by him shall, if any, be deducted from the gross increment of the value of his land.

Chapter V. Tax on Improvements on Land

Article 185: Constructional improvements may be taxed annually according to their assessed values, and the maximum tax rate shall not exceed one per cent thereof.

Article 186: The tax on constructional improvements shall be levied simultaneously with the land value tax, and the provisions of Article 172 shall apply *mutatis mutandis.*

Article 187: Where constructional improvements are used as the owner's dwelling house, they shall be exempted from taxation.

Article 188: Agricultural improvements shall not be subject to taxation.

Article 189: In localities where the value of land is generally less than 500 (silver) dollars per *mow**, all constructional improvements shall be exempted from taxation.

Article 190: The entire tax on improvements on land shall be a local tax.

Chapter VI. Reduction and Remission of Land Tax

Article 191: Public lands and public constructional improvements shall be exempted from the land tax and the tax on improvements, unless they are used by government enterprises or are not used for public purposes.

Article 192: The tax on private lands used for any one of the following purposes may be reduced or remitted upon approval by the Executive Yuan of a joint request made by the Ministry of Finance and the Central Land Administration:

(1) Premises for schools and academic institutions.

(2) Parks and public athletic grounds.

(3) Experimental stations for agriculture, forestry, fishery, and animal husbandry.

(4) Forest land.

(5) Premises for public hospitals.

(6) Public cemeteries.

(7) Other lands used by non-profit undertakings for the promotion of public welfare.

***Mow** is a Chinese unit for the measurement of area, equivalent to 0.1647 acre.

Article 193: On the occurrence of a calamity in any localiy or for the purpose of making social and economic readjustments, the Ministry of Finance and the Central Land Administration may jointly request the Executive Yuan to approve the remission or reduction of the land tax in the affected area for the duration of the said calamity or readjustment.

Article 194: Any land which is reserved for compulsory purchase or whose use is restricted by law shall be exempted from taxation, unless the said land can be used for its original purpose during the period in which it is reserved for compulsory purchase.

Article 195: Any land which is not utilizable owing to its physical condition or for technical reasons, or which is in process of being reclaimed, shall be exempted from the land value tax upon approval by the Executive Yuan of a joint request made by the Ministry of Finance and the Central Land Administration.

Article 196: No land value increment tax shall be levied on any land when the transfer of its ownership is necessitated by compulsory purchase or land replotting.

Article 197: No land value increment tax shall be levied on any lands owned by a farmer which are used for his own cultivation and residence, if they remain untransferred after the lapse of ten full years since the assessment of their value.

Article 198: No land value increment tax shall be levied on any farm land, when its value appreciates as a result of the application of labor and capital by the farmer.

Article 199: Any land on which tax has been reduced or remitted shall be taxed as usual, when the cause or circumstance which justifies such reduction or remission changes or disappears.

Chapter VII. Tax Delinquency

Article 200: If any land value tax is not paid when due, a fine of no more than 2 per cent of the amount overdue shall be imposed for every month of delinquency, beginning from the date when it is overdue, and, for this purpose, a fraction of a month shall be considered as a full month.

Article 201: When the cumulative amount of the land value tax overdue is equal to the amount of the said tax leviable in two years, the competent Municipal or County financial authorities may notify the Municipal or County Land Office to turn over to the judicial authorities for sale by auction both the land on which the tax is overdue and a portion or the whole of the improvements thereon. The proceeds therefrom shall be used to offset the amount of the tax overdue and the surplus, if any, shall be handed back to the delinquent taxpayer.

Article 202: In case any land is to be sold by auction according to the provisions of the preceding Article, the judicial authorities shall serve a written notice thereof to the owner of the said land thirty days before the auction.

Article 203: If, on receipt of the notice referred to in the preceding Article, the landowner furnishes adequate security for the payment of the tax overdue, the judicial authorities may order a postponement of the auction.

The period of the postponement referred to in the preceding paragraph shall not be longer than one year.

Article 204: Where the land on which the land value tax is overdue yields incomes, the competent Municipal or County financial authorities may notify the Municipal or County Land Office to collect such incomes for the purpose of offsetting the amount of the tax overdue, instead of selling the land by auction.

The collection of incomes referred to in the preceding paragraph shall be effected only when the cumulative amount of the tax overdue is equal to the amount of the said tax leviable in one year.

The amount of the incomes collected according to the provisions of Paragraph one shall be limited to such a sum as is enough to offset the amount of the tax overdue.

Article 205: If any land value increment tax is not duly paid according to law, a fine shall be imposed according to the provisions of Article 200.

Article 206: When any land value increment tax is overdue for one full year, the competent Municipal or County financial authorities may notify the Municipal or County Land Office to turn over the land and a portion or the whole of the improvements thereon to the judicial authorities for sale by auction. The proceeds therefrom shall be used to offset the amount of the tax overdue and the surplus, if any, shall be handed back to the delinquent taxpayer.

The provisions of Articles 202 and 203 shall apply to the auction referred to in the preceding paragraph.

Article 207: The provisions of the various Articles in this Chapter concerning the land value tax overdue shall, *mutatis mutandis,* apply to any tax overdue on constructional improvements.

Part V. Compulsory Purchase of Land

Chapter I. General Provisions

Article 208: To meet the requirements of the following public undertakings the State may compulsorily purchase private land according to the Provisions of this Law, but the area of land to be compulsorily purchased shall be limited to what is strictly required for the said undertakings:

(1) Installations of national defense.

(2) Communication enterprises.

(3) Public utility enterprises.

(4) Water conservancy enterprises.

(5) Public health.

(6) Government office buildings, office buildings of local self-governing bodies and other public buildings.

(7) Educational, academic, and philanthropic undertakings.

(8) Enterprises operated by the Sate.

(9) Other undertakings sponsored by the Government in the public interest.

Article 209: For the implementation of national economic policies, the government may compulsorily purchase private land, provided that such compulsory purchase is provided for by law.

Article 210: Scenic spots and historic remains shall not, as far as possible, be compulsorily puschased.

Scenic spots and historic remains that have been included in the area to be compulsorily purchased shall, as far as possible, be preserved.

Article 211: In applying for the compulsory purchase of land, the applicant shall show evidence that the undertaking sponsored has been authorized by law or decree.

Article 212: Zone purchase may be effected in the compulsory purchase of land for any one of the following purposes:

(1) For the implementation of national economic policies.

(2) For the creation of new cities and municipalities.

(3) For the promotion of undertaking specified in Section (1) or (3) of Article 208.

Zone purchase referred to in the preceding paragraph shall mean the compulsory purchase of all the lands within a given area, whereof replanning and replotting are required.

Article 213: Lands may be reserved for compulsory purchase for any one of the following undertakings:

(1) The opening of communication lines.

(2) The promotion of public utility enterprises.

(3) The creation of new cities and municipalities.

(4) The installation of national defense.

Lands reserved for compulsory purchase, as referred to in the preceding paragraph, shall mean those lands that are to be required by the said undertakings for their future use and are prior to their actual use approved, upon the request of the organizations responsible for the said undertakings, and publicly announced by the competent authorities as lands that are subject to compulsory purchase in future and shall not be put to any use that hinders their eventual compulsory purchase.

Article 214: The period in which any land is reserved for compulsory purchase according to the provisions of the preceding Article shall not exceed three years. Failure to effect compulsory purchase within the said time limit shall result in the cancellation of the reservation. But in the case of any undertaking mentioned in Section (1) or (4) of the preceding Article, the period in which any land is reserved for compulsory purchase may be extended with the approval of the competent authorities upon the request of the agency responsible for the said undertaking, provided that the period thus extended be no longer than five years.

Article 215: When any land is compulsorily purchased, all improvements thereon shall also be so purchased, unless the owner of the said improvements requests to remove them and to effect the removal himself.

Article 216: In case the use of a compulsorily purchased land produces such adverse effects on the adjacent land as to make it unfit for its original utilization or to impair the efficiency of its original utilization, the owner of the adjacent land may demand due compensation from the user of the compulsorily purchased land.

The compensation referred to in the preceding paragraph shall not exceed the amount of depreciation in the value of the adjacent land caused by the use to which the compulsorily purchased land is put.

Article 217: In case the remaining portion of a compulsorily purchased land is unsuitable for proper use owing to the smallness of its size or the irregularity of its shape, its owner may request that it be compulsorily purchased altogether.

Article 218: When the lands acquired by the Government by zone purchase are offered for sale or lease, after they have been replanned and replotted, the original owner or obligee thereof shall have preferential right to accept that offer.

Article 219: In case a compulsorily purchased private land is not used according to the approved plan, or is not used at all one year after it has been so purchased, its original owner may redeem it at the purchase price originally paid him.

Article 220: Land that is being currently used for any of those undertakings enumerated in the different Sections of Article 208 shall not be compulsorily purchased, unless its compulsory purchase is unavoidable for the promotion of some more important undertaking. However, this provision shall not prevent the compulsory purchase of a small portion of the land so used, if such purchase does not hinder in any way the continued development of the present undertaking.

Article 221: The liabilities borne by any land under compulsory purchase shall be liquidated, and the amount of the liabilities so liquidated shall be limited to the amount of compensations payable for the said land and shall be paid off by the competent Municipal or County Land Office when the said compensations are paid.

Chapter II. Procedure of Compulsory Purchase

Article 222: The compulsory purchase of land under any one of the following conditions shall be subject to the approval of the Executive Yuan:

(1) If the applicant requiring the use of the land to be compulsorily purchased is one of the five Yuan of the National Government or any governmental office under their direct jurisdiction, any Provincial Government, or any Municipal Government under the direct jurisdiction of the Executive Yuan.

(2) If the undertaking to be promoted is under the direct control or supervision of any one of the Yuan, Ministries, or Commissions of the National Government.

(3) If the land to be compulsorily purchased lies within the territorial limits of two or more Provinces.

(4) If the land to be compulsorily purchased lies within the territorial limits of a Municipality under the direct jurisdiction of the Executive Yuan.

Article 223: The compulsory purchase of land under any one of the following conditions shall be subject to the approval of the Provincial Government:

(1) If the applicant requiring the use of the land to be compulsorily purchased is any one of the Departments of the Provincial Government or any governmental office under them, any Municipal or County Government, any governmental office under it, or any local self-governing body.

(2) If the undertaking to be promoted is under the control or supervision of any local Government.

All cases approved by the Provincial Government according to the provisions of the preceding paragraph shall be reported to the Executive Yuan for reference.

Article 224: In applying for the compulsory purchase of land, the applicant shall prepare a detailed project of compulsory purchase, a map with explanatory notes of the land to be compulsorily purchased and a blueprint showing how the land is to be used, and submit them for approval according to the provisions of the preceding two Articles.

Article 225: Upon the approval of any application for the compulsory purchase of land, the Executive Yuan or the Provincial Government shall transmit all the details of the case to the Land Office of the competent Municipality or County where the land is situated.

Article 226: In case two or more applicants apply for the compulsory purchase of the same land, the comparative importance of the undertakings sponsored shall be the criterion whereby approval is to be granted. In case the nature of the undertakings sponsored happens to be of equal importance, the order in which the applications have been made shall be the criterion whereby approval is to be granted.

Article 227: On receipt of instructions from the Executive Yuan or the Provincial Government concerning the approval of any application for the compulsory purchase of land, the Municipal or County Land Office shall make a public announcement thereon and notify the owner of the said land and other obligees having rights over it accordingly.

The period of the public announcement referred to in the preceding paragraph shall be 30 days.

Article 228: In case the land to be compulsorily purchased is a land whereof the registration of ownership is not yet completed, the holders of other rights over it shall, within 30 days after the expiration of the period of public announcement*, apply to the competent Municipal or County Land Office for the official recording of their rights. In case the land to be compulsorily purchased is a land whereof the registration of ownership is completed, only such other rights over it shall be recognized as are recorded in the land register on the last day when the period of public announcement expires.

---

*The phrase "within 30 days after the expiration of the period of public announcement" is a correct translation of the Chinese text, but it is apparent from the

(Continued on next page)

Article 229: In case the land to be compulsorily purchased is a land whereof the registration of ownership is not yet completed according to law and over which the holders of other rights fail to apply for the recording of their rights according to the provisions of the preceding Article, such rights shall not be regarded as liabilities borne by the land under compulsory purchase.

Article 230: The applicant requiring the use of the land to be compulsorily purchased may, after the public announcement has been made, go unto the land to make inspections or serveying.

In making inspections or surveying as referred to in the preceding paragraph, the applicant shall notify the landowner or the holder of other right over the land to remove obstacles on the said land or have the obstacles removed for him.

Article 231: The applicant requiring the ues of the land to be compulsorily purchased shall not go unto the said land to begin construction work before the compensation for the land value and other compensations have been fully paid.   But this provision shall not apply to the implementation of national economic policies nor to undertakings mentioned in Section (1), (2), or (4) of Article 208, if special permission is given by the Executive Yuan to use the said land before payment of the compensations therefor.

If the applicant who uses the said land with the special permission of the Executive Yuan as provided for in the preceding paragraph fails to pay the compensation for the land value according to law, the orginal owner of the said land may appeal for redress according to law.

Article 232: After public announcement has been made of the impending compulsory purchase of any land, its obligee shall not add any improvement thereon, and the construction of any improvements which is in progress at the time of the public announcement shall be immediately stopped.   But if the competent Municipal or County Land Office considers that the addition or continued construction of such improvements will not hinder the execution of the compulsory purchase project, special permission may be given, at the request of the obligee concerned, for the addition or continued construction of such improvements.

Article 233: Compensation for the value of a compulsorily purchased land and other compensations therefor shall be paid within 15 days after

provisions of Articles 229, 221, and 233 that the phrase should read "within 30 days beginning from the date of public announcement."

the expiration of the period of public announcement. But in the case of lands compulsorily purchased for the implementation of national economic policies or for those undertakings mentioned in Section (1), (2), or (4) of Article 208, the compensations may be paid, upon approval of the Executive Yuan, partly with land bonds.

Article 234: After all the compensations for a compulsorily purchased land have been duly paid, the Municipal or County Land Office may fix a time limit within which the said land shall be vacated by the original obligee or user thereof.

Article 235: The rights and obligations of the original owner in respect of his land that is compulsorily purchased shall terminate when the compensations he is entitled to are paid in full. Pending the full paymant of the said compensations, he shall have the right to continue to use the said land except in those cases covered by the last sentence of Paragraph one of Article 231.

Chapter III. Compensations for Compulsory Purchase

Article 236: Compensation for land value, other compensations, and removal fees to be paid for the compulsorily purchased land shall be fixed by the competent Municipal or County Land Office.

Compensation for land value, other compensations, and removal fees referred to in the preceding paragraph shall all be borne by the applicant requiring the use of the land to be compulsorily purchased and shall be paid through the competent Municipal or County Land Office.

Article 237: In effecting the payment of the compensation for land value and other compensations, the Municipal or County Land Office may deposit the sum of money in the local court in either of the following cases:

(1) In case the rightful recipient refuses or is unable to accept the payment.

(2) In case the whereabouts of the rightful recipient is unknown.

Article 238: Under any one of the following conditions, the Municipal or County Land Office may remove the improvements on a compulsorily purchased land on behalf of their owners or purchase them together with the land:

(1) If the rightful recipient of the removal fee refuses or is unable to accept the payment.

(2) If the whereabouts of the rightful recipient of the removal fee is unknown.

(3) If the rightful recipient of the removal fee fails to remove the said improvements within the prescribed time limit.

Article 239: The compensation for land value payable for the land to be compulsorily purchased shall be determined according to the following provisions:

(1) Where the value of the land to be compulsorily purchased has been assessed according to law and the ownership thereof has undergone no transfer, the compensation therefor shall be based on its statutory value.

(2) Where the value of the land to be compulsorily purchased has been assessed according to law and the ownership thereof has been transferred, the compensation therefor shall be based on its value at the last transfer.

(3) Where the value of the land to be compulsorily purchased has not been assessed according to law, the compenation therefor shall be based on the land value as assessed by the competent Municipal or County Land Office.

Article 240: The compensation for the value of land reserved for compulsory purchase shall be based on its value at the time of compulsory purchase.

Article 241: The compensation for improvements on land that are compulsorily purchased shall be based on their value as assessed by the competent Municipal or County Land Office.

Article 242: Where the agricultural improvements on a compulsorily purchased land are also compulsorily purchased and where the fruits thereof are due to ripen within one year from the date of compulsory purchase, the compensation for such improvements shall be based on the assessed value of the ripened fruits.

Article 243: Due compensation shall be paid to the owner of the adjacent land whereto damage is caused by the removal of obstacles on the compulsorily purchased land according to the provisions of Paragraph two of Article 230.

Article 244:   A due amount of removal fee shall be paid for the removal of the improvements on any land if such improvements thereon have to be removed elsewhere as a result of the compulsory purchase of the said land.

Article 245:   In case all the improvements on any land have to be removed elsewhere owing to the compulsory purchase of a part of the said land, the owner of the said improvements may request that removal fee be paid him for all the improvements.

Article 246:   Where graves and other commemorative objects on a compulsorily purchased land have to be removed elsewhere, the removal fee payable therefor shall be the same as that payable for the removal of improvements therefrom.

The applicant requiring the use of the land to be compulsorily purchased shall have all ownerless graves thereon safely removed and re-interred elsewhere, and make a detailed statement in tabulated form thereanent and submit it to the competent Municipal or County Land Office for record.

Article 247:   In case any objection should be raised as to the amount of compensation fixed according to the provisions of Article 239, 241 or 242, the competent Municipal or County Land Office shall refer the matter to the Committee on Standard Land Values for decision.

LAW GOVERNING THE APPLICATION
OF THE LAND LAW

(Promulgated by the National Government, May 8, 1935;
enforced, March 1, 1936; amended April 29, 1946)

Part I.   General Principles

Article 1: This Law is hereby enacted according to the provisions of Article 9 of the Land Law.

Article 2: The Land Law and this Law shall both come into force from the day on which this Law is promulgated.

Article 3: All work relating to land administration that was carried out in the various localities before the enforcement of the Land Law shall be subject to review by the Central Land Administration, and the said Administration shall give instructions to rectify any part of the work found to have been improperly carried out.

Article 4: In respect of the categories into which the different types of land are subdivided according to Article 2 of the Land Law, as well as their descriptive symbols, the competent County or Municipal Land Office shall find out the designations customarily used in the locality and submit them to the Provincial Land Administration for approval and official adoption and for transmission to the Central Land Administration for reference. In any municipality under the direct jurisdication of the Executive Yuan, the Land Office shall adopt such designations on its own authority and report them to the Central Land Administration for reference.

Article 5: The "certain limits" referred to in Sections (1) to (4) inclusive, Article 14 of the Land Law shall be definitely determined by the competent Municipal or County Land Office in collaboration with the competent water conservancy authorities.

Article 6: When any enterprise operated by the State requires the use of public land, the location and size of the land shall be determined by the highest authority in charge of the said enterprise and the required land shall be allotted gratis for the designated use by the competent Municipal or County Government, provided that the allocation is duly approved by the Executive Yuan.

Article 7: The limits on the maximum area of land referred to in Article 28 of the Land Law shall be severally prescribed for the different categories of land: land for dwelling houses shall be limited to 10 *mow;* agricultural land to an area from which the net income is sufficient to provide sustenance for a family of ten; and land for the use of other undertaking to an area commensurate with the size of each individual undertaking.

Article 8: Where land bonds are used to pay for private land compulsorily purchased according to article 29 of the Land Law, the period during which such bonds shall be liquidated shall not exceed five years.

Part II. Cadastration

Article 9: Where the cadastral survey that was undertaken in any locality before the enforcement of the Land Law is in conformity with the provisions of Article 44 of the Land Law, the Provincial Government or the Municipal Government under the direct jurisdiction of the Executive Yuan may report the work to the Central Land Administration for approval, which, if granted, shall exempt the said locality concerned from undertaking another cadastral survey.

Article 10: The period of application for registration proclaimed according to the provisions of Article 48 of the Land Law shall be reported to the Central Land Administration for reference.

Article 11: Localities which have, before the enforcement of the Land Law, completed the registration of land according to local regulations approved by superior authorites, may be exempt from undertaking another registration, but those localities where the registrations is incomplete in its scope shall take steps to complete the registration according to law and submit a report thereon to the Central Land Administration for reference.

Article 12: Localities, wherein cadastral survey has been completed, formal registration of land has not been undertaken, but a provisional registration of land and the issuance of provisional certificates of land-ownership have been carried out under authorization, shall proceed to undertake, according to law, the general registration of land and the issuance of formal certificates of landownership and of other rights over land; but the fees previously paid by the holders of provisional certificates shall be counted as part of the certificate and registration fees now payable.

Article 13: In localities where the general registration of land is being undertaken, the courts of law shall, beginning from the first day of the general registration, suspend the registration of immovable property. But lands which have already been registered by the courts shall be registered anew without charge.

Article 14: In localities where the general registration of land is being undertaken, the office in charge of recording the transfer of immovable property shall suspend its operations beginning from the first day of the general registration.

Article 15: The period of the public announcements made according to the provisions of Articles 55 and 57 of the Land Law shall be submitted by the competent Municipal or County Land Office to the Central Land Administration for approval.

Article 16: During the period of the general registration of land, holders of untaxed old title deeds may be allowed to pay the title-deed tax at a later date and shall not be subject to fines.

Article 17: The shapes and sizes of forms and books to be used in land registration shall be prescribed by the Central Land Administration.

Article 18: The collection of registration and certificate fees shall not be delayed even if objection has been raised in respect of the standard land value. But as soon as such standard value has been duly fixed according to law, the amount of the said fees shall be adjusted accordingly.

Article 19: In undulating areas where the configuration of farm land is such as to break it into very tiny fields, all such fields belonging to the same owner that are adjacent to one another and are of the same category may be combined to form a single plot and the configuration of the tiny fields shall be shown on the plot map, but they shall be registered as a single plot.

Part III. Land Use

Article 20: After the classification of lands into different categories for specific uses is announced according to Article 84 of the Land Law, separate notifications thereof shall be sent to landowners, and a report thereof shall be submitted to the Central Land Administration for reference.

Article 21: The minimum units for the different categories of land prescribed according to Article 31 of the Land Law and the size of collective farms prescribed according to Article 86 of the same Law shall be submitted to the Executive Yuan for approval.

Article 22: The compensation for lands purchased at their declared values according to Article 89 of the Land Law may be paid in installments, but the period of payment shall not be longer than five years.

Article 23: The formulation of city planning projects and any change therein shall be submitted to the Executive Yuan for approval.

Article 24: In newly created cities, the areas to be offered for development one after another shall be defined in the city planning project, and the time for offering each of such areas for development shall be fixed by the competent Municipal or County Government in the light of local needs and subject to the approval of the Executive Yuan.

Article 25: In computing the total value of the land and buildings thereon as referred to in Article 97 of the Land Law, the value of land shall be its statutory value and the value of buildings shall be the value as assessed by the competent Municipal or County Land Office.

Article 26: In localities where farm rent is payable in farm products according to local custom, the rate at which the farm products are to be converted into cash shall be fixed by the competent Municipal or County Land Office according to the average market prices of such products prevailing in the last two years in the said localities.

Whenever land value is re-assessed, the value of the aforesaid farm products shall be also re-appraised in the light of actual fluctuations therein.

Article 27: The provisions of Sections (1), (2), (6) and (7) of Article 114 of the Land Law shall, *mutatis mutandis,* apply to farm lease contracts for a definite period.

Article 28: Where the lessee claims from the lessor the repayment of the outlay for special improvements according to the provisions of Article 120 of the Land Law, the cost of that part of the special improvements which has not lost its utility may be appraised by the competent Municipal or County Land Office.

Article 29: The decisions on the reduction or remission of farm rent made according to the provisions of Article 123 of the Land Law shall be subject to the approval of the Central Land Administration.

Article 30: The provisions of Articles 115, 122 and 123 of the Land Law shall, *mutatis mutandis,* apply to lands subject to perpetual lease *(yungtien).*

Article 31: Projects for the utilization of uncultivated land in different localities shall be formulated by the competent Provincial or Municipal Government, and submitted to the Central Land Administration and the central reclamation authorities for reference; but projects for the utilization of vast tracts of uncultivated land covering 100,000 *mow* or more may be formulated by the Central Land Administration and the central reclamation authorities in collaboration with the Provincial Government.

Article 32: The provisions of the Land Law and of this Law concerning owner-cultivators shall, *mutatis mutandis,* apply to the use, management, transfer and inheritance of those lands under reclamation where of the settlers have acquired ownership after the completion of the reclamation work.

Article 33: Projects of land replotting in cities and municipalities shall be subject to the approval of the Central Land Administration.

Article 34: Projects for the replotting of farm lands shall be formulated by the competent Municipal or County Government in the light of farming techniques and local needs, and submitted to the Central Land Administration for reference.

Article 35: If the value of land in the area to be replotted has not yet been assessed, it shall be assessed according to law before replotting begins.

Part IV. Land Tax

Article 36: In localities where the value of land has been assessed according to law, the competent Municipal or County Government shall immediately fix the basic rate* of the land value tax according to Article 169 of the Land Law, the initial point of land value subject to progressive rates accroding to Article 171, the multiplier for the vacant land tax according to Artilcle 173, the multiplier for the uncultivated land tax according to Article 174, the amount of remission of the land value in-

---

*It will be noted by the discerning reader that the basic rate of the land value tax is already fixed at 1.5 per cent of the statutory land value by Article 169 of the Land Law.

crement tax according to Article 180, and the rate of the tax on constructional improvements according to Article 186; submit the said rate, point multipliers, and amount through the regular channels of official communication to the Execultive Yuan for approval; and proceed to levy the land value tax, the land value increment tax, and the tax on constructional improvements accordingly.

Article 37: Before levying the "construction benefit charge," the Municipal or County Government shall submit through the Provincial Government to the Executive Yuan for approval the rules governing such levy together with the engineering project and the budget.

Article 38: Where the engineering work for the improvement of land referred to in Article 147 of the Land Law is not undertaken by the competent Municipal or County Government itself, the "construction benefit charge" shall be levied on behalf of the sponsoring agency by the Municipal or County Government in whose territory such engineering work is carried on.

Article 39: The "construction benefit charge" may be paid in a lump sum or in installments. The payer of the said charge shall be determined in conformity with the provisions of Article 172 of the Land Law. Cases of failure to pay the said charge shall be dealt with according to the provisions relating to delinquency in the payment of the land value tax.

Article 40: Rules governing the investigation and assessment of the value of land and those governing the assessment of the value of constructional improvements on land shall be formulated by the Central Land Administration.

Article 41: Where land is compulsorily purchased or purchased at its statutory value according to the provisions of Articles 29, 33, 34, 89, or 157, the constructional improvements thereon shall be purchased together with the land, unless the owner of such improvements undertakes to remove them elsewhere.

Article 42: After the basic rate of the land value tax, the initial point of the land value subject to progressive rates, the multiplier for the vacant land tax or for the uncultivated land tax, the amount of remission of the land value tax and the rate of tax on constructional improvements have been fixed and enforced, any increase or decrease in such rate, point, multiplier, or amount, if called for, shall be effected according to the procedure prescribed in Article 36 of this Law, and announced before the beginning of the next fiscal year.

Article 43: "The land value tax leviable on the said land" referred to in Article 173 and Article 174 of the Land Law shall mean the land value tax leviable on the vacant land or uncultivated land according to the basic rate.

Article 44: The Municipal or County Government shall make an annual investigation of the lands owned by absentee landlords within its jurisdiction and compile a register thereof to be submitted to the Provincial Government for the purpose of levying the increased amount of the land value tax on such lands according to law.*

The Municipal Government under the direct jurisdiction of the Executive Yuan shall make an annual investigation of the lands owned by absentee landlords within its jurisdiction, and levy the increased amount of the land value tax on such lands according to law.*

Article 45: When a landowner ceases to be absentee landlord, he shall report the fact to the competent Municipal or County Land Office, but he shall be exempted from the increased levy prescribed in Article 175 of the Land Law only after one full year has elapsed from the day when his report is submitted.

Article 46: The criteria and procedure for the reduction and remission of the land tax shall be governed by rules to be formulated by the Central Land Administration and the central financial authorities.

Article 47: When a land originally exempt from taxes becomes taxable, the land tax thereon shall be levied beginning from the year following.

Article 48: When a taxable land becomes exempt from taxes, the land tax thereon shall be remitted beginning from the year when the cause of exemption begins to be operative. But the said land shall not be exempt from taxes if it is not put to such use as to qualify it for exemption.

Part V. Compulsory Purchase of Land

Article 49: The compulsory purchase of land shall, in so far as the objective of the compulsory purchase can be attained, be effected in places where the least damage will be done and where, as far as possible, no farm land is involved.

Article 50: The project of compulsory purchase referred to in Article

---

*See Article 175 of the Land Law.

224 of the Land Law shall specify the following items:

(1) Reasons for the compulsory purchase.

(2) The location, extent, and area of the land to be compulsorily purchased.

(3) The nature of the undertaking to be promoted.

(4) The law or decree on which the undertaking to be promoted is based.

(5) Incidental purchase or zone purchase; and its area.

(6) Condition of improvements on the land to be compulsorily purchased.

(7) Description of the present use of the land, and the name and address of the user.

(8) Description of the present use of the adjacent lands, and condition of improvements thereon.

(9) Scenic spots and historic remains, if any, within the area to be compulsorily purchased, a statement of their history and present condition.

(10) A statement as to whether negotiations have been made with the landowner and the results thereof.

(11) Name and address of the landowner or the custodian of the land.

(12) Detailed project of the use of the land to be compulsorily purchased.

(13) Outline plan of the undertaking to be promoted.

(14) The total amount of the compensations required and the distribution thereof.

(15) The total amount of the reserve fund and the distribution thereof.

Article 51: The map with explanatory notes of the land to be compulsorily purchased referred to in Article 224 of the Land Law shall indicate the following items:

(1) Extent and boundaries of the land to be compulsorily purchased.

(2) Boundaries of the different plots within the area to be compulsorily purchased, and a description of their present use.

(3) Location and names of neighboring streets, village *(tsun)*, districts and townships.

(4) Location of improvements such as houses, etc., within the area to be compulsorily purchased.

(5) The scale of the map.

Article 52: The detailed project of compulsory purchase, the map with explanatory notes of the land to be compulsorily purchased, and the blueprint showing how the land is to be used, as referred to in Article 224 of the Land Law, shall each be made in triplicates and submitted to the competent authorities for approval.

Article 53: The blueprint showing how the land is to be used, as referred to in Article 224 of the Land Law, shall mean the "ground plan of construction" in the case of public enterprises, the "city-planning project" in the case of newly created cities, and the "replotting project" in the case of land replotting.

Article 54: All cases of compulsory purchase approved according to the provisions of Article 222 of the Land Law shall, after full payment has been effected for the compulsorily purchased land, be reported in detail to the Executive Yuan for approval. All cases of compulsory purchase approved according to the provisions of Article 223 of the Land Law shall, after full payment has been effected for the compulsorily purchased land, be reported in detail to the Provincial Government for approval.

Article 55: The public announcement made according to the provisions of Article 227 of the Land Law shall specify the following items:

(1) The full name of the applicant requiring the use of the land to be compulsorily purchased.

(2) The type of undertaking to be promoted.

(3) A detailed statement of the specific area of the land to be compulsorily purchased.

(4) The amount of compensations to be paid for the compulsorily purchased land.

The public announcement referred to in the preceding paragraph shall be accompanied with a map of the land to be compulsorily purchased, and posted in front of the competent Municipal or County Land Office as well as at the place where the land to be compulsorily purchased is located.

Article 56: The notification referred to in Ariticle 227 of the Land Law shall be made according to the following provisions:

(1) Where the land to be compulsorily purchased has been duly registered, a written notification shall be sent to that owner of the said land and to those other obligees having rights over it whose names appear on the general register.

(2) Where the land to be compulsorily purchased has not been duly registered, a notification shall be published in the local newspaper for seven days.

Article 57: The period in which any land may be reserved for compulsory purchase shall be calculated from the day on which a public announcement to that effect is made.

Article 58: The computation and disbursement of compensations for any compulsorily purchased land shall be made, on behalf of the applicant requiring the use of the land, by the competent Municipal or County Land Office.

Article 59: The liabilities borne by any land under compulsory purchase shall be settled by the competent Municipal or County Land Office out of the compensations for the said land, when such compensations are paid, and the surplus, if any, shall be handed over to the owner of the said land.

Article 60: "Its value at the last transfer" referred to in Section (2), Article 239 of the Land Law, shall be such value as has been duly registered.

Article 61: In removing ownerless graves according to the provisions of Paragraph two, Article 246 of the Land Law, a public announcement to that effect shall be made ten days prior to their actual removal, and the period of the said announcement shall not be shorter than seven days.

THE FARM RENT REDUCTION TO 37.5% ACT

(Passed by the Legislative Yuan, May 25, 1951; promulgated by the President of the Republic of China, June 7, 1951)

Article 1: The lease of farm land shall conform to the provisions of this Act. Matters not provided for in this Act shall be governed by the provisions of the Land Law and the Civil Code.

Article 2: The amount of farm rent shall not exceed 37.5 per cent of the total annual yield of the principal product of the main crop. If the rent originally agreed upon exceeds 37.5 per cent, it shall be reduced to 37.5 per cent; and if it is less than 37.5 per cent, it shall not be increased.

In the preceding paragraph, the term "main crop" shall mean the crop most commonly grown or the rotation crop actually grown according to local farming practices, and "principal product" shall mean the chief article for which the crop is grown.

Article 3: A Land Commission shall be established by each County or Municipal Government and by each District, Township or Urban Disitrict Office. The number of members representing tenant farmers on the Committee shall be no fewer than the total number of members representing landlords and owner-farmers. Rules for the organization of such Committees shall be drawn up by the Provincial Government and submitted to the Executive Yuan for approval.

Article 4: The standard amount of the total annual yield of the principal article of the main crop of a farm land shall be appraised, with reference to the grade to which it belongs, by the Land Commission of the District, Township or Urban District Office, and the amount appraised shall be submitted to the Land Commission of the County or Municipal Government for confirmation, and to the Provincial Government for final approval.

Article 5: The period for which any farm land is leased shall not be shorter than six years. If the period originally agreed upon is longer than six years, it shall remain unchanged.

Article 6:   After the enforcement of this Act, all farm lease contracts shall be made in writing, and the lessor and the lessee shall jointly apply for the registration of the signing, revision, termination, or renewal of their farm lease contract.

Rules governing the registration referred to in the preceding paragraph shall be drawn up by the Provincial Government and submitted to the Executive Yuan for approval.

Article 7:   The amount, kind, quality and standard of farm rent, the date and place of payment and other relevant matters shall be specified in the lease contract.   If the rent payable in kind is to be delivered by the lessee, the lessor shall pay for the cost of delivery according to the distance covered.

Article 8:   The lessee shall pay the rent when due.   On accepting the rent paid in kind, the lessor shall make measurement thereof only with officially certified measures of volume or weight.

Article 9:   If some other crop is planted instead of the stipulated main crop during its growing season, the lessee shall nevertheless pay the rent in terms of the stipulated main crop; but he may, with the consent of the lessor, pay the rent either in cash or in terms of the crop actually planted, by duly converting it at the local market price at the time of payment.

Article 10:   If the lessor refuses, without adequate cause, to accept the rent paid according to the provisions of this Act and the terms of the lease contract, the lessee may, with the cognizance of the Village *(tsun)* and Precinct *(li* or *pao)* Chiefs and of the farmers' association, deliver the crop rent to the District, Township or Urban District Office for safekeeping, and notify the lessor to pick it up within ten days.   If he fails to do so, the said Office may, if necessary, sell the crop by tenders at the current local market price, and hold the proceeds therefrom in safekeeping for the lessor.   This procedure shall have the same validity as a formal lodgement in a court of law.

Article 11:   If a crop failure on any farm land is caused by natural disaster or other *force majeure,* the lessee may request the Land Commission of the District, Township, or Urban District Office to investigate and ascertain the extent of the crop failure and to decide on measures for the reduction of rent, and the Commission must take action within three days.

If a general crop failure occurs in any given area, the Commission shall immediately investigate and ascertain the extent of the crop failure in the area affected and submit a report thereon to the Land Commission of the County or Municipal Government with the request that measures for the reduction of rent be adopted.

If, owing to crop failure, the total yield is less than 30 per cent of the normal yield, the entire rent payment shall be remitted.

Article 12: The farmhouse of the lessee which has been originally provided unconditionally by the lessor shall continue to be used by the lessee after the enforcement of this Act, and the lessor shall not, under whatever pretext, refuse such use or charge any fee therefor.

Article 13: The lessee may freely make special improvements on the leased farm land, but shall give the lessor a written notice of the particulars and the amount of the outlay incurred. When the farm land is returned to the lessor on the termination of the lease contract, he shall repay to the lessee the cost of that part of the improvements which has not yet lost its utility.

The "special improvements on farm land" referred to in the preceding paragraph shall mean improvements resulting from the increased application of labor and capital which, besides preserving the original qualities and utility of the land, increases its productivity or facilitates its cultivation.

Article 14: The lessor shall not collect the farm rent in advance or demand any security deposit. Any security deposit already paid before the enforcement of this Act shall be returned to the lessee in installments or deducted in installments from the rent payable by the lessee.

If the deposit referred to in the preceding paragraph has been paid in cash, it shall be converted into terms of farm products by the Land Commission of the County or Municipal Government at the local market price of the time when the deposit was paid.

Article 15: If a farm land is offered for sale or *dien**, the lessee shall have the preferential right to accept the offer and the lessor shall give him

---

* According to the provisions of the Chinese Civil Code, **dien** means the right to take possession of another person's real estate and to use it and to enjoy the incomes accruing therefrom by paying a price for it (Article 911), and the **dien**-holder acquires the ownership of the property in case its owner fails to redeem it within two years after the expiration of the contractual period (Article 923).

a written notice of the terms thereof. If the lessee makes no written reply to the said offer within 15 days, he shall be deemed to have waived his preferential right.

If the said farm land is offered for sale or *dien* for the second time at a lower price because no one has accepted the sale or *dien* at the original price, the lessor shall be again required to comply with the provisions of the preceding paragraph.

If the lessor signs a contract with a third party in violation of the provisions of the preceding two paragraphs, the contract shall be invalid as against the lessee.

Article 16: The lessee shall cultivate the leased land himself and shall not sublease the whole or part thereof to another person.

If the lessee violates the provisions of the preceding paragraph, the lease contract shall become null and void, and the lessor may take back the leased land for his own cultivation or lease it to another person. If such violation occurred before the enforcement of this Act, the actual cultivator of that part of the land which has been subleased and the original lessee cultivating the other part which has not been subleased shall, individually and separately, sign new lease contracts with the original lessor, and these new contracts shall expire on the date when the original contract expires.

If, during the period of the lessee's military service which causes a shortage of farm labor, he entrusts the whole or part of the leased farm land to another person for cultivation, the land so entrusted shall not be regarded as having been subleased.

Article 17: Farm lease contracts shall not be terminated before the expiration of the period of the contracts, except under any one of the following conditions:

(1) If the lessee dies without leaving an heir.

(2) If the lessee waives his right of cultivation by migrating elsewhere or changing his occupation.

(3) If the cumulative amount of the farm rent the lessee has failed to pay is equivalent to the total of two years' rent.

Article 18: The termination of a farm lease contract shall take place after the harvest season and before the next planting season, unless there are special local customs to the contrary.

Article 19: The lessor shall not take the leased land for his own cultivation on the expiration of the period of the lease contract under any one of the following conditions:

(1) Where the lessor is unable to cultivate the land himself.

(3) Where the lessor's total income is sufficient to support his family.

(3) Where the lessor's action in taking back the land will deprive the lessee's family of its subsistence.

In case the lessor's total income is insufficient to support to his family and at the same time the situation mentioned in Section (3) of the preceding paragraph is bound to arise, he may request the Land Commission of the District, Township or Urban District Office for conciliation.

Article 20: If, on the expiration of the period of the farm lease contract, the lessee is willing to continue the lease, the contract shall be renewed, unless the lessor takes back the land for his own cultivation in accordance with the provisions of this Act.

Article 21: The lessor who forces the lessee to waive his right of cultivation by violence or duress shall be punished with imprisonment for a term of three years or less.

Article 22: In any one of the following cases, the lessor shall be punished with imprisonment for a term of one year or less or with detention:

(1) If he terminates the lease contract in violation of the provisions of Article 17.

(2) If he takes back the land for his own cultivation in violation of the provisions of Article 19.

(3) If he refuses to renew the lease contract in violation of the provisions of Article 20.

Article 23: In any one of the following cases, the lessor shall be punished with detention, or a fine of 200 dollars or less:

(1) If he collects excessive rent in violation of the provisions of Article 2.

(2) If he collects rent in advance or demands security deposit in violation of the provisions of Article 14.

Article 24: The lessee shall be punished with detention or a fine of 200 dollars or less, if he violates the provisions of Paragraph one of Article 16.

Article 25: If the lessor transfers the ownership of the leased land to, or creates a *dien* over it in favor of, a third party before the expiration of the period of the lease contract, the contract shall remain valid in respect of the transferee or *dien*-holder, and the transferee or *dien*-holder shall, jointly with the original lessee, apply for the registration of the revision of the said contract.

Article 26: If any dispute concerning the lease of a farm land arises between the lessor and the lessee, it shall be submitted to the Land Commission of the District, Township or Urban District Office for conciliation. In case of the failure of conciliation, the dispute shall be submitted to the Land Commission of the County or Municipal Government for reconciliation. In case of the failure of re-conciliation, the latter Committee shall transfer the dispute to the judicial authorities, who shall immediately deal with it without charging any judicial fees therefor.

No judicial action shall be taken in regard to the dispute referred to in the preceding paragraph, before it has been submitted to conciliation and re-conciliation. If the dispute is settled by conciliation or re-conciliation, a written statement to that effect shall be issued by the Land Commission of the County or Municipal Government.

Article 27: If either of the parties to a dispute, for which a conciliation or re-conciliation has been effected according to the provisions of the preceding Article, fails to fulfill his obligations, the other party may request the competent local judicial authorities for compulsory enforcement and he shall not be required to pay any enforcement fee.

Article 28: The provisions of this Act shall, *mutatis mutandis,* apply to farm lands subject to perpetual lease *(yungtien).*

Article 29: After the enforcement of this Act, the Provincial Government shall, with due consideration of local conditions, formulate measures for the protection of farm hands and submit them to the Executive Yuan for approval.

Article 30: The regions in which this Act shall be enforced shall be announced by the Executive Yuan by decree.

Article 31: This Act shall come into force from the date of its promulgation.

REGULATIONS GOVERNING THE SALE OF PUBLIC FARM LANDS TO ESTABLISH OWNER-FARMERS IN TAIWAN PROVINCE

(Approved by the Executive Yuan, June 4, 1951; promulgated by the Taiwan Provincial Government, June 15, 1951)

Article 1: To govern the sale of public farm lands (hereinafter referred to as public lands) to establish owner-farmers, the present Regulations are hereby drawn up by the Taiwan Provincial Government.

Article 2: Public lands for sale shall be limited to those farm lands lying within the Province of Taiwan that are owned by the National Government or the Provincial Government.

Article 3: Where the public lands for sale are owned by the National Government the annual proceeds therefrom shall be turned over to the National Treasury as an Owner-Farmers Promotion Fund; and the Taiwan Provinical Government shall, at the end of each fiscal year, make the necessary transfers of accounts according to law. Where the public lands for sale are owned by the Provincial Government, all proceeds therefrom in excess of the farm rent originally collected shall also be credited to the Owner-Farmers Promotion Fund. Rules for the administration of the said Fund shall be separately prescribed.

Article 4: In the sale of public lands, the Land Bureau of the Department of Civil Affairs, Taiwan Provincial Government, shall be the responsible authority and the different County and Municipal Governments shall be executive agencies.

Article 5: A Committee for the Establishment of Owner-Farmers shall be set up by each County or Municipal Government to assist in the sale of public lands to promote owner-farmers, and rules for the organization of the said Committee shall be separately prescribed.

Article 6: Public lands shall be sold to applicants according to the following order of priority:

(1) Present tenant cultivator of public land.

(2) Farm hand.

(3) Tenant who is cultivating insufficient land under lease.

(4) Part-owner farmer who is cultivating insfficient land.

(5) Person who was originally an interested party in public land and who, having no land to cultivate now, is in need of some for cultivation.

(6) Person who changes his occupation and becomes a farmer.

If there are several applicants to purchase the same piece of public land, the choice shall be made by the Committee for the Establishment of Owner-Farmers.

Article 7: The standard area of public land to be purchased by a farming family shall be:

(1) One half to two *chia* (1.1988 to 4.7934 acres) of paddy field.

(2) One to four *chia* (2.3967 to 9.5868 acres) of cultivated dry land.

The County or Municipal Government shall group the different grades of public lands of different categories into three classes, and shall, according to the aforesaid standard, fix a definite area for each class of public land to be purchased by a farming family; but if the applicant is a tenant farmer of the public land lawfully leased to him, he may be allowed to purchase such area as is originally leased.

Article 8: The sales price of public land shall be calculated in terms of farm products at 2.5 times the total annual yield of the main crop fixed for each grade of such land.

The sales price referred to in the preceding paragraph shall be fixed by the local Committee for the Establishment of Owner-Farmers and reported through the County or Municipal Government to the Provincial Government for reference.

Article 9: The sales price of public land shall be paid by the purchaser in installments in ten years, and each annual payment plus the farm land tax or the land tax shall not exceed 37.5 per cent of the total annual yield of the main crop of the land purchased, but the purchaser may shorten the period of payment, if he wishes to pay off the total price at an earlier date. Rules for such earlier payment shall be separately prescribed.

Article 10: The purchaser of public land shall make the annual payment of the land price in two half-yearly installments without fail.

The land price shall, in general, be paid in farm products, but may be paid in cash by converting the amount payable in kind into monetary terms according to the market price announced by the local County or Municipal Government.

Article 11: The purchaser of public land shall be exempted from paying rent thereon from the year when the land is purchased, but he shall begin from the same year to pay the farm land tax or the land tax.

Article 12: The purchaser of public land shall acquire its ownership when he has fully paid the total land price within the prescribed period, and a landownership certificate shall be issued to him in exchange for the purchase certificate.

Article 13: The purchaser of public land shall not transfer the purchased land to another person without government approval, except in case of lawful inheritance. If he offers it for sale owing to his inability to undertake its cultivation, the Government may redeem the land at the original purchase price; and if special improvements have been made on such land, he may be compensated for that part of the improvements which has not lost its utility. If the purchaser dies without leaving a lawful heir, the Government shall take back the said land.

Article 14: The procedure for implementing the sale of public lands shall be as follows:

(1) Delimitation of the public lands to be offered for sale.

(2) Public announcement calling for applicants.

(3) Examination of the status of applicants.

(4) Collection of the first installment of the land price and issuance of purchase certificates.

(5) Issuance of landownership certificates in exchange for the purchase certificates, after the total price has been paid.

Article 15: If any purchaser of public land comes under any one of the following conditions, his purchase may be annulled and the land purchased may be taken back by the Government without refunding to him any part of the purchase price he has paid.

(1) If he has purchased the land under the assumed name of another person.

(2) If he does not cultivate the land himself.

(3) If he transfers the land in violation of the present Regulations.

(4) If he fails to pay the land price, the farm land tax, or the land tax without lawful grounds.

(5) If he violates the present Regulations and other relevant regulations.

Article 16: The present Regulations shall come into force from the date of their approval by the Executive Yuan.

THE LAND-TO-THE-TILLER ACT

(Passed by the Legislative Yuan, January 20, 1953, and promulgated
by the President of the Republic of China, January 26, 1953; amended
by the Legislative Yuan, April 6, 1954, and promulgated by the
President of the Republic of China, April 22, 1954)

Chapter I. General Provisions

Article 1: For the implementation of the Land-to-the-Tiller Policy, this Act is hereby adopted.

Matters which are left unprovided for in this Act shall be governed according to provisions of the Chinese Land Law and other related laws.

Article 2: The responsible organs for enforcing this Act shall be the Ministry of Interior for the Central Government, the Land Bureau of the Department of Civil Affairs for the Provincial Government, and the County or Municipal Government for the County or Municipality.

Article 3: After this Act goes into effect, the present Land Commission in each County or Municipal Government and in each District and Township Office shall assist in the execution of this Act.

Article 4: The term "present tillers," as used in this Act, shall mean tenant farmers and farm hands.

Article 5: The term "cultivated land," as used in this Act, shall mean privately owned paddy field and privately owned cultivated dry land.

Article 6: The term "landlord," as used in this Act, shall mean a landowner who rents his land to other person or persons for cultivation. Any land, which the owner does not till by himself or which is tilled largely by the owner's farm hands, shall be deemed to be tenant land, except that portion under the owner's own cultivation. However, orchards, tea plantations, land used for growing industrial materials or land under mechanical cultivation, and land under reclamation, though operated by farm hands, shall not be considered as tenant land.

A landowner or his dependent who entrusts his land to others for cultivation because he or his dependent is in military service, shall be considered as an owner-cultivator during the service period.

Article 7: The landlord from whom land shall be purchased for this Land-to-the-Tiller Program by the Government or by whom part of his land may be retained in accordance with this Act shall be the landowner who has been registered as chief of his household in the government land cadastre as of the first day of April 1952. Land transfers effected after April 1, 1952 shall not be recognized except for the following:

(1) Land transferred by act of succession.

(2) Land transferred as a result of court decision made prior to the effective date of this Act.

(3) Land purchased by its present tiller or tillers.

(4) Land compulsorily purchased by the Government in accordance with law.

Chapter II.   Government Purchase of Cultivated Land

Article 8: Tenant cultivated land of the following categories shall be puschased by the Government for resale to the present tiller or tillers:

(1) Land owned by the landlord in excess of the retention acreage prescribed in Article 10 of this Act.

(2) Land under joint ownership.

(3) Private portion of any land owned jointly by private individuals and the Government.

(4) Land under Government trusteeship.

(5) Land owned by private individuals or family clans for purposes of ancestral worship and land owned by religious institutions.

(6) Land owned by the Shenming Hui* and land owned by other juristic persons and corporate bodies.

---

* Popular religious associations in Taiwan.

(7) Land which the landlord does not wish to retain and requests the Government to purchase.

The land referred to in Sections (2) and (3) above may be retained, upon Government approval, by its lessor in accordance with the retention standards set forth in Article 10 of this Act, if the lessor is old and infirm, widowed, orphaned, or disabled and depends upon the land for his or her livelihood; or if a joint ownership of the land originally under individual ownership is created by act of succession with the joint owners being husband and wife, or brothers and sisters of blood relationship.

The retention acreage for land owned for ancestral worship and land owned by religious institutions referred to in Section (5) above, shall be twice as much as the retention acreage allowed for individual landlord. However, the right to retain such land shall be accorded only to those ancestral worship bodies and religious institutions which are already established prior to the effective date of this Act.

Article 9: Cultivated land of the following categories shall not be subject to purchase by the Government under this Act, when approved by the Provincial Government:

(1) Tenant land within the announced area of city planning.

(2) Newly reclaimed land and land on which crop harvests are obviously unreliable.

(3) Land used for experiment, research, or agricultural extension purposes.

(4) Land needed by educational and philanthropic institutions.

(5) Land required by public and private enterprises for growing necessary raw materials.

The Provincial Government, in granting the approval, shall report such approval to the Executive Yuan.

Article 10: After the effective date of this Act, the acreage of tenant cultivated land to be permitted to be retained by a landlord shall be 3 *chia* (7.1901 acres) of paddy field of 7th to 12th grade, inclusive. Retention acreage for paddy field and dry land of other grades shall be converted according to the following scales:

(1) Every ½ *chia* (1.6983 acres) of paddy field of 1st to 6th grade inclusive shall be equivalent to 1 *chia* (2.3967 acres) of paddy field of 7th to 12th grade inclusive.

(2) Every 1½ *chia* (4.0950 acres) of paddy field of 13th to 18th grade inclusive shall be equivalent to 1 *chia* of paddy field of 7th to 12th grade inclusive.

(3) Every 2 *chia* (4.7934 acres) of paddy field of 19th to 26th grade inclusive shall be equivalent to 1 *chia* of paddy field of 7th to 12th grade inclusive.

(4) Every 1 *chia* of dry land of 1st to 6th grade inclusive shall be equivalent to 1 *chia* of paddy field of 7th to 12th grade inclusive.

(5) Every 2 *chia* of dry land of 7th to 12th grade inclusive shall be equivalent to 1 *chia* of paddy field of 7th to 12th grade inclusive.

(6) Every 3 *chia* of dry land of 13th to 18th grade inclusive shall be equivalent to 1 *chia* of paddy field of 7th to 12th grade inclusive.

(7) Every 4 *chia* (9.5868 acres) of dry land of 19th to 26th grade inclusive shall be equivalent to 1 *chia* of paddy field of 7th to 12th grade inclusive.

The land to be retained shall be examined and defined by the District or Township Land Commission according to the above scales of retention, with the results thereof reported to the County or Municipal Land Commission for clearance and then forwarded to the County or Municipal Government for approval. The Land Commissions, in making the examination and clearance, may set the actual retention acreage at 10% more or less than the prescribed scales, as may be necessitated by the shape and terrain of the land in question.

A landlord who does not wish to retain the land may request the Government to purchase such land.

Article 11: In case a landlord's holdings consist of land leased out and land under self-cultivation, the retained portion of the land leased out, together with the acreage of land under self-cultivation, shall not exceed the retention limit referred to in the previous Article. If the acreage of land under self-cultivation already exceeds the retention limit, no portion of the land leased out shall be retained by the landlord.

Article 12: One year after the effective date of this Act, the present tiller, if he wishes to purchase the landlord's retained land referred to in Article 10 of this Act, may request the Government for loans. Procedures for granting such loans shall be formulated by the Provincial Government and submitted to the Executive Yuan for approval. When a landlord wishes to sell his retained land, the present tiller on such land shall have first priority of purchase. The purchase price of such land shall be negotiated by the parties concerned, or decided by a ruling of the Land Commission in case the negotiation fails.

Article 13: Farmhouses, drying grounds, ponds, fruit trees, bamboos, woods etc., and sites thereof which are accessory to the land under Government purchase and are used by its present tenant farmer shall be purchased by the Government together with the land.

The purchase price of the above accessory properties and their sites shall be appraised by the District or Township Land Commission, agreed upon by the County or Municipal Land Commission, and approved by the Provincial Government. The purchase price of such accessory properties and their sites shall be included in, and paid together with, the purchase price of the land. When local custom requires no compensation for such accessory properties, the local custom shall prevail.

Article 14: The purchase price of the land shall be 2.5 times the amount of its total annual main crop yield for the respective land grades.

The amount of the total annual main crop yield mentioned above shall be calculated according to the standards as appraised and approved in the various localities during the 37.5% rent reduction program period.

Article 15: The purchase price for the land shall be paid 70 per cent in land bonds in kind and 30 per cent in Government enterprise stock shares.

Article 16: Land bonds in kind shall be issued by the Provincial Government in accordance with law. They shall bear interest at the rate of 4 per cent in kind per annum and shall be redeemable in equal annual amounts over a period of ten years. The actual handling of the issuance, redemption, and interest payment of the land bonds shall be entrusted to the Land Bank in the province.

Holders of these said bonds shall be exempt from paying the stamp tax, the income tax on interests, and the household tax as a special tax.

Article 17: The procedures for Government purchase of cultivated land shall be as follows:

(1) The County or Municipal Government shall investigate the land to be purchased, prepare a list thereof and announce it to the public for a period of 30 days.

(2) Upon discovering any errors in the said list, the owner of any land, which is to be purchased by the Government, and other parties concerned may, within the stipulated period of public announcement, request the local Government to correct the errors.

(3) After the expiration of the period of public announcement, the County or Municipal Government shall notify the landowner to surrender, within a prescribed period, the ownership certificate and other relevant documents. If the landlord fails to surrender such certificate and relevant documents, they shall be declared null and void.

(4) The landowner, after surrendering the ownership certificate and relevant documents, or after such certificate and relevant documents have been declared null and void, shall pick up the purchase price in accordence with this Act. For any landowner, who fails to pick up the purchase price within a prescribed period, the Government shall, according to law, deposit the price in the local court.

The procedures for the purchase of accessory properties and their sites, referred to in Article 13 of this Act, shall be the same as those mentioned above.

Article 18: Other rights originally created on the cultivated land shall be liquidated after the purchase of the land by the Government in accordance with the following provisions:

(1) Rights of servitude and superficies shall be transferred together with the land.

(2) Rights of perpetual lease, *dien** and mortgage shall automatically become null and void; but such rights shall be compensated and paid for to the holder thereof by the County or Municipal Gov-

---

*See note on p. 193.

ernment on behalf of the landowner, in stock shares and land bonds, from the amounts to be paid to that owner as the Government purchase price for the land, in the same ratio of stock shares to land bonds as the landowner receives. However, the price paid for the liquidation of such rights shall not exceed the total purchase price of the land in question.

Chapter III. Resale of Government Purchased Land

Article 19: Cultivated land purchased by the Government shall be resold to the present tiller. The accessory properties and their sites purchased together with the land referred to in Article 13 of this Act shall also be resold to the present tiller.

Article 20: The resale price of the land shall be computed according to standards set up in Article 14 of this Act. The resale price, together with the price of accessory properties and their sites, shall bear interest at the rate of 4 per cent in kind per annum. Beginning from the season in which the land is purchased, the purchaser shall pay the price and its interest in 10 annual equal installments in kind, or in those land bonds in kind falling due in the same period. The average annual burden to be borne by the purchaser shall not exceed the burden on the same grade of land presently borne by the tenant farmer under the 37.5% rent reduction program. The purchaser may pay a part or the whole of the price and interest in advance. Measures encouraging such earlier payment shall be formulated by the Provincial Government and submitted to the Executive Yuan for approval.

Article 21: Procedures for reselling the cultivated land purchased by the Government shall be as follows:

(1) The County or Municipal Government shall investigate the names and status of the present tillers to whom the land is to be sold, and shall compile a purchasers' list thereof.

(2) The purchasers' list shall be examined by the District or Township Land Commission, agreed upon by the County or Municipal Land Commission, and shall be announced by the County or Municipal Government to the public for a period of 30 days.

(3) Upon discovering any errors in the purchasers' list, the purchaser and other parties concerned may, within the stipulated period of public announcement, request the local Government to correct the errors.

(4) The land purchaser shall submit a purchase application within 20 days after expiration of the period of public announcement. The County of Municipal Government shall, after examining the application, notify him to fulfill the required procedures of purchase within a prescribed period and to pay the first installment of the purchase price.

(5) Any purchaser, who fails to observe the provisions of Section (4) of this Article, shall lose his right of purchase.

Article 22: After the purchaser has completed the purchase procedures, the County or Municipal Government shall register the transfer of the ownership title and shall issue a landownership certificate to the purchaser.

In registering the ownership title transfer referred to in the preceding paragraph, the land purchaser shall be exempt from paying the property transfer tax and witness fees.

Article 23: The Government shall, after selling the land to the present tillers, establish a special production fund from which to extend cheap loans to them in order to improve land use and to increase farm production.

Article 24: The Government shall, after selling the land, encourage the purchasers to operate the land on a cooperative basis with improved techniques.

Article 25: Through proper channels, the purchaser may request the Provincial Government to grant certain reduction or exemption of the unliquidated portion of the purchase price on the land he has purchased, when such land has lost, due to *force majeure,* a part or the whole of its usability.

Reduction or exemption of the purchase price as approved by the Provincial Government under the preceding paragraph shall be reported annually to the Ministry of Interior for reference.

Article 26: After investigation and approval by the Government, the purchaser may be allowed to postpone for one or more payment periods the installment payments of the purchase price when, during such periods, the land has suffered seriously from catastrophe or harvest loss. Immediately after expiration of the amortization period of the total purchase price, the installment payments thus postponed shall be made up in the same number of payments as those for which the postponement was granted.

Article 27: Installment payments of the principal of the land bonds and interest that fall due shall be paid to the bond holders through the Land Bank from the installment payments of the purchase price and interest paid by the land purchaser. However, they may be paid from the Land Bond Redemption Guaranty Fund under any one of the following conditions:

(1) When the land purchaser is permitted to reduce or to postpone the amount of payment or to be exempt from payment.

(2) When the land purchaser defaults in the payment of the price.

Measures for establishing the Guaranty Fund shall be formulated by the Provincial Government and submitted to the Executive Yuan for approval.

Chapter IV. Restrictions and Penal Provisions

Article 28: Any purchaser who has acquired land under this Act shall not transfer it to any other person before its purchase price is fully paid; transfers of land, after its purchase price is fully paid, shall be permitted only when the transferee can cultivate it himself or it can be used for industrial or constructional purposes.

Any transfer of landownership in violation of the provisions of the preceding paragraph shall be null and void.

Article 29: In the event that the purchaser cannot till the land himself before its purchase price is fully paid, he may request the Government to purchase the land for resale to other farmers. The Government shall, in such case, reimburse to the purchaser in one lump sum the purchase price already paid.

Article 30: The Government shall take back the land sold to a purchaser and shall not refund any purchase price already paid, if he is found to have committed any of the following acts:

(1) Used the name of another person to purchase the land;

(2) Leased out the land after purchase;

(3) Failed to make an installment payment for more than four months

after falling due.

Article 31: Any person committing any of the following acts shall be punished by the court for a term of imprisonment not to exceed three years:

(1) Interference with the purchase of land by the Government under this Act, by violence, duress, or fraud;

(2) Interference with the resale of land under this Act, by violence, duress, or fraud;

(3) Damaging the land subject to Government purchase under this Act to such an extent as to render it unusable or less productive;

(4) Demolishing or removing the properties accessory to the land subject to Government purchase under this Act.

Article 32: Any purchaser who fails to pay any installment that falls due, shall be fined according to the following scales:

(1) A fine of 2% of the installment amount for a delay of less than one month;

(2) A fine of 5% of the installment amount for a delay of over one month but less than two month;

(3) A fine of 10% of the installment amount for a delay of over two months but less than three months;

(4) A fine of 15% of the installment amount for a delay of over three months.

In addition to the provisions of Article 30 of this Act, any purchaser who fails to pay any installment for more than four months shall be reported to the court for enforcing payment.

Chapter V. Supplementary Provisions

Article 33: Regulations governing the implementation of this Act shall be formulated by the Provincial Government of the province wherein this Act shall be effective and shall be submitted to the Executive Yuan for approval.

Article 34: The disposition of private cultivated land located within municipalities under the direct jurisdiction of the Executive Yuan, shall follow the same procedures as provided in this Act.

Article 35: The area in which this Act shall be effective shall be decided and announced by an order of the Executive Yuan.

Article 36: This Act shall become effective on the day of its promulgation.

REGULATIONS GOVERNING THE ISSUANCE OF LAND IN KIND, TAIWAN PROVINCE

(Passed by the Legislative Yuan, January 20, 1953, and promulgated by the President of the Republic of China, January 26, 1953; amended by the Legislative Yuan, June 19, 1953, and April 6, 1954, and promulgated by the President of the Republic of China, July 4, 1953, and April 22, 1954)

Article 1: For the purpose of implementing the Land-to-the-Tiller Program in Taiwan, the Central Government hereby authorizes the Taiwan Provincial Government to issue, in accordance with the present Regulations, bonds entitled "Land Bonds in Kind, Taiwan Province" (hereinafter to as the bonds) to be used for paying for the land to be purchased by the Government from landlords according to law.

Article 2: The bonds shall be issued according to areas with each County or Municipality as one area; and the name of each County or Municipality shall be stamped on the bonds for that area.

The Yangminshan Administration area shall be included in the Taipei County area.

Article 3: The procedures for issuing the bonds, the amortization of principal and the payment of interest shall be entrusted by order of the Provincial Government to the Land Bank of Taiwan.

Article 4: The commodity that the bonds stand for shall be one of two kinds of food crops, namely, rice or sweet potatoes:

(1) The amoount of rice bonds to be issued shall be for 1,260 million kilograms (2,777,821,200 lbs.) to be used for paying fields purchased by the Government, including double-crop land, single-crop land, "weather-depending field," and rotation land (including specially irrigated fields).

(2) The amount of sweet potato bonds to be issued shall be for 440 million kilograms (970,032,800 lbs.) to be used for paying for dry land purchased by the Government.

The two kinds of bonds referred to above shall be issued in 1953 at face value by the Provincial Government.

Article 5:   The bonds shall be secured by the proceeds from the resale to the tenants of government purchased land in accordance with the Land-to-the-Tiller Act and shall be further guaranteed by the Provincial Treasury of Taiwan.

Article 6:   The Provincial Government shall, in accordance with Article 27 of the Land-to-the-Tiller Act, set up a Land Bond Redemption Guaranty Fund for the bonds.   The fund shall be kept in custody by the Land Bank of Taiwan and, with the approval of the Provincial Government, used for making payments to landlords in case the land purchasers delay in installment payments or are exempt from making such payments for the land they have purchased due to crop failures or other causes.

The procedures for setting up the Guaranty Fund shall be formulated by the Provincial Government and shall be approved by the Executive Yuan.

Article 7:   The face value of the rice and sweet potato bonds shall be of six denominations, respectively: 50 kilograms (110 lbs.), 100 kilograms (220 lbs.), 500 kilograms, 1,000 kilograms, 5,000 kilograms, and 10,000 kilograms for rice; and 100 kilograms, 500 kilograms, 1,000 kilograms, 5,000 kilograms, 10,000 kilograms, and 30,000 kilograms (66,139 lbs.) for sweet potatoes.

Article 8:   The bonds shall be in the form of bearer bonds.

Article 9:   The bonds shall bear interest at the rate of four per cent in kind per annum.

Article 10:   The principal of the bonds together with interest shall be amortized in 10 years in 20 equal semi-annual installments.   The schedule of amortization of principal and payment of interest is shown in the attached table.

Article 11:   The principal and interest of the bonds shall be paid, upon maturity, to the bondholders as follows:

(1)   Rice bonds shall be paid in rice.   However, rice bonds intended to pay for the government purchased rotation land (including specially irrigated fields) shall be paid in cash by converting the rice into cash at the current market rice price in the locality at

the time of maturity of the installment, and rice bonds intended to pay for the government purchased single-crop land and "weather-depending field" shall be paid 50% in cash by converting the rice into cash at the current market rice price in the locality at the time of maturity of the installment.

(2) Sweet potato bonds shall be paid in cash by converting the sweet potatoes into cash at the market sweet potato price at the time of maturity of the installment.

The principal and interest in cash referred to above shall be paid through the local branches of the Land Bank of Taiwan and the principal and interest in rice shall be paid by the Provincial Food Bureau upon request of the Land Bank through local warehouses designated by the Bureau. The quality of rice to be paid for the rice bonds shall be in conformity with the standards as set up in the Regulations Governing Inspection and Collection of Land Tax in Kind in Taiwan.

Article 12: The current price of rice and sweet potatoes referred to in the preceding Article shall be decided by the County or Municipal Government on the basis of average wholesale quotations in important rice-producing townships in each County or Municipality during a period of ten days starting from the twentieth day before the beginning of the first day of collecting the installment purchase price paid by the land purchasers in that County or Municipality.

Article 13: The Land Bank of Taiwan shall make public announcement of the date for the beginning of making installment payments of the principal and interest of the bonds one month before the date of maturity of the bonds for that period.

Article 14: The bondholder shall collect the principal and interest upon presenting the matured bonds within a period of three years. The principal and interest to be paid in rice shall be collected by the bondholders upoon presenting, in addition, their Citizen's Certificates within six months after maturity. Failure to collect such rice within this period shall result in payment in cash according to Article 12 of the present Regulations.

Article 15: The bonds may be transferred and sold in open market and may be used as a guaranty for public obligations. The coupons on which principal and interest are due for any given installment may be used to pay for the corresponding installment of the purchase price of the land in the same County or Municipality in whose name the bonds have been issued.

Article 16:   Holders of the bonds shall be exempt from paying the stamp tax, the income tax on interests, and the household tax as a special tax.

Article 17:   Any act of counterfeiting or tampering with the bonds shall be punished by the court according to law.

Article 18:   The present Regulations shall become effective on the day of promulgation.

SCHEDULE OF AMORTIZATION OF PRINCIPAL AND PAYMENT OF INTEREST

Land Bond in Kind (Face Value in RICE), Taiwan Province   1 kg.=2.20462 lbs.

(Total Issue: 1,260,000,000 kilograms)

Year and Installment		Principal Outstanding	Installment No.	Details of Amortization		
				Principal	Interest	Total
1953	1 st	1,260,000,000.00	1	75,600,000.00	23,688,000.00	75,600,000.00
	2 nd	1,184,400,000.00	2	51,912,000.00	22,649,760.00	75,600,000.00
1954	1 st	1,132,488,000.00	3	52,950,240.00	21,590,100.00	75,600,000.00
	2 nd	1,079,537,760.00	4	54,009,900.00	20,510,280.00	75,600,000.00
1955	1 st	1,025,527,860.00	5	55,089,720.00	19,409,040.00	75,600,000.00
	2 nd	970,438,140.00	6	56,190,960.00	18,285,120.00	75,600,000.00
1956	1 st	914,247,180.00	7	57,314,880.00	17,138,520.00	75,600,000.00
	2 nd	856,932,300.00	8	58,461,480.00	15,969,240.00	75,600,000.00
1957	1 st	798,470,820.00	9	59,630,760.00	14,777,280.00	75,600,000.00
	2 nd	738,840,060.00	10	60,822,720.00	13,560,120.00	75,600,000.00
1958	1 st	678,017,340.00	11	62,039,880.00	12,319,020.00	75,600,000.00
	2 nd	615,977,460.00	12	63,280,980.00	11,053,980.00	75,600,000.00
1959	1 st	552,696,480.00	13	64,546,020.00	9,762,480.00	75,600,000.00
	2 nd	488,150,460.00	14	65,837,520.00	8,445,780.00	75,600,000.00
1960	1 st	422,312,940.00	15	67,154,220.00	7,102,620.00	75,600,000.00
	2 nd	355,158,720.00	16	68,497,380.00	5,733,000.00	75,600,000.00
1961	1 st	286,661,340.00	17	69,867,000.00	4,335,660.00	75,600,000.00
	2 nd	216,794,340.00	18	71,264,340.00	2,910,600.00	75,600,000.00
1962	1 st	145,530,000.00	19	72,689,400.00	1,456,560.00	75,600,000.00
	2 nd	72,840,600.00	20	72,840,600.00		74,297,160.00
GRAND TOTAL			20	1,260,000,000.00	250,697,160.00	1,501,697,160.00

NOTES: 1 As the first installment of amortization is due in the first year of issuance, no interest accrues.

2 From the second to the twentieth installments, amortization is paid in equal amounts.

SCHEDULE OF AMORTIZATION OF PRINCIPAL AND PAYMENT OF INTEREST

Land Bond in Kind (Face Value in SWEET POTATO), Taiwan Province

(Ttal Issue: 440,000,000 kilograms)

1kg. = 2.20462lbs.

Year and Installment	Principal Outstanding	Installment No:	Details of Amortization		
			Principal	Interest	Total
1953 1 st	440,000,000.00	1	26,400,000.00		26,400,000.00
2 nd	413,600,000.00	2	18,128,000.00	8,272,000.00	26,400,000.00
1954 1 st	395,472,000.00	3	18,490,560.00	7,909,440.00	26,400,000.00
2 nd	376,981,440.00	4	18,860,600.00	7,539,400.00	26,400,000.00
1955 1 st	358,120,840.00	5	19,237,680.00	7,162,320.00	26,400,000.00
2 nd	338,883,160.00	6	19,622,240.00	6,777,760.00	26,400,000.00
1956 1 st	319,260,920.00	7	20,014,720.00	6,385,280.00	26,400,000.00
2 nd	299,246,200.00	8	20,415,120.00	5,984,880.00	26,400,000.00
1957 1 st	278,831,080.00	9	20,823,440.00	5,576,560.00	26,400,000.00
2 nd	258,007,640.00	10	21,239,680.00	5,160,320.00	26,400,000.00
1958 1 st	236,767,960.00	11	21,664,720.00	4,735,280.00	26,400,000.00
2 nd	215,103,240.00	12	22,098,120.00	4,301,880.00	26,400,000.00
1959 1 st	193,005,120.00	13	22,589,880.00	3,860,120.00	26,400,000.00
2 nd	170,465,240.00	14	22,990,880.00	3,409,120.00	26,400,000.00
1960 1 st	147,474,360.00	15	23,450,680.00	2,949,320.00	26,400,000.00
2 nd	124,023,680.00	16	23,919,720.00	2,480,280.00	26,400,000.00
1961 1 st	100,103,960.00	17	24,398,000.00	2,002,000.00	26,400,000.00
2 nd	75,705,960.00	18	24,885,960.00	1,514,040.00	26,400,000.00
1962 1 st	50,820,000.00	19	25,383,600.00	1,016,400.00	26,400,000.00
2 nd	25,436,400.00	20	25,436,400.00	508,640.00	25,945,040.00
GRAND TOTAL		20	440,000,000.00	87,545,040.00	527,545,040.00

NOTES: 1. As the first installment of amortizaton is due during the first year of issuance, no interest accrues.

2. From the second to the 20th installments, amortizaton is paid in equal amounts.

3. Amortization of the land purchase price in Penghu County, where all land belongs to the dry land category and where only one crop can be harvested in a year, shall be made once every year. The issuance of bonds and the amortization of principal and payment of interest shall also be made once every year.

REGULATIONS GOVERNING THE TRANSFER OF GOVERNMENT ENTERPRISES TO PRIVATE OWNERSHIP

(Passed by the Legislative Yuan, January 20, 1953, and promulgated by the President of the Republic of China, January 26, 1953)

Article 1: Transfer of government enterprises to private ownership, unless otherwise provided for by law, shall be conducted according to provisions of the present Regulations.

Article 2: The term "government enterprises" referred to in the present Regulations shall mean the following enterprises:

(1) Enterprises solely financed and operated by the Government.

(2) Enterprises jointly financed and operated by governments on various levels.

(3) Enterprises jointly invested in and operated by civilians and governments in accordance with special laws establishing such enterprises.

(4) Enterprises jointly invested in and operated by civilians and governments in accordance with the "Law of Corporations" where the government capital exceeds 50 per cent of the total capital value of each of the enterprises.

Article 3: Enterprises of the following categories shall be operated only by the Government or governments and shall not be transferred to private ownership under the present Regulations:

(1) Enterprises directly affecting national defense and military security.

(2) Government monopoly enterprises and enterprises of a monoplistic nature.

(3) Enterprises for the large-scale operation of public utilities or for other specific purposes.

Article 4: The competent authorities of the Government to which enterprises operated by governments on various levels are responsible shall, except those enterprises provided for under Article 3 of the present Regulations, adopt either one of the following two formulas to work out plans and budget estimates for transferring such enterprises and shall submit such plans and estimates through proper channels to their superior organs for approval and action.

(1) Sale of government stocks in one operation or in installments:

    (a) Any enterprise solely invested in and operated by the Government of jointly invested in and operated by governments on various levels shall first re-evaluate its capital value and the government stocks invested in such enterprise shall then be sold either in one operation or in installments until all the stocks are sold. After sale, an enterprise which was not originally incorporated as a corporate body shall be reorganized according to the "Law of Corporations."

    (b) Any enterprise jointly invested in and operated by the Government or governments and civilians shall first re-evaluate its capital value and the government stocks invested in such enterprise shall then be sold either in one operation or in installments until all the government stocks are sold.

(2) Sale of one or more factories or the entire enterprise by auction in accordance with law.

Article 5: Before the auction of government enterprises, a re-evaluation Committee shall be organized jointly by the competent authorities of the Government and other government agencies concerned. The re-evaluation shall be made on the basis of the following standards:

(1) Original capital value.

(2) Current capital value.

(3) Possible profit returns in the future.

Article 6: The transfer of government enterprises to private ownership shall be valid only when the transfer of such enterprises is made to Chinese citizens or overseas Chinese or foreigners who are citizens of countries with which the Republic of China has concluded agreements for private investments.

Article 7: The government stocks of any enterprise sponsored and partially invested in by the Government or governments and of any one created by further investment by other government enterprise or enterprises from their earnings may be sold and transferred to private ownership according to the provisions, *mutatis mutandis,* of the present Regulations.

Article 8: The sales proceeds of government enterprises transferred to private ownership shall be used specifically for production and reconstruction purposes.

Article 9: The present Regulations shall become effective on the day of promulgation.

RULES GOVERNING THE PAYMENT FOR THE PRICE OF CULTIVATED LANDS PURCHASED BY FARMERS FROM THE GOVERNMENT UNDER THE LAND-TO-THE-TILLER PROGRAM IMPLEMENTED IN TAIWAN PROVINCE

(Promulgated by the Taiwan Provincial Government, June 22, 1953;
and amended, September 26, 1953 and May 26, 1954)

Article 1: Payment for the price and its interest of cultivated lands, the immovable fixtures and their sites resold by the Government to the farmer under the Land-to-the-Tiller Program implemented in Taiwan Province shall, unless otherwise provided for by law or ordinance, be made according to the provisions of the present Rules.

Article 2: Payment for the price of cultivated land resold by the Government shall be made in rice or in cash by converting the food crops payable into cash. The collection of both kinds of payment shall be conducted by the Land Bank of Taiwan and its branches and sub-branches, but the rice paid shall be collected by the Food Bureau and its branches and sub-branches.

Article 3: The price of cultivated lands resold by the Government shall be calculated and paid for according to the provisions of Article 20 of the Land-to-the-Tiller Act and the relevant provisions of the Regulations Governing the Implementation of the said Act in Taiwan Province.

Article 4: Payment for the price of dry land, immovable fixtures and their sites resold by the Government shall be made in cash calculated in terms of the current value of sweet potato. Payment for the price of paddy fields shall be made in rice; but in the case of single-crop paddy fields and paddy fields depending on weather, the installment due in the season when no rice is planted shall be made in cash calculated in terms of the current value of rice, and in the case of rotation fields (including the specially irrigated fields), the entire payment shall be made in cash calculated in terms of the current value of rice.

Article 5: If the payment for the installment of the land price is effected with coupons for installment payment of the principal and interest of land bonds in kind which are redeemable in the same period and in the same county or municipality as the installment of land price is payable, the following provisions shall be observed:

(1) Coupons of rice bonds payable in rice (including coupons for the installment payment in rice of rice bonds payable 50% in rice and 50% in cash) shall be used to pay the installment of the land price which is payable in rice, provided that such payment is made for the price of land which is situated in the urban district, township or urban district designated in such bonds.

(2) Coupons of rice bonds payable in cash (including coupons for the installment payment in cash of rice bonds payable 50% in rice and 50% in cash) shall be used to pay the installment of the land price which is payable in cash.

Article 6: The standard for converting the value of sweet potato and rice into cash shall be fixed by the competent County or Municipal Government in the light of average wholesale quotations on the markets or important centers of production in the districts and townships of the county or municipality, in the period lying between the twentieth day and eleventh day before the date on which payment for the installment of the land price begins. The County or Municipal Government shall make public announcement of such standard, and notify the local Land Bank of Taiwan of such standard on the tenth day before the date on which payment for the installment of the land price begins.

Article 7: In case the cultivated land resold by the Government becomes partially or entirely unusable owing to *force majeure,* the purchaser of such land may, through proper channels, request the Provincial Government to grant a reduction or remission of the unliquidated portion of the price of such land.

Article 8: In case a crop failure occurs on the cultivated lands resold by the Government, the postponement in the payment of the price and interest thereof shall be regulated according to the following provisions:

(1) A 30% postponement in the payment shall be permitted in cases in which the crop failure is not less than 30%; a 50% postponement in cases in which the crop failure is not less than 40%; and a 100% postponement in cases in which the crop failure is over 50%.

(2) The percentage of crop failure shall be estimated plot by plot on the lands purchased by farmers.

(3) Within ten days after the occurrence of a crop failure on the cultivated land resold by the Government, the purchaser thereof shall submit to the District or Township Office a written application for the postponement of the payment for the land price. The District or Township Office shall transmit the application to the competent County or Municipal Government, which shall then dispatch an officer to make a preliminary on-the-spot investigation, plot by plot, in cooperation with members of the District or Township Office. If the results of the investigation confirm the statements in the application, a written report thereof shall be submitted to the County or Municipal Government. At the same time, the County or Municipal Government shall report the case by telegram to the Provincial Government, which shall then dispatch an officer to make a second on-the-spot investigation with reference to the report of the preliminary investigation and in cooperation with the county or municipal officer who has made the preliminary investigation. The results of the second investigation shall be embodied in a written report to be submitted, together with three copies of the List of Recommended Postponements in the Payment of the Land Price, to the Provincial Government for approval. A fourth copy of the List shall be sent to the local branch or sub-branch of the Land Bank of Taiwan. When the recommended postponements are approved by the Provincial Government, one copy of the above-mentioned List, together with any attachment showing whatever corrections, if any, are to be made therein, shall be sent to the competent County or Municipal Government, and another copy to the Land Bank of Taiwan to serve as the basis for action.

Article 9: When the reduction or remission of the payment of the land price as specified in Article 7 of the present Rules, or the postponement in the payment of the land price as specified in Article 8 of the present Rules is approved, the competent County or Municipal Government shall, not later than the tenth day before the date on which the installment payment for the land price begins, compile a list of purchasers whose installment payments of the land price falling due are reduced, remitted or postponed, and send a copy of such list each to the Land Bureau, the local Food Office, and the local Land Bank of Taiwan.

Article 10: Payment for the price of cultivated land resold by the Government shall be made once a year in Penghu County and twice a year in all other counties and municipalities, provided that wherever only one crop is grown in a year on the said land owing to natural limitations, the purchaser thereof may request the District or Township Office to report the case to the competent County or Municipal Government. If the case is found to be true after a preliminary investigation, the County or Municipal Government shall submit a report to the Provincial Government for a second investigation. If the results of the second investigation confirms the statements in the preliminary report, the Provincial Government shall notify the Land Bank of Taiwan to permit the payment for the price of the said land to be made once in the year at the harvesting season.

The period for the payment of each installment of the land price shall be a month. The date on which the payment for each installment begins in each county or municipality shall be regulated according to the attached table *(See next page);* and in case any date specified in the table has to be altered owing to actual needs, the competent County or Municipal Government, the local Food Office and the local Land Bank of Taiwan shall jointly make a decision of the alteration, and report the alteration to the Provincial Government for approval:

Article 11: After the resale of cultivated lands is completed, each County or Municipal Government shall compile a list of lands resold and send it to the local Land Bank of Taiwan.

Article 12: The procedures for paying the land price in cash shall be as follows:

(1) The local Land Bank of Taiwan shall prepare a "specified sheet" for payment of the land price in cash, whereof the first part, a notice of payment, is to be sent to the purchaser, and the second part, a receipt of payment, to be used for collecting payment. In addition, the local Land Bank of Taiwan shall prepare a detailed list of cash payments of the land price to be collected in each district or township, send a copy of such list to the competent County or Municipal Government and keep another copy in file.

(2) When the purchaser presents the notice of payment and makes cash payment for the land price, the local Land Bank of Taiwan or its designated agency shall record the date of receipt thereof in each part of the specified sheet, chop each part with proper seals, keep the first part in file and give the second part back to the purchaser.

(3) The local Land Bank of Taiwan or its designated agency shall com-

pile a five-day report of cash payments of the land price collected, keep a copy thereof in file and bind another copy together with the first part of the aforesaid specified sheet. If the cash payments are received by a designated agency of the local Land Bank of Taiwan, another copy of the report shall be prepared and kept in file by such agency.

(4) On the basis of the aforesaid five-day reports, the local Land Bank of Taiwan shall, every ten days, compile a ten-day report, in four copies, of cash payments of land price collected, one copy to be

Area	Counties and Municipalities	Date on which first semi-annual install-ment payment begins	Date on which second semi-annual install-ment payment begins
Kaohsiung Area	Kaohsiung County Kaohsiung Municipality Pingtung County	June 21	November 21
Tainan Area	Tainan County Tainan Municipality Chiayi County Yunlin County	July 11	November 21
Taichung Area	Taichung County Taichung Municipality Nantou County Changhua County	July 11	November 21
Taitung Area	Taitung County	July 11	November 21
Hsinchu Area	Hsinchu County Taoyuan County Miaoli County	July 11	December 1
Taipei Area	Taipei County Taipei Municipality Yangmingshan Administration Keelung Municipality Ilan County	July 21	December 1
Hualien Area	Hualien County	July 21	December 1
Penghu Area	Penghu County		September 1*

* Owing to special circumstances, the installment payment is made once a year in Penghu County.

kept in file, one copy to be sent to the competent County or Municipal Government and the other two copies to be sent to the Head Office of the Land Bank of Taiwan, which shall keep a copy in file and send another copy to the Land Bureau.

(5) The Head Office of the Land Bank of Taiwan shall every month gather together the aforesaid ten-day reports submitted by its branches and sub-branches, and compile a Monthly report, in three copies, of cash payments of land price collected: one copy to be kept in file, and the other two copies to be sent to the Finance Department and the Land Bureau.

Article 13: The procedures for paying the land price in rice shall be as follows:

(1) The local Land Bank of Taiwan shall prepare a specified sheet for the payment of the land price in rice, whereof the first part, a notice of payment, is to be sent to the purchaser, the second part, a receipt of payment, and the third part, a duplicate receipt of payment, are to be sent to the local Food Office, which shall transmit them to the designated warehouse for collecting the payment. At the same time, the local Land Bank of Taiwan shall prepare a detailed list, in four copies, of rice payments of the land price to be collected in each district and township: one copy to be kept in file, one copy to be sent to the competent County or Municipal Government, and the other two copies to be sent togeher with the second and third parts of the aforesaid specified sheet to the local Food Office, which shall keep a copy in file, and transmit another copy to the designated warehouse together with the second and third parts of the specified sheet.

(2) When the purchaser presents the notice of payment and makes rice payment for the land price, the designated warehouse shall record the date of the receipt of such payment in each part of the specified sheet, chop each part with proper seals, transmit the first part to the local Food Office for filing, give the second part back to the purchaser, and send the third part to the local Food Office for transmission to the local Land Bank of Taiwan.

(3) Each designated warehouse shall compile a five-day report, in four copies, of rice payments of the land price collected, keep a copy in file and submit the other three copies together with the first and third parts of the specified sheet to the local Food

Office.

(4) On the basis of the aforesaid five-day reports received, each local Food Office shall, every ten days, compile a ten-day report, in seven copies, of rice payments of the land price collected: one copy to be kept in file, two copies to be submitted to the Food Bureau, and four copies to be sent to the local Land Bank of Taiwan together with two copies of the aforesaid five-day reports and the third part of the specified sheet. The local Land Bank of Taiwan shall send a copy of the ten-day report to the competent County or Municipal Government, keep a copy in file together with a copy of the five-day report (another copy of the five-day report shall be bound together with the third part of the specified sheet), and submit the other two copies of the ten-day report to the Head Office of the Land Bank of Taiwan, which shall keep a copy in file and send another copy to the Land Bureau.

(5) The Head Office of the Land Bank of Taiwan shall, every month, gather together the ten-day reports submitted by its branches and sub-branches, and compile a Monthly Report, in three copies, of rice payments for the land price collected: one copy to be kept in file, two copies to be sent to the Finance Department and the Land Bureau.

(6) The standard for inspecting and testing the rice paid shall be regulated according to the provisions of the Regulations Governing the Inspection and Collection of the Land Tax in Kind.

Article 14: The procedures for paying the land price with land bonds in kind shall be as follows:

(1) Matured coupons for the installment payment for the principal and interest of rice bonds payable in cash and sweet potato bonds payable in cash may be used to pay the installment of land price which is payable in cash by converting the designated amount of rice or sweet potato into cash according to the standard of conversion fixed in the area of issuance of such bonds.

(2) Matured coupons for the installment payment for the principal and interest of rice bonds payable in rice may be used to pay the installment of the land price which is payable in rice, unless such coupons are presented after the lapse of six months from the date publicly announced as the date on which the redemption of such coupons begins.

(3) If the face value of land bonds presented by the purchased for paying the land price is smaller than the payment due, the deficit shall be paid off in cash or rice, as the case may require. If the face value of such bonds is bigger than the payment due, the surplus shall be set off against the unliquidated portion of the land price, and the purchaser shall not demand immediate payment of such surplus in cash or rice.

(4) When land bonds are presented by the purchaser for paying the land price, the local Land Bank of Taiwan or the local Food Office shall, after finding the bonds upon examination to be in due and proper form and not included in the list of land bonds for which payment should be withheld, record in the proper columns in the bonds, the account number for the payment, the address of the purchaser, and the number of his citizenship certificate; and the purchaser shall then put his signature and seal on the bonds.

(5) The purchaser who wishes to pay the land price with land bonds payable in cash, shall present such bonds together with the notice of payment and his citizenship certificate and personal seal to the local Land Bank of Taiwan to effect the payment.

(6) The purchaser who wishes to pay the land price with rice bonds payable in rice shall present such bonds together with the notice of payment and his citizenship certificate and personal seal to the local Food Office. After finding the bonds to be in due and proper form, the local Food Office shall keep the bonds and issue a "delivery order" for the payment of the land price to the purchaser, who shall then present such order together with the notice of payment to the designated warehouse to complete the payment procedures.

(7) The local Land Bank of Taiwan, or the local Food Office and the designated warehouse, shall record on each part of the specified sheet for payment of the land price, the respective amounts of land bonds, and of cash or rice, received as payments for the land price. In the five-day report of rice payments for land price collected, the respective amounts of land bonds and of cash or rice received in each case shall also be recorded.

(8) After receiving rice bonds as payment for the land price, the local Food Office shall compile a List of Redeemed Rice Bonds in six copies: one copy to be kept by the Food Office in file, two copies to be submitted to the Land Bureau, and the other three copies

to be sent to the local Land Bank of Taiwan together with redeemed rice bonds and other relevant lists and tables.

Article 15: The forms of lists, reports, and other documents mentioned in the present Rules and the measures for coordination and cooperation in operation shall be jointly prescribed by the Land Bank of Taiwan, the Food Bureau and the Land Bureau.

Article 16: After having completed the purchase procedures, the purchaser shall present the receipt of payment of the first installment of the land price to the local Land Office, and request it to register the change of landownership and issue him a certificate of landownership.

Before the land price is fully paid, the purchaser shall not transfer the land, as provided for by law; and when the land price is fully paid, the Land Bank of Taiwan shall put a chop on the certificate of landownership, stating that "the price of land is paid in full."

Article 17: The Land Bank of Taiwan shall keep special accounts for the receipts of cash payments and rice payments for the land price and the fines for defaulted payments; such receipts shall be appropriated for the redemption of the principal and interest of the land bonds in kind and for the repayment to the Government of the value of government enterprise stocks sold out.

Article 18: In case the installment payment for the land price already collected is found to be deficient or excessive owing to certain reasons, the deficit shall be made up when the next installment is due, and the amount in excess shall be set off against the next installment payment.

Article 19: Any purchaser who fails to pay the installment of the land price that falls due shall be fined according to the following scale:

(1) A fine of 2% of the installment payment for a delay of less than a month;

(2) A fine of 5% of the installment payment for a delay of over a month but less than two months.

(3) A fine of 10% of the installment payment for a delay of over two months but less than three months.

(4) A fine of 15% of the installment payment for a delay of over three months but less than four months.

If any purchaser fails to pay any installment of the land price for over four months, the case shall be brought before the court for compulsory execution, the land purchased by him shall be taken back by the Government; and the installments of the land price already paid by him shall not be refunded.

Article 20: The competent County or Municipal Government shall, in cooperation with the Disitrict, Township or Urban District Office, press for the payment for the price of lands resold by the Government.

Article 21: The present Rules shall come into force from the date of their promulgation.

RULES GOVERNING THE COMPENSATION FOR THE PRICE OF CULTIVATED LANDS COMPULSORILY PURCHASED BY THE GOVERNMENT UNDER THE LAND-TO-THE-TILLER PROGRAM IMPLEMENTED IN TAIWAN PROVINCE

(Promulgated by the Taiwan Provincial Government,
June 22, 1953, and amended, September 26, 1953)

Article 1: Compensation for the price of cultivated lands compulsorily purchased by the Government under the Land-to-the-Tiller Program implemented in Taiwan Province shall, unless otherwise provided for by law or ordinance, be made according to the present Rules.

Article 2: The price of cultivated lands compulsorily purchased by the Government from landlords shall be separately calculated for each landlord, and compensated 70% with land bonds in kind and 30% with government enterprise stocks according to the provisions of Article 15 of the Land-to-the-Tiller Act and Articles 4 and 11 of the Regulations Governing the Issuance of Land Bonds in Kind, Taiwan Province. In case the odd sums out of the 70% compensation payable in land bonds are smaller than the smallest face value of the bonds, such sums shall be paid in government enterprise stocks, and the remaining odd sums which are smaller than the smallest face value of such stocks shall be paid in cash.

A temporary certificate to exchange for the aforesaid government enterprise stocks shall be jointly issued, in the first instance, by the Ministry of Interior, the Ministry of Economic Affairs and the Taiwan Provincial Government, and its face value shall be expressed in kilograms of rice and sweet potato. When the certificate is presented in exchange for government enterprise stocks, the odd sums out of its face value which are smaller than the smallest face value of the stocks shall be paid in cash by conversion according to the provisions of Article 12 of the Regulations Governing the Issuance of Land Bonds in Kind, Taiwan Province.

Article 3: Compensation for the immovable fixtures and their sites compulsorily purchased by the Government together with the cultivated land according to the provisions of the Land-to-the-Tiller Act shall be paid in sweet potato bonds, as provided for by Article 41 of the Regulations

Governing the Implementation of the said Act in Taiwan Province.

Article 4: To each former landowner who is entitled to receive land bonds in kind and government enterprise stocks as compensation, the bonds and stocks of the biggest face value shall be allocated in the first instance, and if the amount of the compensation payable in bonds or stocks is smaller than the biggest face value of the bonds or stocks, those of smaller face values shall be successively allocated to meet the requirement.

Article 5: The land bonds in kind and the temporary certificates to be used for exchange for government enterprise stocks which are allocated for compensating the land price shall be delivered to former landowners through the Land Bank of Taiwan and its branches and sub-branches.

Article 6: Procedures for paying the compensation for the land price shall be as follows:

(1) On the expiration of the period of public announcement for the compulsory purchase of cultivated lands, the competent County or Municipal Government shall send a list of cultivated lands subject to compulsory purchase to the local Land Bank of Taiwan. After the owner of the land subject to compulsory purchase has surrendered his certificate of landownership and other relevant documents, the competent County or Municipal Government shall send him a notice of payment of the land price together with the public announcement issued by the Land Bank of Taiwan for payment of land price, and notify him to pick up the payment at the local Land Bank of Taiwan (a note shall be inserted in the notice to the effect that the list of land subject to compulsory purchase which has been previously sent to him shall be also presented, when the payment of the land price is requested). The aforsaid notice shall be chopped with the official seal of the competent County or Municipal Government and the personal seal of the officer in charge.

(2) When the former landowner presents the aforesaid notice to the local Taiwan Land Bank and requests the payment of the land price, the Bank shall pay him the price he is entitled to get, after the official seal chopped on the notice has been found to be in due and proper form and the items stated in the notice to be correct upon comparison with the detailed list of payments for the land price compiled by the Bank on the basis of the list of lands subject to compulsory purchase and other relevant documents, and after the former landowner has put his personal seal on the notice.

Article 7: The period for payment of the land price shall be a month; and the dates when such payment begins and ends, and the place where it is to be effected shall be publicly announced by the local Land Bank of Taiwan.

Article 8: In case the notice of payment for the land price presented by the former landowner or the official seal chopped on the notice is found upon examination to be in doubtful or improper form, the local Land Bank of Taiwan may suspend payment, until the landowner has requested the competent County or Municipal Government to make necessary corrections and produced evidence thereof.

Article 9: The compensation for the price of land under joint ownership shall be paid to the representative of the joint owners as specified in the list of land subject to compulsory purchase, and the compensation paid shall be distributed by the joint owners among themselves.

Article 10: In case the land subject to compulsory purchase has been encumbered with such other rights as specified in Section 2, Article 18 of the Land-to-the-Tiller Act or with such money deposit as specified in Article 62 of the Regulations Governing the Implementation of the said Act in Taiwan Province, the competent County or Municipal Government shall record the items of such rights or money deposit in the list of land subject to compulsory purchase and issue a notice of liquidation of such rights or money deposit to the person holding such rights or entitled to recover such money deposit, who shall present the notice to the local Land Bank of Taiwan within the period for payment of the land price and request it to pay for the liquidation of such rights or money deposit out of the land price payable to the former landowner.

Procedures for issuing the aforesaid notice and for the Land Bank of Taiwan to make payment to the person holding other rights or entitled to recover his money deposit shall be regulated *mutatis mutandis* by the provisions of Article 6 of the present Rules.

In case the value of other rights is expressed in terms other than New Taiwan Dollars, it shall, according to general rules and precedents, be converted into New Taiwan Dollars for the purpose of liquidation, unless owing to the rise of disputes over the value of such rights, the obligor has brought the case before the court according to law and requested the Land Bank of Taiwan to suspend the payment of the land price, or unless the government has prescribed different provisions for the liquidation of such rights. The calculation of the value of other rights in terms of land bonds in kind shall be regulated by the provisions of Article 12 of the Regulations

Governing the Issuance of Land Bonds in Kind, Taiwan Province.

Article 11: If the former landowner has faild to pay the farmland tax due or the surplus rice requisitioned by the government from big and medium landlords, the competent authorities shall request the Land Bank of Taiwan to collect, on their behalf, the overdue payments of such tax or surplus rice out of the land price payable to the former landowner.

Article 12: The several payments to be deducted from the land price payable to the landowner as respectively specified in Articles 10 and 11 of the present Rules shall be deducted therefrom according to the following order of priority, and effected with land bonds in kind and government enterprise stocks according to the following ratioes:

(1) Payment for farmland tax overdue: The payment for farmland tax overdue which is payable in cash shall be effected with rice bonds payable in cash or sweet potato bonds payable in cash as the case may require, and in case the amount of the aforesaid bonds payable to the landowner are insufficient to cover the total payment, the deficit shall be made up with rice bonds payable 50 per cent in cash and rice bonds payable in rice. The payment for the tax overdue which is payable in rice shall be effected entirely with rice bonds payable in rice.

(2) Payment for liquidation of other rights: Such payment shall be effected according to the provisions of Article 18 of the Land-to-the-Tiller Act and Article 39 of the Regulations Governing the Implementation of the said Act in Taiwan Province; and in respect of that part of the payment which should be effected with land bonds in kind, sweet potato bonds payable in cash, rice bond payable in cash, rice bonds payable 50 per cent in cash and rice bonds payable in rice shall be allocated successively.

(3) Payment for surplus rice requisitioned by the Government: Such payment shall be effected with rice bonds payable in rice, and in case the amount of such bonds payable to the landowner is insufficient to cover the total payment, the deficit shall be made up with rice bonds payable 50 per cent in cash.

(4) Payment for money deposit: Such payment shall be effected on the same basis as the payment specified in Section 2 of this paragraph.

In case the amount of the land bonds in kind payable to the former landowner is not sufficient to cover the amount of the bonds required for effecting the several payments referred to in the preceding paragraph, the deficit, except in the case of the payment for farmland tax or surplus rice, shall be made up as far as possible with government enterprise stocks payable to the landowner, and the remaining deficit, if any, shall be left unpaid. The Land Bank of Taiwan shall notify the authorities concerned to deal with such case of deficit payments by themselves.

Article 13: If the former landowner fails to pick up the payment of the land price he is entitled to receive within the period prescribed in Article 7 of the present Rules, such payment shall be deposited in a court according to law, and the necessary expenses incurred shall be paid out of such payment.

If the person holding other rights or entitled to recover his money deposit fails to pick up the payment for such rights or money deposit within the aforesaid period, such payment shall be disposed of according to the provisions of the preceding paragraph.

Article 14: Lists, tables and notices relating to the several payments to be deducted from the land price as specified in Articles 10 and 11 of the present Rules shall be sent to the local Land Bank of Taiwan not later than June 25, 1953.

Article 15: Procedures for exchanging the temporary certificate for government enterprise stocks and for paying the odd sums, as specified in Paragraph 2, Article 2 of the present Rules, shall be separately prescribed by the Ministry of Economic Affairs.

Article 16: When the work of paying the land price is completed, the Land Bank of Taiwan and the Land Bureau shall jointly submit a report thereof to the Provincial Government for transmission to the Executive Yuan for approval.

Article 17: The present Rules shall come into force from the date of their promulgation.

RULES GOVERNING THE TRANSFER OF GOVERNMENT ENTERPRISES TO PRIVATE OWNERSHIP UNDER THE LAND - TO - THE - TILLER ACT

(Promulgated by the Ministry of Economic
Affair, December 22, 1953)

Article 1: To pay the 30% compensation for the price of cultivated lands compulsorily purchased by the Government from landlords, as provided by Article 15 of the Land-to-the-Tiller Act, all government stocks of the following four Corporations shall be sold: the Taiwan Cement Corporation, the Taiwan Paper and Pulp Corporation, the Taiwan Agricultural and Forestry Development Corporation, and the Taiwan Industrial and Mining Corporation.

Article 2: The Cement Corporation and the Paper and Pulp Corporation shall be sold in one operation and managed as integral units. The Agricultural and Forestry Development Corporation and the Industrial and Mining Corporation shall be sold unit by unit according to the categories of its undertakings, and each unit shall be put under a separate management.

Article 3: As a principle, the above-mentioned four Corporations shall be entirely sold to private investors. All government stocks of the Cement Corporation and the Paper and Pulp Corporation shall be allocated in due proportions to pay the total amount of the 30% compensation for the land price to landlords, and, if such stocks are insufficient to pay the total compensation, the stocks of the Agricultural and Forestry Development Corporation and the Industrial and Mining Corporation shall be allocated in due proportions to make up the deficit.

The stocks of the Argicultural and Forestry Development Corporation and the Industrial and Mining Corporation allocated according to the preceding paragraph may be exchanged by the holders thereof for any unit of such Corporations which is separately sold.

Article 4: The government stocks of the Agricultural and Forestry Development Corporation and the Industrial and Mining Corporation that still remain after the total amount of compensation to landlords has been paid up shall continue to be sold, and may be exchanged by any person for land bonds in kind. Further government stocks remaining in the hands of the Government shall be sold by bids according to law, until they are entirely sold out.

Article 5:   A Committee for the Allocation of Government Stock Shares to Landlords shall be set up with a representative each from the Ministry of Economic Affairs, the Ministry of Interior, the Taiwan Provincial Government, the Land Bank of Taiwan and the four Corporations concerned.   The actual work of allocation shall be entrusted by the four Corporations to the Land Bank of Taiwan, and the necessary expenses incurred shall be apportioned among the four Corporations in proportion to the amount of government stocks sold by each of them.

The representative of the Ministry of Economic Affairs shall be the chairman of the Committee, and the representative of the Taiwan Provincial Government, the deputy chairman.

Article 6:   The amount of government stocks payable to each landlord shall be calculated by converting the amount of farm crops stated in the temporary certificate for government enterprise stocks issued by the Land Bank of Taiwan, into monetary terms at a rate based on the average market price of farm crops for the whole province in December 1952, i.e., at the rate of NT$160 to 100 kilograms (NT$72.57 to 100 lbs.) of unhulled rice, and of NT$38.85 to 100 kilograms (NT$17.62 to 100 lbs.) of sweet potato.

Article 7:   If, on allocating the government stocks of the four Corporations to a landlord according to the provisions of Article 3 of the present Rules, the odd sums out of the amount of compensation payable with the stocks of each of the four Corporations are, in each instance, smaller than the value of a stock share, such sums shall be added up, and the added total, if greater than the value of a stock share, shall be paid with the stocks of the Agricultural and Forestry Development Corporation and those of the Industrial and Mining Corporation in succession, and further odd sums remaining shall be paid in cash.

The formula to be used in calculation shall be as follows:

I. Percentage of stocks of four Corporations to be allocated:

1. Percentage of Cement Corporation stocks=

$$\frac{\text{Total amount of C. C. stocks} \times \text{NT\$10}}{\text{Total amount of 30\% compensation for land price payable in whole province}} = P_1\%$$

2. Percentage of Paper and Pulp Corporation stocks=

$$\frac{\text{Total amount of P.P.C. stocks} \times \text{NT\$10}}{\text{Total amount of 30\% compensation for land price payable in whole province}} = P_2\%$$

3. Percentage of Agricultural and Forestry Development Corporation stocks=

$$\frac{\text{Total amount of A.F.D.C. stocks}}{\text{Total amount of A.F.D.C. stocks and I.M.C. stocks}} \times (100 - P_1 - P_2)\% = P_3\%$$

4. Percentage of Industrial and Mining Corporation stocks=

$$\frac{\text{Total amount of I.M.C. stocks}}{\text{Total amount of A.F.D.C. stocks and I.M.C. stocks}} \times (100 - P_1 - P_2 - P_3)\% = P_4\%$$

NOTE: $P_1 + P_2 + P_3 + P_4 = 100$

II. Amount of stocks of four Corporations to be allocated to each landlord:

1. Amount of Cement Corporation stocks=

$$\frac{\text{Amount of 30\% compensation for land price payable to each landlord} \times P_1\%}{10} = Q_1 + \text{odd sums } q_1$$

2. Amount of Paper and Pulp Corporation stocks=

$$\frac{\text{Amount of 30\% Compensation for land price payable to each landlord}}{10} \times P_2\% = Q_2 + \text{odd sums } q_2$$

3. Amount of Agricultural and Forestry Development Corporation stocks=

$$\frac{\text{Amount of 30\% compensation for land price payable to each landlord}}{10} \times P_3\% = Q_3 + \text{odd sums } q_3$$

4. Amount of Industrial and Mining Corporation stock=

$$\frac{\text{Amount of 30\% compensation for land price payable to each landlord}}{10} \times P_4\% = Q_4 + \text{odd sums } q_4$$

5. $\dfrac{q_1 + q_2 + q_3 + q_4}{10} = Q_5 + \text{odd sums } q_5$

    (1) If $Q_5 = 1$, one A.F.D.C. stock shall be allocated.

    (2) If $Q_5 = 2$, one A.F.D.C. stock and one I.M.C. stock shall be allocated.

    (3) If $Q_5 = 3$, two A.F.D.C. stocks and one I.M.C. stock shall be allocated, and the odd sums q_5 shall be paid in cash.

Article 8: The stocks allocated to landlords shall be denominated stocks, recording the full name of the landlord stated in the temporary certificate for government enterprise stocks. If the landlord takes the form of several joint owners, only the full name of their representative shall be recorded in the stock, and his full name and residence shall be also recorded in the Stockholders Register. A copy of his personal seal bearing his full name shall be kept in the file.

Article 9: The agencies for allocating the stocks shall be the eighteen district branches of the Land Bank of Taiwan by which the temporary certificates for government enterprise stocks have been issued. In case of necessity, additional agencies may be designated.

Article 10: While the work of allocating the stocks is in progress, the Land Bank of Taiwan shall every month submit a progress report to the Committee for the Allocation of Government Enterprise Stocks; and when the work is completed, the Bank shall submit a report of the results of allocation to the said Committee for approval. The said Committee shall submit a report of the approved results to the Ministry of Economic Affairs, the Ministry of Interior and the Taiwan Provincial Government, respectively, for their joint transmission to the Executive Yuan for final approval.

Article 11: Any difficult problems encountered by the Land Bank of Taiwan in the course of allocating the stocks, may be reported to the Committee for Allocation of Government Enterprise Stocks for solution.

Article 12: The present Rules shall come into force after they are approved by the Executive Yuan.

REGULATIONS GOVERNING THE IMPLEMENTA-
TION OF THE LAND-TO-THE-TILLER ACT
IN TAIWAN

(Promulgated by the Taiwan Provincial Government, April 23, 1953;
amended and promulgated by the Taiwan Provincial Government,
February 25 and May 26, 1954)

Chapter I.   General Provisions

Article 1:   The present Regulations are drawn up in accordance with
the provisions of Article 33 of the Land-to-the-Tiller Act, which is
hereinafter referred to as this Act.

Article 2:   The term "tenant farmer," referred to in Article 4 of
this Act, shall mean any farmer who is presently actually cultivating a farm
land leased from another person.   Any farmer who has concluded no
written lease contract but has leased land from a landlord in the capacity
of a lessee shall also be taken as a tenant farmer.   The term "farm hand"
shall mean hired laborer employed in farm work.

Article 3:   The terms "paddy field" and "dry land," referred to in
Article 5 of this Act, shall mean those paddy fields and dry land that are
registered in the land register.   Land that was not originally registered as
paddy field or dry land, but has been used as such since the registration,
shall be dealt with as such in accordance with this Act, and the necessary
changes in land categories shall be made in the land register accordingly.

Article 4:   The paddy field referred to in Article 5 of this Act which
is alternately used, according to the original custom, one season for rice-
growing and another for pisciculture by different persons, shall continue
to be so used and shall not be subject to purchase and resale by the
Government.

Article 5:   "The landlord from whom land shall be purchased for
this Land-to-the-Tiller Program by the Government and by whom part
of his land may be retained in accordance with this Act," referred to in
Article 7 of this Act, shall include any landowner whose land is partly leased
to others for cultivation and partly tilled by himself.

Article 6:   The phrase "as of the first day of April, 1952," referred to in Article 7 of this Act, shall include the whole day of April 1, 1952. The phrase "after April 1, 1952" shall mean beginning from April 2, 1952. The effective date of land transfers shall be the day on which the applications relating to such transfers are received by the County or Municipal Land Offices for registration.

Article 7: The retention and Government purchase of those cultivated lands, which shall not be recognized as having been duly transferred according to Article 7 of this Act, shall be regulated according to the following provisions:

(1) If the area of the cultivated land which the landlord has not yet transferred comes up to the prescribed retention limit, all of his cultivated lands which are not recognized as having been duly transferred shall be purchased by the Government

(2) If the area of the cultivated land which a landlord has not yet transferred does not come up to the prescribed retention limit, such untransferred land shall be retained by him and the difference, if any, between the retention limit and the untransferred land shall be made up for from the cultivated lands which he has transferred, up to the prescribed retention limit according to the order in which the tranferees are registered, and the area of such transferred lands in excess of the retention limit shall be purchased by the Government.

(3) If the cultivated land which has been transferred to the transferee under the preceding section is within the original landlord's retention limit and the said transferee also possesses cultivated land of his own, the area of both kinds of land shall be computed together in fixing the retention area for him, and any area in excess of the prescribed retention limit shall be purchased by the Government with the first choice falling on the land the landlord has transferred to him.

Article 8: All re-transfers of cultivated land that has been transferred after April 1, 1952, and to which any one of the provisions of Article 7 of this Act is applicable, shall be regulated according to the following provisions:

(1) All such cultivated lands shall be recognized as having been duly transferred, provided the last retransfer comes under either Section (2) or Section (3), or Section (4) of the said Article.

(2) If the last re-transfer comes under Section (1) of the said Article, the reasons of the successive transfers shall be carefully examined and the case shall be regulated according to the provisions of the preceding section.

Article 9: All cultivated lands which Government organizations have purchased by agreement in order to undertake the enterprises specified in Articles 208 and 209 of the Land Law shall be regarded as having been compulsorily purchased under the provisions of Section (4), Article 7 of this Act.

Article 10: After the promulgation and enforcement of this Act, the smallest unit in terms of area for private cultivated land shall be 0.05 *chia* (0.1198 acre) for paddy field and 0.10 *chia* (0.2396 acre) for dry land. Any cultivated land which is smaller than this unit shall not be subdivided.

Article 11: Any cultivated land of the same plot number under separate cultivation by more than one individual before the promulgation and enforcement of this Act, whose area is smaller than the smallest unit prescribed in the preceding Article, shall be regulated, after its purchase by the Government and resale to a new owner, according to the provisions of Article 24 of this Act.

Chapter II.　Government Purchase of Cultivated Land

Article 12: In the case of cultivated land under joint ownership, referred to in Sections (2) and (3), Paragraph one, Article 8 of this Act, its purchase by the Government shall be effected through that representative in whose name the joint ownership has been registered.

Article 13: All cultivated land which was originally leased to tenants and under individual ownership but has become jointly owned as a result of its sale, exchange, or donation, shall be purchased and resold by the Government.

Article 14: In case the lessee of any cultivated land under joint ownership happens to be one of its joint owners, the entire land may be subject to purchase and resale by the Government all the same.

Article 15: The terms, "old and infirm, widowed, orphaned, or disabled," referred to in Paragraph two, Article 8 of this Act, shall denote lessors of any one of the following descriptions:

(1) Those over sixty years of age.

(2)   Those under eighteen years old and fatherless.

(3)   Widows.

(4)   Those who are mentally deranged, or physically deformed in respect of their senses and limbs, or suffering from chronic diseases.

Article 16:   The clause "if the lessor depends upon the land for his or her livelihood," referred to in Paragraph two, Article 8 of this Act, shall mean that the lessor qualifies under either of the following conditions:

(1)   If the household tax (not including that part of the household tax on land) paid by the lessor in 1952 totals less than one hundred dollars (New Taiwan Currency).

(2)   If the lessor has no one to depend upon.

Article 17:   Owners of cultivated land under joint ownership who are old and infirm, widowed, orphaned, or disabled, and depend upon the land for their livelihood, who are qualified to apply for the retention of their land under the provisions of Paragraph two, Article 8 of this Act, shall file, within the prescribed time limit, their applications together with all relevant documents at the land office of the locality where they are domiciled.

The period for filing the above-mentioned applications shall be 30 days. Failure to file the application within the prescribed time limit shall mean the forfeiture of the right of retention.

Article 18:   Any landlord who does not wish to retain the land which he is entitled to retain and requests the Government to purchase it, according to the provisions of Section (7), Paragraph one, Article 8 of this Act, shall file an application at the District, Township, or Urban District *(Chu)* Office of the locality where his land is situated. The said application, after being investigated by the District, Township or Urban District Office and found to be fit and proper, shall be sent to the County or Municipal Government concerned for final approval.

Article 19:   If graves are located within the area of the cultivated land to be purchased by the Government under the provisions of Article 8 of this Act, they shall be investigated, marked off, and retained by the land-owner and the change in land categories involved shall be registered forthwith.

In case the said graves do not belong to the owner of the land on which they are located, the matter shall be settled by agreement between the purchaser and the owner or owners of the graves.

Article 20: The phrase "religious institutions," referred to in Section (5), Paragraph one, Article 8 of this Act, shall mean Buddhist, Taoist, Mohammedan, Catholic, Christian, and other lawful religious institutions and organizations, which have been duly approved and registered before the promulgation and enforcement of this Act.

Article 21: The announced area of city planning, referred to in Section (1),Paragraph one, Article 9 of this Act, shall mean districts where construction has been carried out as part of such city planning. But all leased land under private ownership lying outside of the districts where construction has been carried out as part of such city planning shall be subject to purchase and resale by the Government according to the provisions of this Act.

The districts where construction has been carried out as part of such city planning, referred to in the preceding paragraph, shall be subject to investigation by the Department of Reconstruction and the Land Bureau in conjunction with the County or Municipal Governments concerned and the results of the investigation shall be tabulated and submitted to the Provincial Government for approval.

Article 22: The cultivated land that shall not be subject to purchase by the Government, according to the provisions of Section (3), Paragraph one, Article 9 of this Act, shall mean non-leased land that has been used, before the promulgation and enforcement of this Act, for purposes of experimentation, research, or agricultural extension by organizations that have been duly approved and registered before the promulgation of this Act.

Article 23: The cultivated land that shall not be subject to purchase by the Government, according to the provisions of Sections (2) and (3), Paragraph one, Article 9 of this Act, shall be investigated by the County or Municipal Governments concerned and the results of the investigation shall be tabulated and submitted to the Provincial Government for approval.

Article 24: The educational institutions, referred to in Section (4), Paragraph one, Article 9 of this Act, shall mean those that have been established and duly approved by the competent educational authorities before the promulgation and enforcement of this Act.

Article 25: The charitable institutions, referred to in Section (4), Paragraph one, Article 9 of this Act, shall be limited to those that have been established and duly approved and registered before the promulgation of this Act.

Article 26: The public and private enterprises, referred to in Section (5), Paragraph one, Article 9 of this Act, shall be limited to those that have been established and duly approved and registered before the promulgation and enforcement of this Act.

Article 27: The cultivated land, referred to in Section (5), Paragraph one, Article 9 of this Act, shall be limited to that which is mentioned in the last sentence of Paragraph one, Article 6 of this Act.   If such land is leased to tenants, it shall be subject to Government purchase and resale according to the provisions of this Act.

Article 28: Applications for exemption from Government purchase of cultivated lands coming within the scope of Sections (4) and (5), Paragraph one, Article 9 of this Act, shall be made within the prescribed time limit to the proper authorities concerned.

The above-mentioned applications shall be referred by the authorities concerned to the Land Bureau for consideration together with the Department of Education, the Bureau of Social Affairs, and the Department of Reconstruction, and the results thereof shall be submitted to the Provincial Government for final approval.

Article 29: In calculating the area which a landlord is entitled to retain, such land as is exempt from Government purchase under the provisions of Sections (1) and (5), Paragraph one, Article 9 of this Act, shall be considered together with his other lands that are under his own cultivation and under lease.   In case such land of his as is exempt from Government purchase under the provisions of Sections (1) and (5), Paragraph one, Article 9 of this Act, comes up to, or exceeds, the prescribed area which he is entitled to retain, all his other lands under lease shall be purchased by the Government.

Article 30: In authorizing the retention of cultivated land according to the provisions of Article 10 of this Act, the criteria to be followed shall be the distance between the land in question and the landlord's place of residence, the economic condition of the tenants, the conditions of land utilization, etc.   The order in which the cultivated lands are to be retained shall be as follows:

(1) Cultivated land whose owner is resident in the township;

(2) Cultivated land whose owner is resident in the County but non-resident in the township;

(3) Cultivated land whose owner is non-resident in the County.

The order prescribed in the preceding paragraph may be changed to avoid the breaking up of cultivated land and preserve its shape and terrain.

Article 31: In recommending, according to the provisions of Paragraph two, Article 10 of this Act, any departure from the prescribed standards of retention by a 10% margin or less either in excess or falling short of them, as may be necessitated by the shape and terrain of the land in question, the following provisions shall be observed:

(1) The result of the recommended departure from the prescribed standards of retention either way shall be as close to the standards as possible. In case the result works out exactly the same either way, the choice shall fall on that figure which is lower than the prescribed standards of retention.

(2) In case the results of any departure from the prescribed standards of retention either way cannot achieve the purpose of preserving the shape and terrain of the land in question, the prescribed standards of retention shall be strictly followed and no departure either way is to be recommended or authorized.

Article 32: Before approving the retention of cultivated land according to the provisions of Article 10 of this Act, the County and Municipal Governments concerned shall make a preliminary calculation on the basis of all available data and of the prescribed standards of retention, and the results of this preliminary calculation shall be subject to another check before they are handed over for examination and clearance.

Article 33: All cultivated lands under lease that are retained by the landlords according to the provisions of Article 10 of this Act, shall continue to be regulated by the provisions of the Farm Rent Reduction to 37.5% Act.

Article 34: The cultivated land under the landlord's own cultivation in addition to his land leased to tenants, referred to in Article 11 of this Act, shall be that whose area was duly registered in the cadastre on April 1,

1952, and any transfers thereof made after April 1, 1952 shall be regulated according to the provisions of Article 7 of this Act.

Article 35: In case the contractual relationship between the landlord and his tenant is terminated as a result of the Government purchase of his land, the house that the tenant has been using shall be disposed of according to the following provisions:

(1) In case the house has been subject to a house tax, it shall be purchased by the Government at a price to be determined by the Land Commission by capitalizing the annual house tax minus the investment of capital and the application of labor made by the tenant. But wherever local custom prescribes no additional payment for such houses when the land is offered for sale, the local custom shall prevail.

(2) In case the use of the house has been shared by the landlord and the tenant in the past, its future disposal shall be regulated by agreement between the two parties.

In case the house referred to in the preceding paragraph has been used all along by the landlord for purposes of ancestral worship by his family and clan, it may be exempt from Government purchase along with the land, on which it is situated, upon the request of the landlord. But any part of the house concerned that has been used by the tenant all along shall continue to be disposed of according to the original arrangements.

Article 36: In case the contractual relationship between the landlord and his tenant continues to be in force after a part of his land is purchased by the Government, such immovable fixtures as houses, drying ground, ponds, fruit trees, bamboos, woods, etc. and sites thereof which have been used by the tenant all along shall continue to be so used according to the original arrangements and the landlord shall not refuse.

Article 37: Water sources, wells, channels and ditches, and other water conservancy facilities that have been used all along for the irrigation and drainage of those lands which are now purchased by the Government, shall continue to be so used according to the original practice and the owners thereof shall not refuse.

Article 38: Water pumps and accessory equipment which have been used all along for the irrigation of those lands that are now purchased by the Government, and which are not the property of the prospective purchasers of the lands concerned, may be purchased by the Government together with the lands according to the provisions of Article 13 of this Act.

Measures governing the Government purchase, compensation, and administration of the articles, referred to in the preceding paragraph, shall be drawn up by the Water Conservancy Bureau and submitted to the Provincial Government for approval.

Article 39: The provisions in Article 15 of this Act that "The purchase price for the land shall be paid seventy per cent in land bonds in kind and thirty per cent in Government enterprise stock shares" shall refer to the total price of the land which each landowner is entitled to receive from the Government as compensation. But in making actual payments to each landowner, all odd sums out of the seventy per cent payable in land bonds which are smaller than the smallest face value of the bonds shall be paid in Government enterprise stocks. Similarly, all odd sums out of the purchase price payable in Government enterprise stocks which are smaller than the smallest face value of the stocks shall be paid in cash.

The payment for the monetary value of such rights as are to be compensated and paid for to the holders thereof by the Government on behalf of the landowner, as specified in Section (2), Article 18 of this Act, shall be regulated by the provisions of the preceding paragraph.

Article 40: Where the land bonds in kind issued according to Article 16 of this Act are to be redeemed on an annual basis according to the tables attached to the Regulations Governing the Issuance of Land Bonds in Kind, Taiwan Province, only the principal but no interest shall be paid for the first annual installment; and where the said bonds are to be redeemed on a semi-annual basis according to the same tables, only the principal but no interest shall be paid for the first semi-annual installment. All interest on the purchase price of land shall begin with the second annual installment or the second semi-annual installment, as the case may be, of the respective bonds.

All interest on the resale price to be paid by the purchaser according to the provisions of Article 20 of this Act, shall be regulated by the provisions of the preceding paragraph.

Article 41: The compensation for all articles that are subject to Government purchase along with the land to which they belong shall be evaluated in terms of sweet potatoes and shall be paid for in sweet potato bonds.

Article 42: The price of three-year rotation fields shall be calculated in terms of rice and sweet potato according to the following formula:

Price of three-year rotation field=part of price expressed in rice+part of price expressed in sweet potato $= \dfrac{2 \times \text{(Standard yield of two crops of rice)} \times .5}{3} + \dfrac{\text{(Standard yield of one crop of sweet potato)} \times 2.5}{3}$

That part of the price expressed in sweet potato, referred to in the foregoing formula, shall be converted into terms of rice, according to the ratio between the current prices of rice and sweet potato on the local market in the respective county or municipality, and shall be paid with rice bonds.

Article 43: The price of single-crop paddy fields shall be estimated at 2.5 times the standard yield of one crop of rice plus the standard yield of one crop of sweet potato.

That part of the price expressed in sweet potato, referred to in the preceding paragraph, shall be calculated according to the provisions of Paragraph two of the preceding Article.

Article 44: The price of paddy fields depending on weather and of the specially irrigated fields shall be estimated at 2.5 times the standard yield originally agreed upon between the parties concerned.

In case the standard yield originally agreed upon is expressed in terms of sweet potato, it shall be converted into terms of rice, according to the ratio between the current prices of rice and sweet potato on the local market in the respective county or municipality, and shall be paid according to the provisions of Articles 4 and 11 of the Regulations Governing the Issuance of Land Bonds in Kind, Taiwan Province.

Article 45: The compensation for land under joint ownership that is purchased by the Government shall be paid, according to the customary practice, to that person whose name appears as the first one on the list of joint owners as registered, but if any one of the joint owners applies for the payment to himself of his share of the compensation, the amount shall be calculated and paid to him accordingly.

Article 46: Compensation for the Government purchase of cultivated land not recognized as having been duly transferred shall be made to the transferee.

Article 47: The public announcement, referred to in Section (1), Paragraph one, Article 17 of this Act, shall be made according to the following provisions:

(1) A list shall be prepared by the County or Municipal Government concerned and shall be exposed to public view in the District, Township, and Urban District Office under whose jurisdiction the cultivated lands are situated.

(2) The list to be publicly announced shall include names of landlords, their addresses, particulars of the lands to be purchased by the Government, purchase price, other articles to be purchased by the Government along with the land, and other rights involved. Other articles to be purchased by the Government along with the land may, however, form the subject of a separate public announcement.

(3) Before the public announcement is made, a notice shall be posted for the general public, indicating when the public announcement will begin and when it will end.

Article 48: In filing a request for the rectification of any error in the public announcement during the prescribed period, according to the provisions of Section (2) Paragraph one, Article 17 of this Act, the landowner or other interested parties shall present a written application and submit it, together with all relevant documents, to the District, Township, and Urban District Office under whose jurisdiction the cultivated land is situated. Within three days on the receipt of this written application, the District, Township, and Urban District Office shall make a thorough investigation of the case and submit it to the County or Municipal Government concerned for approval.

Article 49: When the landowner has surrendered the ownership certificate and other relevant documents, according to the provisions of Section (3), Paragraph one, Article 17 of this Act, the Land Office shall register the transfer of landownership accordingly. When any ownership certificate and relevant documents have been declared null and void, the transfer of the ownership of the land involved shall be registered forthwith.

Th declaration that any ownership certificate and relevant documents are null and void, referred to in the preceding paragraph, shall be made in the form of a public notice by the County or Municipal Government under whose jurisdiction the land involved is situated.

Article 50: The County and Municipal Governments shall require the landowners to surrender their ownership certificates and other relevant documents, according to the provisions of Section (3), Paragraph one, Article 17 of this Act, within ten days after the expiration of the prescribed period of public announcement.

Article 51: When the transfer of the ownership of any land purchased by the Government is duly registered, the County or Municipal Government concerned shall notify, by means of a written notice, the former landowner to pick up the purchase price at the Land Bank.

Article 52: In surrendering the ownership certificate and other relevant documents according to the provisions of Section (3), Paragraph one, Article 17 of this Act, the landowner shall submit the lease contract of the land purchased by the Government for revision or cancellation, as the case may require.

Article 53: The landowner shall pick up the purchase price according to the provisions of Section (4), Paragraph one, Article 17 of this Act, within one month beginning from the day when such payments commence.

The date on which payments of the purchase price begin, referred to in the preceding paragraph, shall be publicly announced by the Land Bank.

Article 54: Other rights to be liquidated, according to the provisions of Article 18 of this Act, shall be those which are duly registered in the land register. In case any one of those rights has been changed or extinguished, the obligee shall, during the period of public announcement, make a joint application with the obligor at the Land Office of the locality where the cultivated land involved is situated and request that the change or the extinction be duly registered.

Article 55: In liquidating other rights, according to the provisions of Article 18 of this Act, the County and Municipal Governments concerned shall record specific items of those rights in the list of the lands subject to Government purchase and shall have both publicly announced at one and the same time.

Article 56: Rights of servitude and superficies that are to be transferred together with the land, referred to in Section (1), Article 18 of this Act, shall be registered as having been duly transferred, immediately after the Government purchase of the land, by the Land Office which shall notify the obligee of this fact.

Article 57: In effecting payments for the liquidation of other rights, referred to in Section (2), Article 18 of this Act, the County and Municipal Governments concerned shall, after the public announcement is made definitive, send a complete list to the Land Bank with the request that payments be made to the holders of those rights out of the amounts which the obligor receives from the Government as the purchase price for his land.

Article 58: In case disputes arise concerning the value of those rights to be paid for and liquidated, according to the provisions of Section (2), Article 18 of this Act, the obligee and the obligor may bring the case directly before a court of law and may, during the period of public announcement on the presentation of written evidence issued by the court that the care is *sub judice,* request the Land Bank to suspend payment on the purchase price of the land or on the value of the rights involved. If no such request is made before the expiration of the period of public announcement, the Land Bank shall proceed to make the payments according to the value of such rights publicly announced.

Article 59: In effecting payments with land bonds in kind for the values of other rights expressed in monetary terms, the conversion shall be made on the same basis as cases coming under the provisions of Article 12 of the Regulations Governing the Issuance of Land Bonds in Kind, Taiwan Province.

Article 60: In the case of land on which a *dien** has been created, the present tiller shall be the prospective buyer of the land.

Article 61: Any tenant whose rent payments are in arrears owing to causes other than *force majeure,* shall, during the period of public announcement of the resale, sign a written agreement for the repayment of those arrears in installments. The original landowner may enforce payment for any defaults thereon according to law.

Article 62: Any deposit money which the tenant has paid to the landlord as a guarantee may be paid back to him out of the purchase price which the landlord is entitled to receive from the Government, on the same basis as cases coming under the provisions of Section (2), Article 18 of this Act, if the tenant makes to the Government a due application to that effect. This provision shall not apply to cases in which the two parties concerned have already, before the Government purchase, entered into an agreement for the repayment of the deposit money.

---

*See note on p. 193.

Chapter III.   Resale of Government Purchased Land

Article 63:   In case there are two or more farm hands tilling the land to be resold by the Government according to the provisions of this Act, the District, Township, and Urban District Land Commission concerned shall carefully choose one of them, on the basis of their ability to till the land, as the prospective purchaser and submit the choice to the County or Municipal Government concerned for approval.

In case the farm hands, referred to in the preceding paragraph, happen to be transient or temporary in character, the land shall be resold by the Government to one of the farming families duly registered as would-be cultivators.

Article 64:   The public announcement, referred to in Section (2), Article 21 of this Act, shall be made according to the following provisions:

(1)   A purchasers' list shall be compiled by the County or Municipal Gonvernment concerned and shall be exposed to public view in the District, Township, and Urban District Office under whose jurisdiction the cultivated lands are situated.

(2)   The list to be publicly announced shall include names of the prospective purchasers, their addresses, particulars of the lands to be resold by the Government, and other articles to be resold by the Government along with the land.   Other articles to be resold by the Government along with the land may, however, form the subject of a separate public announcement.

(3)   The prospective purchaser shall, during the period when the list is exposed to public view, hand the original lease contract to the District or Township Office for revision or cancellation, as the case may require.

(4)   The public announcement for the resale of Government purchased land shall be made simultaneously with the public announcement for the Government purchase of the same.

Article 65:   In filing a request for the rectification of any error in the public announcement during the prescribed period, according to the provisions of Section (3), Article 21 of this Act, the prospective purchaser or other interested parties shall present a written application and submit it, together with all relevant documents, to the District, Township, and Urban District Office under whose jurisdiction the cultivated land is situated. Within three days on the receipt of this written application, the District, Township, and Urban District Office shall make a thorough investigation of the case on the spot and submit it to the competent County or Municipal Government for approval.

Article 66: In case the land subject to Government purchase happens to be leased to two or more tenants, whose names all appear on the lease contract, it shall be resold to them, separately, by the Government. In case the lease contract, though signed by only one of the tenants, specifically states that there are, besides himself, a definite number of other tenants, and if the other tenants are found, upon investigation, to be actual tillers of the land, the same procedure shall also apply.

Article 67: Any cultivated land bought by its present tenant-tiller in the name of his children or grandchildren shall be considered as having been bought by the tiller himself.

Article 68: All cultivated land jointly bought by the present tenant together with other person or persons after April 1, 1952 shall be regulated according to the following provisions:

    (1)   If such land is entirely cultivated by the purchasers themselves, it shall be retained by them without being subject to Government purchase.

    (2)   If the tenant-purchaser cultivates under lease that part of the land which has been jointly bought by him and his associates, in addition to the part bought by himself, the entire land may be purchased by the Government and resold to the tenant-purchaser.

    (3)   If such land as has been jointly bought is partly cultivated by the tenant-purchaser and partly leased to others for cultivation, the entire land may be purchased by the Government and separately resold to the cultivators.

Article 69: After being notified by the Government that his application for the purchase of land has been duly approved, the purchaser shall go to the Land Bank and pay the purchase price by installments, as they fall due.

Article 70: The price of land resold by the Government and the interest thereon shall be paid in equal annual amounts over a period of ten years with farm products or with land bonds in kind which are redeemable at the same time as the installment payment of the land price. The payments shall be made in cash calculated in terms of the current value of sweet potato in respect of dry land and the immovable fixtures thereon and the sites thereof, and in rice in respect of paddy field. But in the case of one-crop paddy fields and paddy fields depending on weather, the installments due in years when no rice is planted shall be paid in cash calculated in terms of the current value of rice; in the case of rotation field's (inculding the specially irrigated fields), the entire purchase price shall be paid in cash calculated in terms of the current value of rice.

Article 71: The current value of sweet potatoes and rice in terms of which cash payments are to be made, as provided for in the preceding paragraph, shall be fixed by the County and Municipal Governments in the light of the average wholesale quotations on the markets of important centers of production in the villages and townships of the respective County or municipalities in the period lying between the twentieth and eleventh day inclusive, before the date on which any given installment payment on the purchase price of land is due to begin in the respective County and Municipialities.

Article 72: The purchaser of cultivated land resold by the Government shall, after having paid the first installment of the purchase price, show the receipt at the local Land Office and request it to register the transfer of land and to issue him the ownership certificate.

Article 73: In issuing the ownership certificate to the purchaser, the Land Office shall make the following notes thereon.

(1) Provisions of Article 30 of this Act.

(2) The purchaser shall not transfer the land to any other person before the purchase price is fully paid, as provided for in Article 28 of this Act. When the purchase price is fully paid, the Land Bank shall put a chop on the ownership certificate, stating that "The purchase price is paid in full."

Article 74: Measures for the implementation of the provisions of Articles 23 and 24 of this Act, concerning the improvement of land use and the encouragement of cooperative operations, respectively, shall be drawn up by the Land Bureau, the Department of Agriculture and Forestry, the Department of Finance, the Cooperatives Administration, the Land Bank, and other authorities concerned and be submitted to the Provincial Government for approval.

Article 75: Requests for reduction in the amount of, or exemption of payments on, the unliquidated portion of the purchase price, as provided for in Article 25 of this Act, shall be regulated according to the following provisions:

(1) The purchaser shall, within ten days after the occurrence of the *force majeure,* make a written request to the District, Township, and Urban District Office, under whose jurisdiction the land is situated.

(2) Within three days on the receipt of this written request, the District, Township, and Urban District Office shall make a thorough investigation of the case and submit it, through the normal channels of official communication, to the Provincial Government for approval.

Article 76: Postponements in the payment of the purchase price and interest thereon in case of crop failure, as provided for in Article 26 of this Act, shall be regulated according to the following provisions:

(1) A 30% postponement in the payment shall be permitted in cases in which the crop failure is not less than 30%; a 50% postponement in cases in which the crop failure is not less than 40%; and 100% postponement in cases in which the crop failure is over 50%.

(2) The percentage of crop failure shall be estimated by plots on the lands resold by the Government.

(3) Within ten days after the occurrence of a crop failure on any land resold by the Government and twenty days before the harvesting of the crop, the purchaser shall submit to the District, Township and Urban District Office a written application for the postponement of the purchase price, except in cases of emergency in which no written application shall be required. On the receipt of such an application, the District, Township and Urban District Office shall transmit it to the competent County or Municipal Government, which shall then despatch a responsible officer to make a preliminary on-the-spot investigation of the situation plot by plot in cooperation with members of the District, Township, and Urban District Office. The results of the investigation, if they confirm the statements contained in the purchaser's application, shall be embodied in a written report to be submitted to the County or Municipal Government. At the same

time, the County or Municipal Government shall report the case, by telegram, to the Provincial Government, which shall then despatch a responsible officer to make a second on-the-spot investigation of the situation in cooperation with the County or Municipal officer, who has made the preliminary investigation, and check over the written report that has been submitted to the County or Municipal Government. The results of the second investigation shall be embodied in a written report to be submitted, together with three copies of a List of Recommended Postponements in the Payment of the Land Purchase Price, to the Provincial Government for approval. A fourth copy of the said List shall be sent to the local branch or sub-branch office of the Land Bank for reference. When the recommended postponements are approved by the Provincial Government, one copy of the above-mentioned List, together with any attachment showing whatever corrections, if any, are to be made therein, shall be sent to the County or Municipal Government concerned, and another copy to the Land Bank, to serve as the basis for official action.

Chapter IV. Restrictions and Penalties

Article 77: The clause "in the event that the purchaser cannot till the land himself," referred to in Article 29 of this Act, shall cover either one of the following cases:

(1) In the event of the death of the purchaser whose heir is incapable of tillage.

(2) In the event of the purchaser being incapacitated for tillage and all of his family members living with him in the same household being incapable of tillage.

Article 78: All cultivated land taken back by the Government, according to the provisions of Articles 29 and 30 of this Act, shall be resold according to the procedure laid down in this Act. When such land is available for resale, the District, Township, and Urban District Office, under whose jurisdiction such land is situated, shall make recommendations from among the farmers in the localities concerned who need land and have the capacity to till it. The land shall be resold to the farmers thus recommended when the recommendations have been examined, cleared, and approved.

Article 79: In the case of cultivated lands lying within an area for which a city planning project has been publicly announced but where no construction has been done as part of such city planning, all such lands that have been purchased and resold by the Government may be rebought by the Government at the original resale price and put to a different use, if any one of the following circumstances obtains after the purchase and resale:

(1) If the lands are required by the Government, for the extension of urban reconstruction or for the use of public enterprises.

(2) If the land resold by the Government is, without Government permission, transferred to another person or persons or encumbered by the purchaser.

(3) If the land is used by the purchaser for purposes other than cultivation without the permisson of the competent County or Municipal Government.

Even though the purchased land is used, with Government permission, for purposes other than cultivation, it shall be rebought by the Government at the original resale price, if its ownership is transferred.

Article 80: In the case of cultivated land taken back from the purchaser by the Government, according to the provisions of Article 30 of this Act, accessories thereon shall not be compensated for.

Chapter V. Supplementary Provisions

Article 81: Rules governing rewards and punishments for, and supervision over, the execution of this Act, shall be drawn up by the Provincial Government and submitted to the Executive Yuan for approval.

Article 82: All tables, literature, and form to be used in the implementation of the Land-to-the-Tiller Program shall be regulated by the Provincial Government by decree.

Article 83: These Regulations shall come into force from the day of their promulgation.

RELIEF MEASURES APPLICABLE TO OLD AND INFIRM, ORPHANED, WIDOWED, OR PHYSICALLY DISABLED JOINT OWNERS OF LAND THAT HAD BEEN COMPULSORILY PURCHASED BY THE GOVERNMENT IN 1954

(Promulgated by the Taiwan Provincial Government,
February 25, 1954.)

Article 1: The present Measures are drawn up according to the instructions given by the Executive Yuan in its letter of No. 756, 1953.

Article 2: The term "Original Regulations" in the present Measures refers to "The Regulations Governing the Implementation of the Land-to-the-Tiller Act in Taiwan Province" promulgated on April 23, 1953, and the term "Amended Regulations" refers to the same Regulation as amended on February 25, 1954.

Article 3: Any joint landowner who would, according to the provisions of Article 15 or 16 of the Amended Regulations, retain a portion of his land which had been compulsorily purchased by the Government according to the provisions of Article 16 or 17 of the Original Regulations may apply for relief according to the provisions of the present Measures.

In any of the following cases, the joint landowner shall not apply for relief:

(1) If the total area of the land under his own cultivation and his leased land already retained by him or exempted from compulsory purchase has reached the prescribed retention limit.

(2) If he has been already permitted to retain his leased land according to the provisions of Article 16 or 17 of the Original Regulations.

(3) If his state of becoming old and infirm, orphaned, widowed, or physically disabled according to the provisions of the Amended Regulations occurs after the expiration of the period of public

announcement for the compulsory purchase of his land in 1953.

Article 4: Any joint landowner who wishes to apply for relief according to the provisions of the present Measures shall, within the prescribed period, present a written application to the Land Office in the locality where he is domiciled, together with the following documents of evidence:

(1) A full copy of the household record.

(2) A certificate issued by the competent tax authorities to prove the total amount of household tax paid by the applicant in the year of 1952.

(3) A certificate issued by a public hospital to prove that the applicant is mentally deranged, physically deformed in respect of senses and limbs, or suffering from chronic diseases. If such state occurs after the expiration of the period of public announcement for compulsory purchase of his land in 1953, a note to that effect shall be added in the certificate.

(4) A certificate issued by the chief of the village or precinct where he is domiciled to prove that the applicant has no one to depend upon. If such state occurs after the expiration of the period of public announcement for compulsory purchase of his land in 1953, a note to that effect shall be added in the certificate.

(5) A list of land under joint ownership which was compulsorily purchased by the Government.

(6) The ownership certificate, the joint ownership certificate or the joint ownership share certificate of the land which was compulsorily purchased by the Government. If such certificate has been surrendered to the Government, a note to that effect shall be inserted in the aforesaid list of land under joint ownership.

The period for the application of relief referred to in the preceding paragraph shall be a month. The dates on which such period begins and ends shall be prescribed by the Provincial Government and publicly announced by the competent County or Municipal Government. If the joint landowner fails to apply for relief within the prescribed period, he is deemed to have given up his application for relief.

Article 5: As the documents of evidence mentioned in the preceding Article serve as basis for weighting the application, the competent authorities issuing such documents shall state therein the true facts obtained through actual investigation, and shall be held legally responsible for any false evidence given in favor of the applicant.

Article 6: The written applications for relief received by the local Land Office shall be transmitted within five days to the competent County or Municipal Government, which shall make a preliminary investigation according to the following provisions:

(1) To find out, in the light of the copy of household record and the public hospital's certificate as presented by the applicant, whether he conforms to the provisions of Article 15 of the Amended Regulations.

(2) To find out, in the light of the certificate of the household tax paid and the certificate proving that the applicant has no one to depend upon as presented by the applicant, whether he conforms to the provisions of Article 16 of the Amended Requlations.

The results of the preliminary investigation together with reasons for approving or disapproving the application shall be recorded in the original application, and the officer in charge of the preliminary investigation shall put his signature and seal thereon.

If, on the preliminary investigation, the documents of evidence presented by the applicant are found to be inadequate, or the statements contained therein are incomplete, the applicant shall be notified to supply the required information within the prescribed period.

Article 7: The notification for the supply of the required information referred to in the preceding Article shall be delivered to the applicant ten days before the expiration of the period for application, and the applicant shall supply the required informtion within the said period. If the notification is delivered to the applicant less than nine days before the expiration of the period for application, he shall supply the required information within ten days from the date on which the notification is delivered. In case the required information is not supplied on the expiration of the prescribed period, the application shall be dismissed.

The supply of required information for an application referred to in the preceding paragraph shall be made only once.

Article 8: The phrase "not including that part of the household tax on land" mentioned in brackets in Section 1, Paragraph 1, Article 16 of the Amended Regulations, shall, in the case of making relief to joint landowners, refer to that portion of the household tax which was paid on the leased land already compulsorily purchased by the Government, and the other portions of the tax which were paid on land cultivated by the owner himself, on leased land retained by him or exempted from compulsory purchase and on land of other descriptions shall be still included in the total amount of the household tax paid.

On certifying the total amount of the household tax paid by the applicant, the competent tax authorities shall, for the convenience of investigation, state separately in the certificate the portion of the tax paid on the land compulsorily purchased by the Government, and the portions paid on other lands and on objects other than land.

Article 9: If the application for relief is found, as a result of the preliminary investigation, not to conform to the provisions of the Amended Regulations, the County or Municipal Government shall notify the applicant of the reasons for disapproving the application; and if the application is found to conform to the provisions of the Amended Regulations, it shall be sent back to the Original Land Office for another checking according to the following provisions:

(1)　The original Land Office shall check to see whether the applicant has already applied for the retention of his land according to the provisions of the original Regulations, and, if so, reject his application for relief.

(2)　The original Land Office shall check to see whether the total area of land now cultivated by the applicant himself and the leased land already retained by him or exempted from compulsory purchase has reached the prescribed retention limit, and if so, reject his application for relief.

(3)　If the land compulsorily purchased by the Government is situated in a village or township under the jurisdiction of the original Land Office, the said Land Office shall check to see whether the descriptions of such land stated in the list of land under joint ownership are consistent with those recorded in the Land Register and the Joint Owners Register, and, if not consistent, make necessary corrections in the list.

(4)　If the aforesaid land is situated in a locality under the jurisdiction of another Land Office or in another County or city, the original Land Office shall send a list of descriptions of the aforesaid land to the other Land Office, or County or Municipal Government, which shall check over the descriptions according to the provisions of the preceding Section, chop the list with proper seals, and send it back to the original Land Office.

After the lists of land under joint ownership presented by the applicants have been collectively checked over according to the provisions of the preceding Paragraph, the original Land Office shall, according to the standard prescribed in Article 14 of the present Measures, estimate the additional compensation payable for that portion of the aforesaid land which may be retained by each applicant, and compile a draft list of old and infirm, orphaned, widowed, and physically disabled joint owners entitled to compensation with government enterprise stocks, and submit the list together with the applications rejected or duly corrected to the competent County or Municipal Government for a further investigation.

Article 10: After the draft list mentioned in the preceding Article has been found upon investigation to be correct, the competent County or Minicipal Government shall submit it to the Provincial Government for approval. After it is approved, the competent County or Municipal Government shall send each applicant a notice of the approved amount of government enterprise stocks payable to him as compensation for relief.

Article 11: If, on receiving the notice mentioned in the preceding Article, the old and infirm, orphaned, widowed, or physically disabled joint owner insists on recovering the retainable portion of land compulsorily purchased by the Government, he shall, within five days, submit a request in writing to the competent County or Municipal Government together with a list of descriptions of the portions of land to be recovered. The County or Municipal Government shall then inquire whether the purchaser of the said land is willing to give up his right of purchase, and if he is unwilling to give it up, the applicant shall be paid with such amount of government enterprise stocks as he is entitled to receive.

In the aforesaid list of descriptions of the portions of land to be recovered, only one group of such portions retainable by him shall be indicated, and no request can be made for an alternative group thereof. Any request submitted after the expiration of the prescribed period shall be rejected.

Article 12: The land whose purchaser has given up his right of purchase according to the provisions of the preceding Article shall be dealt with according to the following provisions:

(1) The said land shall continue to be leased to the purchaser according to the provisions of the Farm Rent Reduction to 37.5% Act.

(2) The old and infirm, orphaned, widowed, or physically disabled joint owner who has received compensation for the price of his share of land compulsorily purchased by the Government shall pay back to the organ which paid the compensation such amount of land bonds and government enterprise stocks as the purchaser is entitled to receive as compensation for the price of the joint owner's share of land whereof the purchaser has given up the right of purchase. If such bonds and stocks have been redeemed for rice or cash, the joint owner shall pay back such rice or cash to the organ which redeemed such bonds.

(3) The purchase price of the aforesaid land which was already paid by the purchaser to the Government shall be returned to him by the Government. The farm land tax, the household tax and the water charges which should have been paid by a landlord and were paid by the purchaser shall be paid back to him by the present landlord, but the purchaser shall pay farm rent, as a tenant is obliged to pay, to the present landlord. In case such rent is, owing to a crop failure, reduced or remitted with the approval of the Government, the relevant provisions of the Farm Rent Reduction to 37.5% Act shall apply.

(4) The purchaser who has given up the land purchased by him shall, according to its category, grade, and acreage, receive as an additional compensation such amount of government enterprise stocks as is payable to him according to the provisions of Paragraph II, Article 14 of the present Measures, and, at the same time, he shall surrender the ownership certificate of the land given up by him.

(5) After the purchaser has surrendered his ownership certificate, the competent County or Municipal Government shall register the transfer of landownership and issue a joint ownership share certificate to the applicant for relief and to the purchaser respectively.

(6) After the procedures referred to in Sections 2,3,4,5, and 6 of this Article have been completed, the applicant for relief and the former purchaser shall jointly conclude a 37.5% rent lease contract in respect of the land recovered by the applicant.

(7) After the registration of the transfer of ownership of the land given up by the former purchaser is completed, the competent Land Office shall make necessary corrections in the following records and documents:

(1) Land Register; (2) Joint Owners Register; (3) Cadastral Record; (4) Joint Owners Record; (5) Land Record Card; (6) List of Joint Owners; (7) Landownership Card; (8) Land Tax Payers Register; (9) List of Lands Subject to Compulsory Purchase; (10) List of Lands Subject to Resale; (11) List of Lands Retained by Landlords; (12) List of Leased Private Lands; (13) Duplicate Copy of Lease Contract; (14) Relevant Statistics.

Article 13: When the old and infirm, orphaned, widowed, or physically disabled joint landowners have been approved, and the purchasers willing to give up their right of purchase have been definitely ascertained after inquiry, the County or Municipal Government shall compile a list, in six copies, of the old and infirm, orphaned, widowed, and physically disabled joint landowners entitled to be compensated with government enterprise stocks, and a list, also in six copies, of the purchasers giving up his right of purchase and entitled to be compensated with government enterprise stocks. One copy of such lists shall be submitted to the Provincial Government, three copies sent to the Land Bank of Taiwan, the Financial Department and the Food Bureau respectively, one copy kept by the County or Municipal Government, and another copy kept by the local Land Office.

Article 14: The old and infirm, orphaned, widowed or physically disabled joint landowner who has been found to conform to the provisions of Article 15 or 16 of the Amended Regulations shall be given relief in the form of an additional compensation based on the total price of his share of land compulsorily purchased by the Government and calculated according to the following provisions:

(1) If the total acreage of his share of land compulsorily purchased by the Government is smaller than the prescribed retention acreage, he shall be compensated with government enterprise stocks amounting to one half of the total price of his share of land calculated according to the categories and grades of the plots and the acreage of his share of land.

(2) If the total acreage of his share of land compulsorily purchased by the Government is greater than the prescribed retention acreage, he shall be compensated with government enterprise stocks

amounting to one half of the average total of the average price of 1st to 6th grade paddy fields of the prescribed retention acreage plus the average price of 7th to 12th grade paddy fields of the prescribed retention acreage.

The purchaser who has given up the land purchased by him according to the provisions of Article 11 of the present Measures shall be similarly compensated with government enterprise stocks amounting to one half of the total price of the land given up by him, calculated according to its category, grade and acreage.

Article 15: The present Measures shall be repealed, when the work of relief is completed.

Article 16: The present Measures shall be promulgated and enforced after they are approved by the Executive Yuan.

ANNEX: Three Principles for the Relief of Old and Infirm, Orphaned, Widowed, or Physically Disabled Joint Owners whose Retainable Lands Were Compulsorily Purchased by the Government. (Issued by the Executive Yuan in 1953 as instructions to the Taiwan Provincial Government.)

I. Relief Measures shall be drawn up. To those who are entitled to relief, a compensation amounting to one half of the price of land compulsorily purchased by the Government should be paid with the surplus stocks of government enterprises, in addition to the compensation for the price of such land.

II. The persons entitled to relief are the old and infirm, orphaned, widowed, or physically disabled joint owners who would, according to the provisions of the Amended Regulations Governing the Implementation of the Land-to-the-Tiller Act, be entitled to retain a portion of their leased land which had been compulsorily purchased by the Government and resold to tenant farmers according to the provisions of the same Regulations before their amendment.

III. The above-mentioned additional compensation should be paid in the first instance to the original owner whose land had been compulsorily purchased by the Government, but if any tenant purchaser should be willing to give up his right to purchase such land, he should be entitled to receive the same additional compensation, and to continue the lease of such land.

MEASURES FOR THE ENFORCEMENT OF THE LAND - TO - THE - TILLER POLICY AND THE PROTECTION OF OWNER - FARMERS IN TAIWAN PROVINCE

(Promulgated by the Taiwan Provincial Government,
November 1, 1960)

Chapter I. General Provisions

Article 1: For furthering the enforcement of the Land-to-the-Tiller policy and the protection and establishment of owner-farmers, the present Measures are formulated by the Taiwan Provincial Government.

Article 2: The organ responsible for the implementation of the present Measures shall be the Provincial Government for the province, and the County or Municipal Government for the county or municipality, and the organs assisting the implementation shall be the Farm Tenancy Committees and the Farmers' Associations on various levels.

Article 3: The term "owner-farmer" referred to in the present Measures shall mean any of the following farmers:

1. Any farmer who has purchased farm land from the Government or from a landlord according to the provisions of the Land-to-the-Tiller Act.

2. Any farmer who has purchased public farm land according to the provisions of the Regulations Governing the Sale of Public Farm Lands to Establish Owner-Farmers in Taiwan Province.

Article 4: The term "owner-cultivated land" shall mean any of the following farm lands:

1. Farm land purchased by a farmer from the Government or from a landlord according to the provisions of the Land-to-the-Tiller Act.

2. Public farm land purchased by a farmer according to the provisions of the Regulations Governing the Sale of Public Farm Lands to

Establish Owner-Farmers in Taiwan Province.

Article 5: To keep the results of the Land-to-the-Tiller Program, the land officers in every county or municipality shall make regular inspection and rechecking. Whenever any case of violation of the provisions of the Land-to-the-Tiller Act or of the present Measures occurs, they shall request, by means of a special report, the competent County or Municipal Government to deal with it according to law.

The County or Municipal Government shall submit a report of its handling of the case referred to above to the Provincial Government for approval, and at the same time notify the organs concerned of such handling.

Article 6: The Government shall make investigations of the burden borne by owner-farmers, and take steps to ameliorate such burden, if it is found to be too heavy for the proper management of the farm land.

Article 7: For the purpose of promoting land utilization and increasing farm production, the Government shall make greater exertions for the construction and improvement of water conservancy works, the reclamation of waste land and the improvement of agricultural technique.

Article 8: After the implementation of the present Measures, the County or Municipal Government shall carry out a registration of would-be owner-farmers. Farm hands, tenant farmers and owner-farmers holding insufficient farm land are all qualified to apply for such registration.

Article 9: Measures for granting loans to tenant farmers for purchasing farm land according to the provisions of Article 33 of the Land Law shall be separately prescribed.

Chapter II. Establishment of Owner-Farmers.

Article 10: A Fund for the Protection and Establishment of Owner-Farmers shall be set up by the Provincial Government and entrusted to the Land Bank of Taiwan for granting the following loans:

1. Loan requested by any tenant farmer for purchasing farm land from a landlord according to the provisions of Article 12 of the Land-to-the-Tiller Act.

2. Loan requested by any farmer for increasing farm production according to the provisions of Article 23 of the Land-to-the-Tiller

Act.

3. Loan requested by any farmer who has purchased public farm land according to the Regulations Governing the Sale of Public Farm Lands and the Establishment of Owner Farmers in Taiwan Province.

4. Loan required for the construction and improvement of water conservancy works and reclamation of waste land as specified in Article 7 of the present Measures.

Article 11: The Fund referred to in the preceding Article shall be derived from the following sources, deposited in the Land Bank of Taiwan under a special account, and used to meet actual needs according to procedures to be separately prescribed:

1. Twenty-five per cent of the Provincial Government's share of the thirty per cent proceeds derived from the resale of farm lands under the Land-to-the-Tiller Act.

2. Part of the proceeds derived from the sale of public farm lands.

3. Special sums earmarked by the Government.

Article 12: The loan specified in Section 2, Article 10 of the present Measures may be granted to a farmer who cultivated his own land before the implementation of the Land-to-the-Tiller Program, possesses an area of land under his own cultivation smaller than the area retainable by a landlord according to the provisions of Article 20 of the Land-to-the-Tiller Act, and is actually in a difficult economic situation.

Article 13: The loan requested by a farmer for purchasing farm land, and the immovable fixtures and their sites on the farm according to the provisions of Section 1, Article 10 of the present Measures shall be granted according to the following provisions:

1. The loan granted to each farmer shall be limited to an amount of 20% to 60% of the total purchase price of farm land to be determined by the Government according to the actual needs of the farmer.

2. The loan shall bear an interest of 5% per annum and be paid in annual installments; the period for payment shall be not shorter than five years, nor longer than ten years.

3. The farmer who requests the loan shall, after the approval of the request, deliver to the loan agency that portion of the purchased price which should be paid out of his own means; and the loan agency shall tranamit such payment to the seller of the farm land together with the loan payment.

Article 14: For the effective enforcement of the provisions of Article 12 of the Land-to-the-Tiller Act, the Government shall take steps to encourage landlords to sell farm lands retained by them.

Article 15: Loan requested by a farmer for increasing farm production according to the provisions of Section 2, Article 10 of the present measures shall be limited to an amount which is necessary for the purchase of materials for farm production and for the improvement of farm land and is to be determined by the Government.

Article 16: Procedures for granting the loans specified in Articles 13 and 15 of the present Measures shall be separately prescribed.

Article 17: When farm lands taken back by the Government according to the provisions of Articles 29 and 30 of the Land-to-the-Tiller Act are offered for resale, the District or Township Farm Tenancy Committee shall select and recommend prospctive purchasers to the competent County or Municipal Government from among the registered would-be owner-farmers, on the basis of such criteria as their capacity to till land, their actual needs for land and the distance between their residences and the farm lands offered for resale. When such recommendations are approved, the County or Municipal Government shall submit a report thereof to the Provincial Government for reference.

On selecting and recommending prospective purchasers according to the provisions of the preceding paragraph, the District or Township Farm Tenancy Committee shall take no account of the original owners or illegal occupiers of the farm lands offered for resale.

Chapter III. Protection of Owner-Cultivated Land

Article 18: Before the purchase price of the land under his own cultivation is fully paid, an owner-farmer shall not use the land for any purpose other than cultivation, except, with the permission of the competent County or Municipal Government, for the construction thereon of farmhouses which are needed for his own residence and for crop improvement.

Article 19: Before its purchase price is fully paid, owner-cultivated land shall not be exchanged with another land for use, unless the exchange conforms to one of the following conditions and is approved by the competent County or Municipal Government:

1. The exchange is necessary for the promotion of any of the public undertakings specified in Article 208 of the Land Law.

2. The exchange had been, for the convenience of farm managment, effected with permission of the Government, before the land was compulsorily purchased and resold to the present owner by the Government.

Article 20: No other rights shall be created on owner-cultivated land except the servitude and superficies which had been created on such land before it was compulsorily purchased and resold to the present owner.

Article 21: An owner-farmer shall not request the Government to take back the land under his own cultivation, unless he conforms to the provisions of Article 77 of the Regulations Governing the Implementation of the Land-to-the-Tiller Act in Taiwan Province.

Article 22: In case any farm land which is permitted by the Government to be used for a purpose other than cultivation as prescribed in Article 79 of the Regulation Governing the Implementation of the Land-to-the-Tiller Act in Taiwan Province is actually put to a different use, the Government may purchase such land at the original resale price.

Article 23: When an owner-cultivated land whose purchase price has been fully paid, or land which was cultivated by its owner before the implementation of the Land-to-the-Tiller program is transferred, the Government shall, before approving the transfer, investigate if the transferee fulfills one of the following conditions:

1 The transferee has the capacity to till the land.

2. In case the land is transferred to the transferee for the purpose of operating an industry approved by the Government, its area does not exceed that required for the industry.

3. In case the land is transferred to the transferee for the construction of buildings thereon, its area does not exceed that required for such construction, and the transferee is capable of completing the construction within the prescribed period after the land is transferred.

Article 24: The provisions of the present Measures relating to the protection of owner-cultivated land shall, *mutatis mutandis,* apply to the immovable fixtures and their sites resold to farmers by the Government along with the farm land according to the provisions of Article 13 of the Land-to-the-Tiller Act.

Chapter IV. Supplementary Provisions

Article 25: After the present Measures come into force, each County or Municipal Government shall submit a monthly report on the progress of the implementation of the present Measures to the Provincial Government for approval.

Article 26: The present Measures shall come into force from the date of their promulgation.

PROVISIONAL BY-LAW GOVERNING THE IMPROVE-MENT OF FARMERS' ASSOCIATIONS OF DIFFERENT LEVELS IN TAIWAN

(Promulgated by the Executive Yuan on August 20, 1952; amended by the Executive Yuan on October 18, 1955 and August 2, 1956)

Chapter I. General Principles

Article 1: These regulations are established with a view to improving the different levels of farmers' associations and to adapting them to the actual conditions in Taiwan. Matters pertaining to the farmers' associations not provided for in these regulations shall be governed by other related laws.

Article 2: The aims and purposes of the farmers' associations are to promote the farmers' interests, advance their knowledge and skill, improve their living conditions, increase agricultural production, and develop rural economy.

Article 3: Farmers' associations shall be considered as legal persons.

Article 4: Farmers' associations of provincial, county or municipal levels shall be governed by corresponding Provincial, County or Municipal Governments, with the agriculture and forestry departments/divisions of the respective governments temporarily in charge of their activities. However, in matters concerning the granting of approval for the establishment and registration of farmers' associations, and the filing of their re-organization and re-election records, etc., actions shall be taken by the said departments/divisions in close coordination with the social affairs departments/divisions of the respective governments.

Article 5: Farmers' associations shall bear all the liabilities relative to their various functions and activities as stipulated in the different laws and government statutes governing such functions and activities (e.g., the liabilities of a farmers' association rendering credit, insurance, consumption and marketing services shall be as stipulated in the Cooperative Law; Insurance Law, etc.) These liabilities shall be stipulated in the constitutional regulations of the farmers' associations.

Chapter II.   Functions and Activities

Article 6: Farmers' associations, in accordance with the demands of their members and in coordination with government policies, may either directly perform or assist other agencies in performing the following functions:

(1) Rendition of advisory, demonstrative and propagative services relative to agricultural production.

(2) Encouragement and promotion of agricultural production.

(3) Improvement of the efficiency of farm labor.

(4) Operation and formulation of extension and training program for the advancement of agricultural technique.

(5) Marketing, warehousing, processing and manufacturing of farm products.

(6) Procurement, allocation, processing and manufacturing of farming and daily necessities for members.

(7) Operation of agricultural warehouses and other communal utilities.

(8) Operation and management of markets for farm products.

(9) Rendition of credit service to members.

(10) Rendition of agricultural insurance service to members.

(11) Advocation of rural avocations and rural industries.

(12) Institution and implementation of land reform program.

(13) Improvement of farm land.

(14) Formulation and execution of water conservancy projects.

(15) Prevention and control of agricultural adversities and disasters.

(16) Encouragement of forest protection efforts and initiation of reforestation projects.

(17) Elevation of rural standard of living and the advancement of rural culture.

(18) Rendition of advice and guidance to rural women and youths on their daily problems and the promotion of general social welfare.

(19) Mediation or arbitration of rural disputes.

(20) Rendition of relief in rural areas.

(21) Execution of consignments placed by government and other official or private organizations or members.

(22) Provision of information and compilation of reports on rural surveys and agricultural statistics.

(23) Initiation of rural health and sanitation projects.

(24) Agency for village and township treasury.

(25) Rendition of deposit service to non-members upon special approval by the Provincial Government and the performance of other functions especially authorized by the Provincial Government.

(26) Performance of other functions in line with the aims and purposes of farmers' associations as set forth in article 2, Chapter I above.

Article 7: In localities where cooperatives for producing and marketing such special products as banana, pineapple, water-melon, orange, tangerine, wentan pomelo, tea, citronella oil, straw-hats and mattings, cassava, rice-paper plant and bamboo pole, etc., have been legally organized, the farmers' associations in those places shall not be permitted to handle the same business. However, in localities where such cooperatives have not yet been established, the respective local farmers' associations shall be allowed to handle the marketing and sales of these special products on behalf of local producers provided that such an arrangement is desired by the producer members of the farmers' associations and the request approved by the respective boards of directors. The local producers then shall not be permitted to organize separate cooperatives for the same purpose. In localities where sales and marketing cooperatives for special products are not in existence and when such businesses are neither handled by local Farmers' Associations, the government agencies in charge of the respective

Farmers' Associations shall decide on the course to be taken as regards this matter, basing their decision on the wishes of local producers.

Article 8: Farmers' Associations shall put aside 10% of their deposits received in a banking institution authorized by the Provincial Government as reserve fund.

Article 9: Farmers' Associations shall not engage in any activities not passed by their members' representatives meetings or by their boards of directors or without the concurrence of the superior farmers' associations. Upon taking up a certain activity, descriptive records of the activity shall be submitted to and filed with the government agency in charge for their reference.

Article 10: Consignments entrusted to and accepted by Farmers' Association from governments, official and private organizations, or members shall be confirmed by written contracts between the parties concerned.

Chapter III. Organization

Article 11: (1) Farmers' Associations may be classified into the following categories:

> (a) District Farmers' Associations—including township, urban district and county-governed city Farmers' Associations.

> (b) County or Municipality Farmers' Associations.

> (c) Provincial Farmers' Association.

(2) District (township, urban district, county-governed city) Farmers' Associations may establish a small agricultural unit in each village or precinct within their respective territories and name the small agricultural unit after the name of the village or precinct in which it is located.

(3) A small agricultural unit may also be established in each cooperative farm which shall be considered as equivalent to a village or precinct.

(4) Where a District (township, urban district and county-governed city) Farmers' Association or a small agricultural unit has an exceptionally small number of members (including associate members), it may be affiliated to other District Farmers' Associa-

tions or other small agricultural units, if such action is deemed necessary by its superior Farmers' Association. A record of such affiliation shall then be filed with the government agency in charge for its reference.

Article 12: (1) The organic territory in which each Farmers' Association may pursue its activities shall be identical to the administrative or autonomous territory under the control of an administrative or autonomous unit in which the Farmers' Association in question is located. Only one Farmers' Association bearing the name of an administrative or autonomous unit shall be established in the territory controlled by the unit.

(2) Provincial and county or municipal Farmers' Associations shall be located at the seats of the respective governments. District (township, urban district and county-governed city) Farmers' Associations shall be located at the seats of the district (township, urban district and county-governed city) office. Locations other than that specified above shall not be chosen as the seats of Farmers' Associations except in cases where such variations are found necessary and have been sanctioned by the government agency in charge.

(3) Farmers' Associations may establish field offices in important areas within its organic territory provided that such actions are resolved by the members' representatives meetings and have been approved by the government agency in charge.

Article 13: (1) A district (township, urban district and county-governed city) Farmers' Association shall be initiated and organized when over fifty farmers in the district (township, urban district and county-governed city) are qualified for a Farmers' Association membership.

(2) A Farmers' Association of a higher level shall be organized when over half of the total number of lower level Farmers' Associations in the territory have been established.

Article 14: The organization of a Farmers' Association shall be preceded by the formation of a preparatory committee consisting of committee members elected from among the initiators. Records of the proceedings of the preparatory committee shall be submitted to the government agency in charge for their reference.

Article 15: The constitutional regulations of a Farmers' Association shall contain the following information:

(1) Name of the Farmers' Association.

(2) Its aim and purposes.

(3) Its organic territory.

(4) Its location.

(5) Its functions and activities.

(6) Its organization.

(7) Rules governing the admission, withdrawal, and dismissal of its members.

(8) Duties and privileges of its members.

(9) Number, authority and term of office of its members' representatives, supervisors and directors and their election and resignation procedures.

(10) Duties and responsibilities of its general manager.

(11) Its meetings.

(12) Its membership fees and capital stocks.

(13) Its budget funds and accounting.

(14) Provision for the amendment and revision of constitutional regulations.

Article 16: Prior to the inauguration meeting of a Farmers' Association, the preparatory committee shall submit a report of the preparation together with a draft of the constitutional regulations of the proposed Farmers' Association to the government agency in charge and request the latter to appoint officials to supervise the elections.

Article 17: Within seven (7) days after the inauguration meeting, the members, newly organized Farmers' Association shall submit a list of its a brief historical account of its supervisors and directors and a copy of adopted constitutional regulations to the government agency in charge for registration. The government agency, after making due registration, shall issue a registration certificate and an official seal to the Farmers' Association.

Chapter IV. Membership

Article 18: Any Chinese national, over 20 years of age, who satisfies the qualifications specified under Article 13 of National Farmers' Association Law and who has derived from farming operations over half of his personal total income and is residing within the organic territory of a farmers' association shall, after careful examination, become eligible to membership in the district (township, urban district and county-governed city) Farmers' Association. For the time being, however, only one person from each household, as appears on the Government Household Register, shall be permitted to join the Farmers' Association; this person does not necessarily have to be the head of the household.

Article 19: Any non-farmer who does not satisfy the qualifications as specified under Article 18 above but who is residing within the organic territory of the Farmers' Association shall be eligible to associate membership. Only one associate member is admitted from each household. The privileges of associate members are the same as that of the members except for their right to elect or to be elected to any office other than that of the supervisor. The number of supervisors to be elected from among associate members is limited to one third of the total number of supervisors. Existing members of Farmers' Associations whose qualifications do not measure up to that specified in Article 18 above shall be redesignated as associate members upon implementation of these regulations.

Article 20: Subordinate Farmers' Associations shall be the members of their respective immediate superior Farmers' Associations.

Article 21: (1) Members' representatives shall be elected from each small agricultural unit to attend the members' representatives meetings of the district (township, urban district and county-governed city) Farmers' Associations. Members' representatives from lower level Farmers' Associations shall also be elected to attend the representatives meetings of their immediate higher level Farmers' Associations. The number of members' representatives to attend the respective meetings are as follows:
  1. To attend the district (township, urban district and county-governed city) Farmers' Associations members' representatives meetings: Two (2) representatives shall be elected from the first thirty (30) members of each small agricultural unit and one more representative shall be elected from each additional thirty (30) members. In case the total membership of a

small agricultural unit does not reach thirty (30) in number,
two (2) representatives shall be elected from the existing number of members.

2. To attend the county or municipal Farmers' Association
   members' representatives meetings: Four (4) representatives
   shall be elected from the first 2,000 basic members of each
   district (township, urban district and county-governed city)
   Farmers' Association and one more representative shall be
   elected from each additional 1,000 members.

3. To attend the Provincial Farmers' Association members' representatives meeting: Four (4) representatives shall be
   elected from the first 30,000 members of each county or
   municipal Farmers' Association and one more representative
   from each additional 15,000 members. If the membership
   falls short of 30,000, still four representatives shall be
   elected.

(2) The total number of members' representatives from lower level
Farmers' Associations attending a meeting of a higher level
Farmers' Association shall not be less than 30 or in excess of 150.
If such shortage or excess occurs, the government agency in charge
shall make adjustments by ordering an increase or decrease in the
number of representatives according to established standards.

(3) The members' representatives of a small agricultural unit to
participate in the members' representatives meetings of a higher
level Farmers' Association shall be elected by the members plenary meeting of the unit. The members' representatives of a
district (township, urban district and county-governed city)
Farmers' Association or a county or municipality Farmers' Association to participate in the members' representatives meetings of
a higher level Farmers' Association shall be elected by the members' representatives meetings of the respective Farmers' Associations in question. The members' representives thus elected shall
hold office for a term of three years, but may continue to officiate
for several consecutive terms if re-elected to the same office
consecutively.

(4) At least two thirds of the members' representatives of a Farmers'
Association shall be owner-farmers and tenant-farmers.

Chapter V. Staff

Article 22: Separate boards of directors and supervisors shall be organized within each Farmers' Association. Directors and supervisors shall be elected by the members of Farmers' Associations. The number of directors and supervisors shall be determined by the government agency in charge within the range as indicated in the following provisoes:

(1) Number of directors for each district (township, urban district and county-governed city) Farmers' Association: 11 to 21.

(2) Number of directors for each county or municipality Farmers' Association: 15 to 25.

(3) Number of directors for the Provincial Farmers' Association: 23 to 33.

(4) The number of supervisors of different levels of Farmers' Associations shall not exceed one third of the total number of directors of the respective Farmers' Associations.

(5) The total number of director-alternatives or supervisor-alternatives shall not exceed one half of the total number of directors or supervisors of the respective Farmers' Associations.

(6) At least two thirds of the directors of a Farmers' Association shall be elected from members with qualifications as specified under Article 13 (1), (2) and (3) of the National Farmers' Association Law and not more than one third of the directors shall be elected from members with qualifications as specified under Article 13 (4) and (5) of the National Farmers' Association Law.

(7) The chairman of the board of directors of a Farmers' Association shall be elected by the directors from among themselves.

Article 23: The candidates for directorship and supervisorship of a Farmers' Association shall be limited to its basic members, but shall not be limited to the members' representatives from lower level Farmers' Associations.

Article 24: (1) The directors and supervisors of a Farmers' Association shall not draw any salary from the Farmers' Association; neither shall they assume concurrently any duty in the operational departments of the Farmers' Association that demands a salary nor are they permitted to hold any remunerative position in any other organization, whether official or private, which is in competition with the Farmers' Association.

(2) Directors and supervisors attending their respective board meetings may draw travel expenses and attendance fees while the meetings are in session.

(3) Directors and supervisors of a farmers' association despatched by its respective boards to attend meetings other than the board meetings, and as representatives of the Farmers' Association, may also draw travel expenses.

(4) At the end of the fiscal year when the Farmers' Association's balance sheet shows a net profit, the directors and supervisors may collectively receive a bonus not exceeding 10% of the total net profit.

Article 25: The term of office of the directors and supervisors of farmers' associations shall be three years. Maximum tenure of office shall be nine consecutive years (three consecutive terms) if consecutively re-elected to the same post. After the expiration of the third term, a respite of three years must elapse before they may be elected again.

Article 26: (1) Each Farmers' Association shall have a general manager, to be engaged by the board of directors. The general manager shall be responsible to the board of directors for the operation of the farmers' association and the management of its business activities. All outgoing documents and correspondence of the farmers' association must be countersigned by the general manager who shall be responsible for the actions taken.

(2) The general manager shall report to the board of directors monthly on the financial and business affairs and annually on the proposed budget for service program as well as service activities and shall submit to the board of supervisors annually the final financial statement and other necessary reports of the Farmers' Association.

(3) The general manager shall secure at least three guarantors acceptable to the board of directors before he may be engaged. The guarantors shall be jointly responsible for any loss, financial or otherwise, suffered by the Farmers' Association through negligence or mismanagment of the general manager.

(4) The general manager may, within the limit of approved budget and staff pattern and as dictated by the need of the Farmers' Associations activities, employ general and technical staff and shall report the employments and termination of employments to the board of dierctors for record. All staff members so employed shall be under the direction and supervision of the general manager.

Article 27: (1) For each small agricultural unit, a chief and a deputy chief shall be elected from among its members. Both the chief and the deputy chief shall draw no salary but shall be equipped with implements or furnished with funds necessary to the execution of their duty.

(2) Both the chief and deputy chief of a small agricultural unit shall hold office for a term of three years, but may continue to officiate for a maximum of three consecutive terms if consecutively re-elected to the same post. After the expiration of the third term, however, a three year respite must intervent before they may be elected again.

Article 28: (1) Directors and supervisors of a higher level Farmers' Association shall not be concurrently directors and supervisors of a lower level Farmers' Association, neither shall the directors and supervisors of a Farmers' Association be concurrently the chief and/or deputy chief of a small agricultural unit.

(2) Legally appointed public functionaries and the heads of autonomous organizations shall not be eligible for the directorship or supervisorship of a Farmers' Association, neither shall they be elected as members' representatives of a Farmers' Association.

Article 29: (1) The board of supervisors shall make regular quarterly audit of the books and accounts of the Farmers' Association and may enlist the service of a certified public accountant for this purpose, if necessary. An auditing report jointly certified by the board of supervisors and the public accountant shall be presented to the members' representatives meeting of the Farmers' Association at least once a year. Likewise, the board of directors are required to submit to the members' representatives meeting, at least once a year, a general report on the Farmers' Association.

(2) The afore-mentioned auditing and general reports shall be submitted, within ten days after ratification by the members' representatives meeting, to the government agency in charge and to the higher level Farmers' Association respectively for their

examination.

(3) When any irregularity is found in the auditing report, the government agency in charge shall make immediate corrections or to take other appropriate actions.

Article 30: Aside from conducting intra-organizational elections in accordance with the prescription of law, the Farmers' Associations shall not permit their officers and their paid staff to use their positions or influence or the name of the Farmers' Association in conducting political campaigns for or against any candidate for public office, neither shall they imply approval nor disapproval of such political candidates.

Article 31: Directors and supervisors of a Farmers' Association and the chiefs and deputy chiefs of a small agricultural unit may be permitted to resign their offices for unreconcilable reasons and upon approval of the members' representatives meeting. They shall, however, be discharged from office upon the resolutions of the members' representatives meeting or the members plenary meeting, for offences against public law or the Farmers' Association regulations or for other serious misconducts.

Article 32: The government agency in charge may order the re-election or termination of any elected officer or employed staff if the latter is found violating the law and regulations or causing serious damage to the Farmers' Association. Approval for such action, however, shall be obtained by the government agency in charge from its immediate superior prior to the issuance of such orders.

Chapter VI. Meetings

Article 33: (1) Members' plenary meetings of small agricultural units and members' representatives meetings of different levels of Farmers' Associations shall each be convened once a year. In both cases, special meetings may be called upon the request of no less than one tenth of the members. Special meetings may also be convened when they are deemed necessary by the respective boards of directors.

(2) Members' plenary meetings of small agricultural units shall be convened and presided over by the chiefs of the respective units. Members' representatives meetings shall be convened and presided over by the chairman of the board of directors of the respective Farmers' Associations.

Article 34: The meetings of the board of directors and the board of supervisors shall be convened by the chairman of the board of directors and the executive-supervisor of the board of supervisors respectively. The time of the respective meetings shall be specified in the constitutional regulations of the individual Farmers' Associations.

Article 35: (1) Meetings of members, members' representatives, board of directors and the board of supervisors shall be held only when over half of the legitimate number of participants of the respective meetings are present. Resolutions shall be passed by the majority af the quorum.

(2) A member, a members' representative or a director may empower another member, members' representative or director in writing to serve as his proxy at the respective meetings. However, each member, members' representative or director may authorize, or accept the authorization of, only one other member, members' representative or director respectively to serve as his proxy.

Article 36: Resolutions on the following matters shall not be adopted unless passed by two thirds of the quorum:

(1) Approval of the constitutional regulations of a Farmers' Association and their amendments.

(2) Readjustment of its organization.

(3) Penalty for members.

(4) Election or dismissal of directors or chiefs of small agricultural units.

(5) Engagement and disengagement of general manager.

(6) Collection of funds.

(7) Disposal of properties.

(8) Determination of the maximum amount of loans to be borrowed or credit to be extended by the Farmers' Association.

If the decision to engage a general manager cannot be made during the meeting, according to item 5 above, another meeting will be called during which a vote will be held to decide which of the two candidates who got the most votes during the previous meeting will be selected. The engagement of the selected candidate will be made with the concurrence of the majority of the attendants to the meeting. If the assenting votes for the two candidates are of equal number, final decision will be made by drawing lots.

Article 37: Board of directors of a Farmers' Association shall work out at their board meeting a schedule for each of the directors to attend by turn the members' representatives meetings, board of directors' meetings of their subordinate farmers' associations and members' plenary meeting of small agricultural units.

Chapter VII. Funds

Article 38: The sources of Farmers' Association funds shall be as follows:

(1) Sales of stocks:

Each share of Farmers' Association stock shall be sold at a face value of NT$10 for district (township, urban district and county-governed city) farmers' associations and NT$100 for provincial and county or municipality Farmers' Associations, each member shall subscribe a minimum of one share and shall be permitted to purchase or own additional shares up to 20% of the total value of all stocks but not in excess of 20%. The purchase of stocks shall be made in one full payment. Interest on Farmers' Association stocks shall be limited to one percent per annum.

(2) Initial fee:

An initial fee of NT$1 shall be paid by each member of a district (township, urban district and county-governed city) Farmers' Association and NT$20 by each member of a county or municipality or the provincial Farmers' Association, in one lump sum, upon his induction into the respective Farmers' Association.

(3) Annual fee:

District (township, urban district and county-governed city) farmers' associations shall decide at their members' representatives meetings, the amount of annual fees to be collected from their members annually. The county or municipality and provincial farmers' associations shall collect 20% of the total annual fees of their respective member associations.

(4) Net profit from economic enterprises undertaken by the Farmers'

association.

(5) Net profit from credit service rendered by the Farmers' Association.

(6) Income from services entrusted to the Farmers' Association by other agencies.

(7) Contributions:

All funds from contributions are confined to the use of rendering advisory, cultural and welfare services and shall be collected by the district (township, urban district and county-governed city) Farmers' Associations after their plans specifying amount, uses and method of collection have been approved by the board of directors of the higher level Farmers' Association.

(8) Government subsidy:

All government subsidies shall be used only for rendering advisory cultural and welfare services and shall be included in the annual expenditure budgets of provincial, county and municipal governments.

(9) Appropriation from agricultural financial agencies:

At least 10% of the net profit of agricultural financial agencies shall be appropriated to the prcvincial Farmers' Association as a subsidy for further equitable distribution among its member associations.

Article 39: (1) Transfer and inheritance of stocks and the use of stocks as security and in payment of debts shall first have the concurrence of the board of directors of the issuing Farmers' Association and the member inheriting the stock shall have the same responsibilities and privileges as did the original stockholder.

(2) For purposes of sale, redemption, transfer, inheritance and security, each share of farmers' association stock shall be taken at its face value only. Member leaving a Farmers' Association may claim for refunds on stocks purchased. But no stock shall be refunded to a member dismissed by the association.

Article 40: Independent and separate bookkeeping and accounting records shall be maintained for each economic enterprise, credit, insurance, production, cultural and welfare service undertaken by the Farmers' Association.

Article 41: The total profit of a Farmer's Association at the end of a year shall consist of the profits of its various economic undertakings and credit and insurance services. After deduction of losses and interests for the shareholders, the balance of this profit shall be divided into one hundred equal portions and allocated as follows:

(1) Twenty (20) portions shall be deposited in a financial institution designated by the government agency in charge as reserve fund and not to be further distributed.

(2) Ten (10) portions shall be for the community chest.

(3) Ten (10) portions shall be awarded to directors, supervisors and employees collectively as remuneration.

(4) Fifty (50) portions shall be used as funds for the rendition of advice and guidance to productive enterprises for the rendition of cultural and welfare services.

(5) Ten (10) portions shall be distributed among members and associate members of the Farmers' Association in proportion to the value of business secured by each individual for the Farmers' Association.

Article 42: All Farmers' Associations shall adopt a single, uniform system of bookkeeping and accounting and shall submit periodic auditing reports to the higher level Farmers' Association and to the government agency in charge.

Article 43: Any member or members' representative, creditor or creditor's legal representative of a Farmers' Association may examine the books and other relevant financial documents of the Farmers' Association within a certain time limit set by the board of supervisors and the Farmers' Association shall not refuse him such inspection.

Article 44: All Farmers' Associations shall deposit their surplus operational funds in banking institutions designated by the respective government agencies in charge.

Article 45: The fiscal-service year of a Farmers' Association shall begin on January 1st and end on December 31st. Before the beginning of each fiscal-service year, the general manager of the Farmers' Association shall have ready the service program, annual budget and a profit-and-loss estimate of its proposed undertakings for the forthcoming year and submit them to the board of directors for approval. The general manager shall also prepare an inventory of the Farmers' Association properties, a statement of assets and debts, a statement of actual profit and loss of its undertakings, an activity report, a final financial statement and a proposal for the distribution of net profits and submit them to the board of directors not later than 30 days after the end of each fiscal year.

Chapter VIII. Supervision

Article 46: The government agency in charge of a Farmers' Association may issue warnings to the Farmers' Association if the latter is found to be negligent in carrying out its duties, endangering public interests or overstepping the bounds of its proper functions.

Article 47: The government agency in charge of a Farmers' Association may order the cancellation of a resolution adopted by the Farmers' Association if the resolution is found violating laws and regulations, endangering public interests or abusing the purposes and responsibilities of the Farmers' Association.

Article 48: (1) The government agency in charge of Farmers' Association may dissolve the Farmers' Association or cancel its registration if the latter is found seriously abusing its purposes and responsibilities. In taking such disciplinary action, however, the government agency in charge must obtain the concurrence of the local people's council.

(2) A new Farmers' Association shall be organized immediately after a faulty one is dissolved.

Article 49: In taking disciplinary actions as specified under Articles 47 and 48, the lower level government agency in charge of Farmers' Associations must have prior approval from its superior administrative authority.

Article 50:..When a Farmers' Association is dissolved or when its registration is cancelled, its properties shall be put under the custody of the official(s) appointed by the government agency in charge for liquidation. The official(s) shall have full authority in repersenting the dissolving Farmers' Association in all matters pertaining to the liquidation of its properties.

Article 51: Farmers' Associations of higher levels shall have the responsibility and authority for guiding, supervising the operation and auditing the accounts of the Farmers' Associations of lower levels. Requests for subsidies submitted by Barmers' Associations of lower levels to the government or other agricultural institutions shall be screened and approved by Farmers' Associations of higher levels.

Chapter IX.   Supplementary Provisions

Article 52: Farmers' Associations may request the respective government agencies in charge or other related government agencies to dispatch to the Farmers' Association either temporary or permanent advisory personnel to offer advice on agricultural technique and other agricultural improvement works.

Article 53: In enforcing these regulations, the Provincial Government of Taiwan may stipulate necessary detailed working procedures basing on these regulations if such procedures are called for by actual need.

Article 54: These regulations shall take effect upon promulgation.

REGULATIONS GOVERNING THE ORGANIZATION OF IRRIGATION ASSOCIATIONS IN TAIWAN PROVINCE

(Promulgated by the Executive Yuan, September 17, 1955)

Chapter I. General Principles

Article 1: These Regulations are drawn up in accordance with Article 3 of the Water Law.

Article 2: The various Irrigation Associations (hereinafter referred to as Association or Associations) of this Province organized under these Regulations shall assist the Government in irrigation matters in their respectively assigned areas.

Article 3: The establishment, amalgamation, separation, abolition, and changes in the organization of Irrigation Associations shall be carried out upon approval by the competent Provincial authorities according to the following stipulations and in the light of the natural environment, the distribution of water sources, the irrigation situation, and economic conditions. Any action taken shall be reported to the competent authorities of the Central Government. The same procedure shall be followed regarding applications requests for action made by individuals.

(1) Areas irrigated by one canal system shall have only one single Irrigation Association in principle.

(2) For areas within a county or municipality irrigated by water from different sources, one Irrigation Association shall be set up in one county or municipality in principle. Individuals who want to establish an Irrigation Association shall submit an application sponsored by over 50 persons who have membership qualifications and signed by over one half of those persons in that area who are qualified for membership, and send it together with charts and explanations on the proposed engineering project in that area for the approval of the competent Provincial authorities.

Chapter II. Membership

Article 4: Any person living in the jurisdictional area of the local

Irrigation Association and possessing any one of the following qualifications may be a member of the local Irrigation Associations;

(1) Agency in charge of public farm land or representative of the agency using it.

(2) Owner of private farm land or its mortgagee.

(3) Lessee or tenant or holder of perpetual lease on public or private farm land.

If any of the obligees referred to in (2) and (3) above is a juristic person or corporate body, the officer in charge or its representative shall be member of the local Irrigation Association.

Article 5: Members shall have the right to vote, the right to be elected, the right to recall officers, and the right to use facilities provided by the Irrigation Association, and to enjoy other privileges according to law.

Article 6: Members shall observe the Water Law and the resolutions of the Irrigation Association, pay membership fees, contribute free labor service, contribute land needed for irrigation facilities required by law, and fulfill other duties according to law.

Chapter III. Functions

Article 7: The Irrigation Associations shall undertake the following matters:

(1) Installation, improvement, maintenance, protection, and management of the irrigation and drainage works.

(2) Regulation and control of water for use in canals and by water pumps and settlement of disputes.

(3) Installation of improvements on land (including facilities for protection against wind, sand, and tide and for soil and water conservation.)

(4) Prevention and elimination of practices destructive of, or hindering farm irrigation.

(5) Operation and management of public property (including irrigation

facilities).

(6) Coordination with and assistance in matters relating to governmental planning for regional irrigation projects contiguous to the Associations jurisdictional areas.

(7) Suggestions and planning for hydraulic development in the Association's jurisdictional area.

(8) Other matters assigned to the Association by competent authorities and matters coming under its jurisdiction according to law.

The Irrigation Associations shall each draw up practical measures of its own for the discharge of the above-mentioned tasks and submit them to the competent authorities for approval.

Article 8: The irrigation small groups shall undertake the following matters:

(1) Maintenance, operation and repair of irrigation laterals and drainage ditches.

(2) Regulation of water for use in the area under the jurisdiction of the small groups.

(3) Planning and establishment of joint seed farms.

(4) Installation of water supply routes in the jurisdictional areas of the small groups.

(5) Installation and operation of water sluice gates for minor irrigation and drainage routes.

(6) Matters delegated by the Irrigation Associations.

In the discharge of the above-mentioned tasks, the irrigation small groups shall be subject to the supervision and guidance of the Irrigation Associations.

Chapter IV.   Organization and Duties and Powers

Section 1.   Deliberative Bodies

Article 9: The Irrigation Association shall have a members' delegates' congress composed of delegates chosen by members in the Association's jurisdictional area. The delegates shall serve without pay other than fees for attending meetings. Their tenure of office shall be three years and they are eligible for reelection. The total number of members' delegates shall be fixed by the competent Provincial authorities according to the following criteria:

(1) For an area to be irrigated and drained that is less than 10,000 *chia* (23,967 acres), there shall be no more than 50 delegates.

(2) For an area to be irrigated and drained that is from 10,000-50,000 *chia* (23,967-119,836 acres), there shall be no more than 100 delegates.

(3) For an area to be irrigated and drained that exceeds 50,000 *chia* (119,836 acres), there shall be no more than 150 delegates.

Two thirds of member of delegates referred to above shall be chosen from among members of the Irrigation Association who do the cultivation themselves.

Article 10: The duties and powers of the members' delegates congress shall be as follows:

(1) To elect and recall the President of the Irrigation Association and the members of the Supervisory Committee.

(2) To decide on irrigation plans for the jurisdictional area.

(3) To approve the budget of the Association and audit its financial statements.

(4) To fix membership fees and other charges to be levied on the members.

(5) To decide on the disposal of public properties.

(6) To approve loans.

(7) To decide on matter proposed for discussion by the President of the Association.

(8) To act on members' petitions.

(9) To hear progress reports by the President of the Association and by the Supervisory Committee and to ask them for additional information.

(10 To give retroactive approval to resolutions of the Supervisory Committee and to urgent matters proposed by the President for discussion.

(11) Other duties and powers authorized by law.

All matters coming under Items (2) to (8) above may be screened by the Supervisory Committee in the first instance and then reported to the members' delegates congress. After being passed by the latter, transmitted through the Irrigation Association to the competent authorities for approval before implementation.

Article 11: When in session, the members' delegates congress shall have a Chairman to be elected from among the delegates by secret ballot.

Article 12: The members' delegates congress shall meet once a year. The first congress shall be convened by the competent authorities one month after the election of all the delegates. An extraordinary delegates congress may be held upon the request of over two-fifths of the delegates or of the Supervisory Committee, or if considered as necessary by the competent authorities. The annual and extraordinary congresses shall be convened by the President of the Association.

Article 13: The members' delegates congress shall set up a Supervisory Committee composed of from seven to 15 members, whose tenure of office shall be three years and who are eligible for reelection. Chosen from among the delegates by secret ballot, the members of the Supervisory Committee shall choose a Standing Member to serve as convenor of the Committee to preside over the Committee meetings. The members of the Supervisory Committee shall serve without pay other than fees for attending meetings. The Standing Member may receive travelling expenses.

Article 14: The duties and powers of the Supervisory Committee shall be as follows:

(1) To supervise the implementation by the President of the Irrigation Association of the resolutions adopted by the members' delegates congress.

(2)   To audit the receipts and disbursements of the Association.

(3)   To see how the work of the Association is proceeding.

(4)   To decide on matters relating to the management of properties.

(5)   To decide on urgent matters proposed by the President of the Association for immediate consideration.

(6)   To hear progress reports by the President of the Association and ask him for additional information.

(7)   To make proposals for improvement and rectification.

(8)   To screen matters coming under Items (2) to (8) in Article 10 above.

(9)   Other matter of a supervisory nature.

Resolutions and rectifications concerning matters coming under Items (2), (4), (5), and (7) above shall be reported by the Irrigation Association to the competent authorities. In case of disputes or difficulties encountered in execution, a full statement of the situation with arguments pro and con shall be submitted to the competent authorities for final decision.

Article 15: Regulations governing the election and recall of members' delegates and members of the Supervisory Committee and conference rules shall be separately prescribed.

Section 2.   Executive Authorities

Article 16: An Irrigation Association shall have a President to be elected from among the members by the members' delegates congress for a term of three years. The President may be reelected for a second term. The regulations governing the election and recall of the President shall be separately prescribed.

Article 17: The duties and powers of the President of the Irrigation Association shall be as follows:

(1)   To represent the Association in its dealings with other agencies.

(2)   To take charge of the matters enumerated in Article 7 above.

(3) To carry out resolutions passed by the members' delegates congress and the Supervisory Committee and to make progress reports.

(4) To appoint and dismiss staff members of the Association and to supervise their services.

(5) To settle disputes between members of the Association.

(6) To carry out assignments by the competent authorities.

Article 18: The Irrigation Association shall have a general manager, to be nominated by the President from among those who are learned and experienced in hydraulic engineering or administration, and appointed by the competent Provincial authorities. The general manager shall assist the President in the administration of the Association and, in the absence of the President, act on his behalf.

Article 19: The Irrigation Association shall have three departments to be in charge respectively, of finance, engineering, and management, and three offices to be in charge, respectively, of secretarial work, accounting, and personnel. Subordinate units on various levels may be set up, whose duties and powers shall be prescribed in detailed rules for the transaction of official business.

The table of organization and number of personnel for the various departments and offices referred to in the preceding paragraph shall be separately prescribed.

Article 20: Small irrigation groups organized with each canal as a unit may be set up by the Irrigation Associations. In case of larger irrigation areas, small groups may be organized with each lateral as a unit. In case of smaller irrigation areas, several neighboring areas may be organized into one single small group. Measures governing the organization of small groups shall be separately prescribed.

Article 21: The Irrigation Associations may hold monthly business meetings attended by key personnel of various departments and offices. When necessary, extraordinary meetings may be convened by the President who will serve as chairman. When necessary, the Standing Member of the Supervisory Committee may be invited sit in at the meetings.

Chapter V. Finance

Article 22: The revenue of the Irrigation Association shall come from the following sources:

(1) Membership fees.

(2) Special assessments.

(3) Incomes from the use of engineering installations.

(4) Incomes from the use of surplus water.

(5) Interest on property.

(6) Proceeds from the sale of property.

(7) Government subsidy.

(8) Indemnities and fines.

(9) Donations and gifts.

(10) Other incomes according to law.

Article 23: The membership fees shall be collected from all members to be used for annual repair and operation and to be set aside as reserve and for depreciation and emergency use. Special assessments may be levied for special engineering projects and improvements, to be paid by members in the areas who will be benefited thereby.

Article 24: The accounting procedures of the Irrigation Associations shall be drawn up for enforcement by the competent Provincial authorities.

Article 25: Membership fees shall be collected according to the degree of benefits accruing to the individual members. The competent Provincial authorities shall set maximum and minimum limits and the different Irrigation Associations may, within the limits thus set, fix their own rates in the light of actual needs and past practices. These rates shall be passed by the members' delegates congress and approved by the competent authorities on different levels before they are enforced.

The membership fees and special assessments shall not be levied in terms of farm products. Rules for their collection shall be separately prescribed. According to Article 6 of these Regulations, members shall pay membership fees. If any member refuses to pay his membership fee, he may be forced to pay according to law *(fieri facies)*.

Chapter VI. Supervision

Article 26: An Irrigation Association whose jurisdictional area lies within one county or municipality shall be supervised in the first instance by the competent county or municipal authorities and, in the second instance, by the competent Provincial authorities. An Irrigation Association whose jurisdictional area lies within two or more than two counties or municipalities shall be supervised by the competent Provincial authorities and be subject to guidance by the competent county or municipal authorities.

The power of supervision referred to in the preceding paragraph may be delegated by the competent Provincial authorities to the Provincial Water Conservancy Bureau, and by the competent county or municipal authorities to the county or municipal Reconstruction Bureaus. But in more important cases, no action may be taken without prior approval by the original competent authorities.

Article 27: Any resolution of the members' delegates congress or of the Supervisory Committee that contravenes laws and regulations or is detrimental to public interests may be subject to correction or rescission by the competent authorities.

Article 28: Any act of negligence, or any act that is detrimental to public interests, on the part of the Irrigation Association, may be subject to effective restraint or correction by the competent authorities.

Article 29: If the President, general manager, or a member of the Supervisory Committe of the Irrigation Association is found to have committed irregularities or to have disobeyed orders, the competent Provincial authorities may take disciplinary action against him according to law.

Article 30: If the Irrigation Association has committed a serious illegal act and all efforts to have it corrected have proved to be ineffective, the Association may be dissolved by the competent Provincial authorities who shall report its dissolution to the competent authorities of the Central Government.

Article 31: All actions taken by the competent county or municipal authorities pursuant to the provisions of Articles 27 and 28 shall have been approved by the competent Provincial authorities.

Article 32: Unless otherwise stipulated, the employment, work evaluation rewards and punishment, retirement, and pensioning of the staff members of Irrigation Associations may be effected according to the laws and regulations applicable to government employees.

Chapter VII. Supplementary Provisions

Article 33: A Joint Office of all the Irrigation Associations may be set up in the Provincial capital. Regulations governing the organization of this Joint Office shall be separately prescribed.

Article 34: By-laws and operational rules for Irrigation Associations shall be separately prescribed.

Article 35: These Regulations shall come into force from the date of their promulgation.

APPENDIX

II. Tables and Sample Documents

304

TABLES

FIGURES

TABLE 1

AREA OF CULTIVATED LAND IN TAIWAN PROVINCE, 1948-59
(Unit: acre)

Year	Area of Cultivated Land	Index Number
1948	2,016,941	100.0%
1949	2,018,760	100.1%
1950	2,024,313	100.2%
1951	2,043,726	100.3%
1952	2,048,997	100.5%
1953	2,073,623	100.8%
1954	2,076,595	100.9%
1955	2,081,789	103.2%
1956	2,091,241	103.6%
1957	2,084,993	103.4%
1958	2,110,204	104.6%
1959	2,104,349	104.3%

Note: Owing to the fact that some of the cultivated land was washed away in the devastating flood of August 7, 1959, the area of cultivated land in that year was smaller than in the previous year.

TABLE 2

POPULATION STATISTICS OF TAIWAN PROVINCE, 1948-59

Year	Total Population	Index Number
1948	6,806,136	100.0%
1949	7,396,931	108.6%
1950	7,554,399	111.0%
1951	7,869,247	115.6%
1952	8,128,374	119.0%
1953	8,438,016	123.9%
1954	8,749,151	128.6%
1955	9,077,643	133.4%
1956	9,390,381	138.0%
1957	9,690,250	142.3%
1958	10,039,435	147.4%
1959	10,431,341	153.2%

TABLE 3

NUMBER OF OWNER-FARMER, PART OWNER-FARMER, TENANT FARMER, AND FARM HAND FAMILIES IN TAIWAN PROVINCE

Year	Owner-Farmers		Part Owner-Farmers		Tenant Farmers		Farm Hands		Total	
	No. of Families	%	No. of Families	%	No. of Families	%	No. of Families	%	No. of Families	%
1940-43 average	140,091	31.2%	138,881	31.0%	169,248	37.8%			448,220	100%
1947	174,937	28.5%	152,716	24.9%	225,655	36.8%	60,177	9.8%	613,485	100%
1948	211,649	33.0%	154,460	24.1%	231,224	36.1%	43,521	6.8%	640,854	100%
1949	224,378	33.7%	156,558	23.5%	239,939	36.1%	44,259	6.7%	665,134	100%
1947-49 average	203,655	31.8%	154,578	24.2%	232,273	36.3%	49,319	7.7%	639,825	100%
1950	231,111	33.9%	162,573	23.8%	244,378	35.8%	44,405	6.5%	682,467	100%
1951	249,850	35.4%	167,962	23.8%	243,313	34.4%	45,070	6.4%	706,195	100%
1952	262,065	36.1%	177,113	24.4%	240,572	33.2%	45,296	6.3%	725,046	100%
1950-52 average	247,675	35.1%	169,216	24.0%	242,754	34.5%	44,924	6.4%	704,569	100%

TABLE 4

INCREASED PRODUCTION OF BROWN RICE AFTER THE IMPLEMENTATION OF RENT REDUCTION IN TAIWAN PROVINCE

(Unit: Short ton)

Year	Quantity of Brown Rice Produced	Index Number
1948	1,143,809	100.0%
1949	1,292,572	113.7%
1950	1,506,515	133.1%
1951	1,567,987	139.0%
1952	1,673,152	147.0%

TABLE 5

COMPARISON OF TENANT FARMER'S INCOME BEFORE AND AFTER RENT REDUCTION IN TAIWAN PROVINCE

(Unit: 1b)

Year	Yield Per *Chia*	Farm Land Rent	Tenant Farmer's Share	Percentage of Tenant Farmer's Share
Before rent reduction	10,249	5,637 (55%)	4,612 (45%)	100%
1949	10,714	3,843 (37.5%)	6,871 (62.5%)	149%
1950	11,360	3,843 (37.5%)	7,517 (62.5%)	163%
1951	11,729	3,843 (37.5%)	7,886 (62.5%)	171%
1952	12,192	3,843 (37.5%)	8,349 (62.5%)	181%

Note: The yield per *chia* in this table is based on the standard production of one *chia* (2,3967 acres) of the ninth-grade paddy field in Taoyuan County.

TABLE 6

DECLINE IN THE VALUE OF FARM LAND AFTER THE 37.5% RENT REDUCTION IN TAIWAN PROVINCE

(Base Period: 1948=100)

Year	7th-Grade Paddy Field	10th-Grade Paddy Field	16th-Grade Paddy Field	22nd-Grade Paddy Field
1948	100	100	100	100
1949	65	71	67	65
1950	67	63	57	41
1951	56	48	42	38
1952	38	43	35	27

TABLE 7

AREA OF FARM LAND BOUGHT BY TENANT FARMERS AND THE NUMBER OF TENANT FARMER FAMILIES BUYING LAND AFTER RENT REDUCTION IN TAIWAN PROVINCE

Year	Area (acre)	Tenant Farmer Families Buying Land
1949	1,853	1,722
1950	8,043	6,989
1951	14,105	11,018
1952	23,636	17,639

TABLE 8

DIFFERENT KINDS OF PUBLIC LAND IN TAIWAN AND THEIR RESPECTIVE AREAS

(Unit: acre)

Kinds of Public Land	Land Categories		Total
	Paddy Field	Dry Land	
State-owned	90,282	126,125	216,407
Province-owned	95,310	102,745	198,055
County or Municipality-owned	4,872	6,045	10,917
District or Township-owned	3,825	5,776	9,601
Grand Total	194,289	240,691	434,980

TABLE 9

STATISTICS ON THE SALES OF PUBLIC LANDS IN TAIWAN PROVINCE

Year	Number of Plots of Farm Land Sold (plots)	Area of Public Land Sold (in acre)				Number of Farming Families Making the Purchase	Land Value (S.T.)	
		Total	Paddy Fields	Dry Land	Others*		Rice	Sweet Potato
1948	11,335	8,108	5,496	2,612		7,572	25,575	27,539
1951	116,688	70,391	31,881	38,491	19	61,782	121,368	285,681
1952	59,225	42,827	21,264	21,554	9	29,814	71,512	186,073
1953, 1st batch	16,014	8,760	5,479	3,281		7,857	23,044	29,064
1953, 2nd batch	35,577	20,957	11,068	9,867	22	14,928	39,231	89,465
1958	36,466	20,720	6,517	14,203		17,735	18,167	107,452
Grand total	275,305	171,763	81,705	90,008	50	139,688	298,897	725,174

*This item denotes farmhouse sites, ditches and ponds.

TABLE 10

AREA OF FARM LAND AND OWNER-CULTIVATED LAND IN TAIWAN PROVINCE BEFORE AND AFTER THE LAND REFORM

(Unit: acre)

Year	Area of Farm Land	Area of Owner-Cultivated Land	Percentage
1948	2,016,941	1,128,357	55.88%
1953	2,073,623	1,718,597	82.87%
1956	2,091,241	1,775,517	84.90%
1959	2,104,349	1,800,867	85.57%

TABLE 11

DIFFERENT KINDS OF FARMING FAMILIES IN TAIWAN PROVINCE BEFORE AND AFTER THE LAND REFORM

Year	Total		Owner-Farmer		Part-Owner-Farmer		Tenant Farmer		Farm Hand	
	Families	%	Families	%	Familier	%	Families	%	Families	%
1948	640,854	100	211,649	33.02	154,460	24.10	231,224	36.08	43,521	6.80
1953	743,982	100	385,286	51.79	169,547	22.79	147,490	19.82	41,657	5.60
1956	785,584	100	448,157	57.05	173,588	22.10	124,573	15.86	39,266	5.00
1959	818,953	100	479,391	58.53	182,121	22.23	118,890	14.51	38,551	4.70

TABLE 12

INCREASE AND DECREASE IN INCOMES OF FARMING FAMILIES BEFORE
AND AFTER THE IMPLEMENTATION OF THE LAND-TO-THE-TILLER PROGRAM

(Unit: lb. of rice)

Year	Annual Yield	Farm Land Rental	Land Price & Interest	Unhulled Rice in Exchange for Fertilizers	Land Tax in Kind	Net Income	Index Number of Net Income
1948	10,249	55%-5,637		251		4,361	100
1949	10,714	37.5%-3,843		829		6,042	138.5
1950	11,360	37.5%-3,843		1,301		6,216	142.5
1951	11,729	37.5%-3,843		1,457		6,429	147.4
1952	12,192	37.5%-3,843		1,713		6,636	152.1
1953	12,604		3,049	1,722	564	7,269	166.7
1954	12,558		3,049	2,090	564	6,855	157.2
1955	13,852		3,049	2,161	564	8,078	185.2
1956	14,542		3,049	2,249	564	8,680	199.0
1957	15,465		3,049	2,297	564	9,555	219.1
1958	15,873		3,049	2,377	564	9,883	226.7
1959	16,001		3,049	2,374	564	10,014	229.6

Note: (a) The annual yield is computed on the basis of the standard amount of production per *chia*
(2.3967 acres) of 9th-grade paddy fields in Taoyuan county.

(b) The amounts of unhulled rice in exchange for fertilizers are based on statistics compiled by
the Taiwan Food Bureau.

TABLE 13

NUMBER OF SCHOOL-AGE CHILDREN AND SCHOOLGOING CHILDREN BEFORE AND AFTER THE LAND REFORM IN TAIWAN PROVINCE

School Year	School-Age Children	Schoolgoing Children	Percentage of Schoolgoing Children
1948	1,090,121	840,783	77.10%
1949	1,129,114	892,758	79.10%
1950	1,133,909	906,950	80.00%
1951	1,149,521	936,709	81.50%
1952	1,107,956	930,719	84.00%
1953	1,116,974	980,160	87.80%
1954	1,141,988	1,037,244	90.80%
1955	1,227,520	1,133,400	92.30%
1956	1,306,058	1,225,317	93.80%
1957	1,449,390	1,371,292	94.60%
1958	1,655,938	1,570,559	94.84%
1959	1,777,748	1,696,641	95.44%

TABLE 14

NUMBER OF HOLDERS OF PUBLIC OFFICES COMING FROM FARM FAMILIES BEFORE AND AFTER THE LAND REFORM IN TAIWAN PROVINCE

Office	1948	1953	1958	1959	1960
Village, Precinct and Neighborhood Chiefs	4,737	6,998	11,206	14,615	14,730
Public Functionaries and Schoolteachers	3,673	6,820	9,778	10,168	10,648
Delegates and Officers of Farmers' Organizations	395	1,823	1,516	5,538	5,865
Members of Farm Tenancy and Conciliation Committees	10	594	840	1,047	1,071
District or Township Chiefs	0	2	7	30	42
Members of County of Municipal Councils	15	58	122	117	114
Members of Provincial Assembly		1	3	2	4

SAMPLE CONTRACT OF PRIVATE FRAM LANDS

FIGURE 1

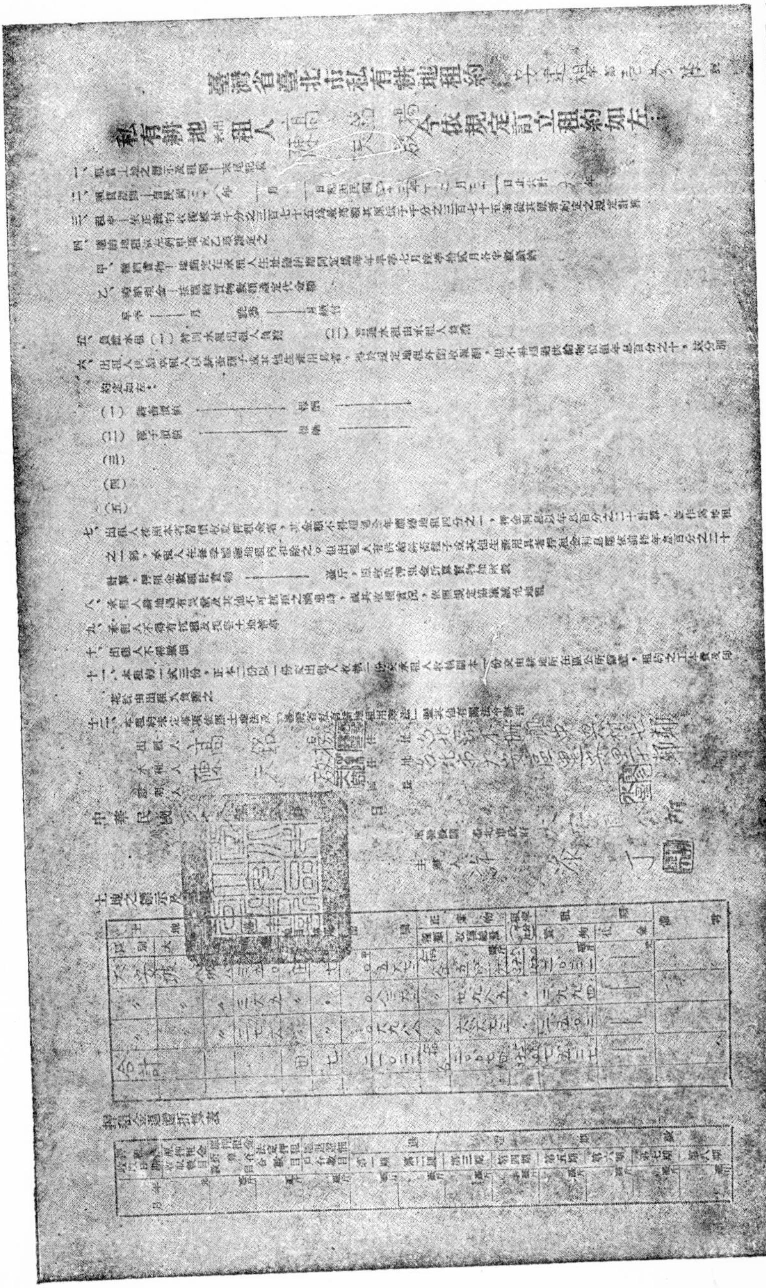

SAMPLE LIST OF FARMER-PURCHASERS OF PUBLIC LAND
OFFERED FOR SALE FOR HSIUSHUI DISTRICT, CHANGHUA
COUNTY, ISSUED BY THE CHANGHUA COUNTY GOVERNMENT

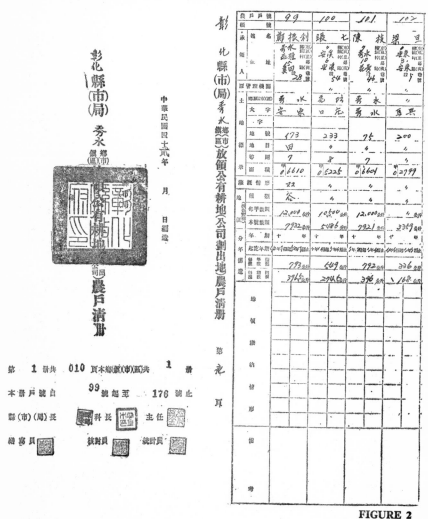

FIGURE 2

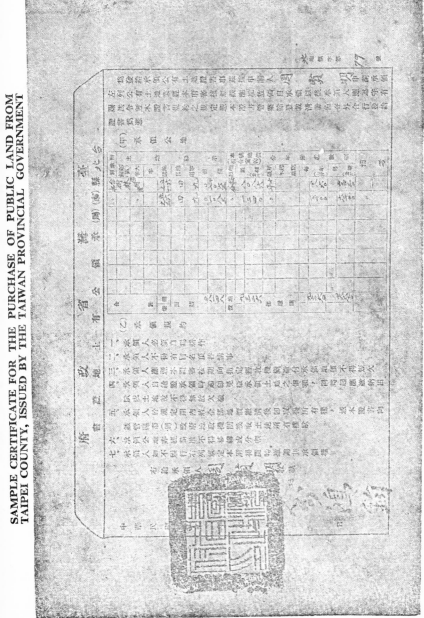

SAMPLE CERTIFICATE FOR THE PURCHASE OF PUBLIC LAND FROM TAIPEI COUNTY, ISSUED BY THE TAIWAN PROVINCIAL GOVERNMENT

FIGURE 3

SAMPLE LIST OF PRIVATE FARM LANDS TO BE COMPULSORILY PURCHASED IN SUNGSHAN DISTRICT, TAIPEI COUNTY

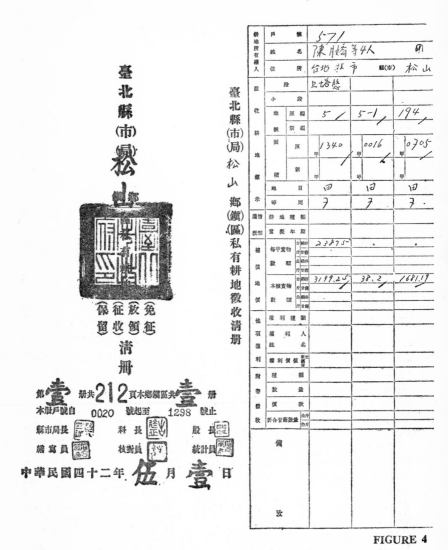

FIGURE 4

SAMPLE LIST OF FARM LANDS TO BE RESOLD TO FARMER-PURCHASERS IN SUNGSHAN DISTRICT, TAIPEI COUNTY

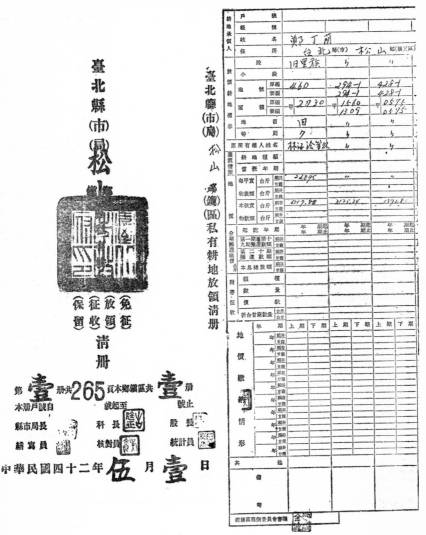

FIGURE 5

LANDOWNERSHIP CERTIFICATE ISSUED BY THE TAIPEI COUNTY GOVERNMENT

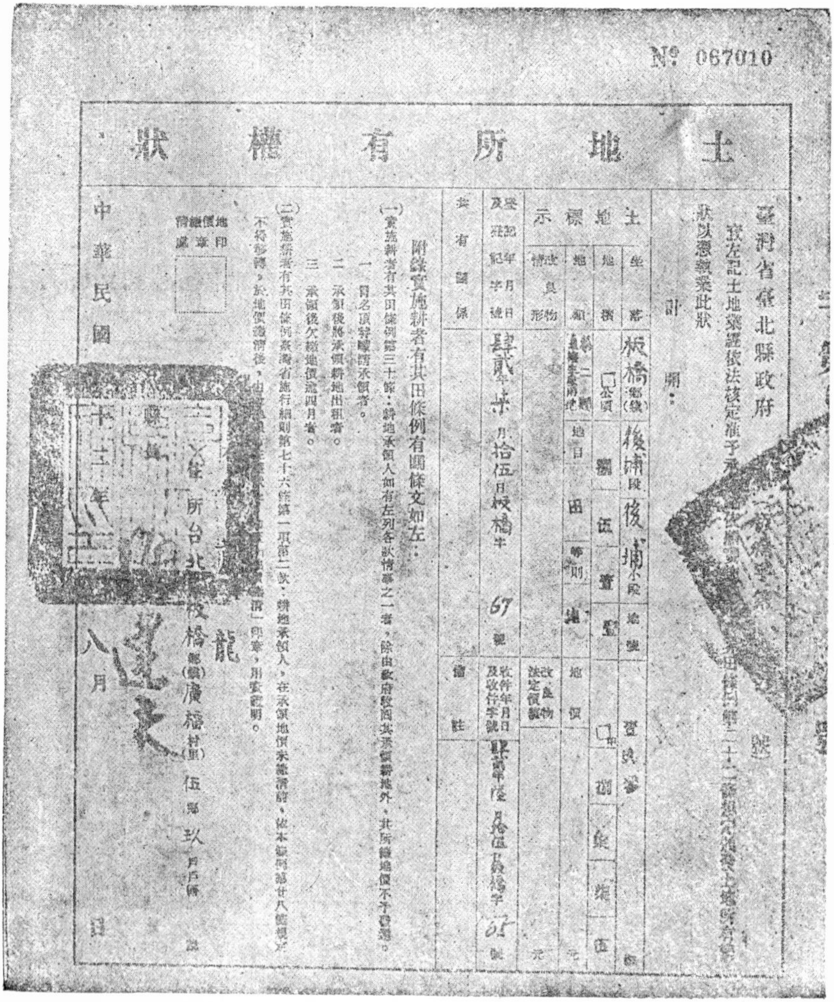

No. 067010

土地所有權狀

臺灣省臺北縣政府

查左記土地業經依法核定准予承領……依照實施耕者有其田條例第二十二條規定發給土地所有權狀以憑執業此狀

計開：

土地標示	
坐落	板橋鄉(鎮) 後埔段 後埔小段
地目	田
登記年月日及登記字號	肆貳年 月拾伍日板橋字 67 號
收件年月日及收件字號	肆貳年 月拾伍日板橋字 65 號

附錄實施耕者有其田條例有關條文如左：

(一)實施耕者有其田條例第三十條：耕地承領人如有左列各款情事之一者，除由政府收回其承領耕地外，其所繳地價不予發還。

一 冒名頂替矇請承領者。

二 承領後將承領耕地出租者。

三 承領後欠繳地價逾四月者。

(二)實施耕者有其田條例臺灣省施行細則第七十六條第一項第二款：耕地承領人，在承領地價未繳清前，依本條例第廿八條規定不得移轉，於地價繳清後，……「清」印章，用資證明。

地價繳清印

所有權人 住所 台北縣板橋鎮(鄉) 廣福村(里) 伍鄰 玖戶

中華民國 四十二年 八月 日

FIGURE 6

SAMPLE RICE BOND

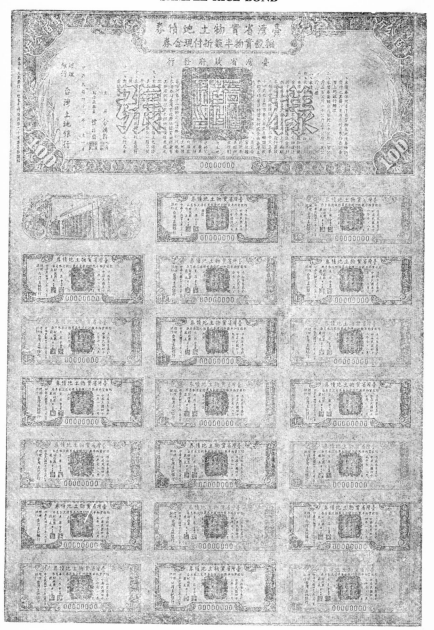

FIGURE 7

FIGURE 7

a. The rice bond is issued on behalf of the Taiwan Provincial Government by the Land Bank of Taiwan.

b. The face value of the rice bond is of six denominations: 50 kg. (110 lbs.) 100 kg. (220 lbs.), 500 kg (1,102 lbs.), 1,000 kg. 5,000 kg. and 10,000 kg. of rice. This sample rice bond stands for 100 kg. of unhulled rice.

c. The rice bond is redeemable in 20 semi-annual installments beginning from July, 1953, and ending in January, 1963.

d. The rice bond bears an interest of four per cent per annum on all later installment payments except the very first one. But for the sake of convenience, both principal and interest for the entire 10-year period were calculated altogether and retired in equal amounts.

e. Each of the coupons for the first 19 semi-annual installments stands for six kg. (13.2 lbs.), of unhulled rice. The coupon for the 20th and last semi-annual installments stands for 5.91 kg. (13.04 lbs.) of unhulled rice.

f. In the upper part of the rice bond there are given the most important provisions of the Regulations Governing the Issuance of Land Bonds in Kind, Taiwan Province.

SAMPLE SWEET POTATO BOND

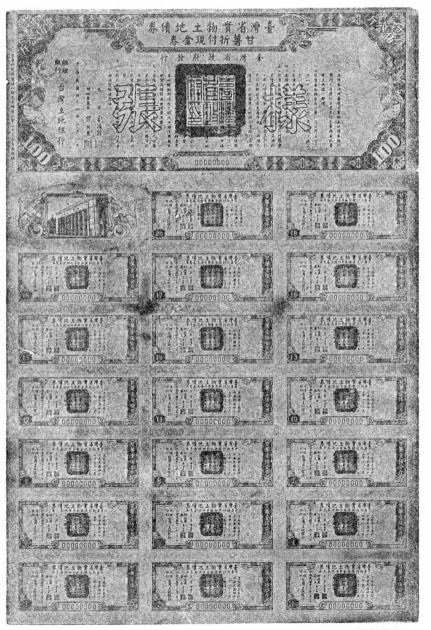

FIGURE 8

FIGURE 8

a. The sweet potato bond is issued on behalf of the Taiwan Provincial Government by the Land Bank of Taiwan.

b. The face value of the sweet potato bond is of six denominations: 100 kg. (220 lbs.), 500 kg. (1,102 lbs.), 1,000 kg. 5,000 kg. 10,000 kg. and 30,000 kg. (66,139 lbs.) of sweet potato. This sample sweet potato bond stands for 100 kg. of sweet potatoes redeemable in cash by converting the sweet potato into monetary terms according to its market value at the time of redemption.

c. The sweet potato bond was redeemable in 20 semi-annual installments beginning from July, 1953, and ending in January, 1963.

d. The sweet potato bond bears interest of four per cent per annum on all installment payments except the first one. But for the sake of convenience, both principal and interest for the entire 10-year period are calculated altogether and retired in equal amounts.

e. Each of the coupons for the first 19 semi-annual installments stands for six kg. (13.2 lbs.) of sweet potatoes payable in cash by converting the sweet potato into monetary terms according to its market value at the time of the installment payment.

f. The coupon for the 20th and last semi-annual installment stands for 5.91 kg. (13.04 lbs.), of sweet potatoes payable in cash by converting the sweet potato into monetary terms according to its market value at the time of payment.

g. In the upper part of the sweet potato bond there are given the most important provisions of the Regulations Governing the Issuance of Land Bonds in Kind, Taiwan Province.

SAMPLE STOCK SHARE OF THE TAIWAN AGRICULTURAL AND FOR-
ESTRY DEVELOPMENT CORPORATION ISSUED TO LANDLORDS IN
PARTIAL PAYMENT FOR THE LAND COMPULSORILY PURCHASED
FROM THEM BY THE GOVERNMENT UNDER THE LAND-TO-THE-
TILLER PROGRAM

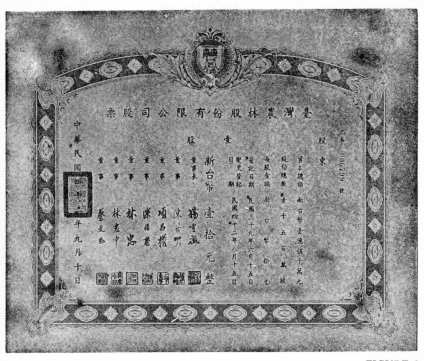

FIGURE 9

a. The total capital value of the Corporation, as finally refixed, is NT$150 million, which is divided into 15 million
shares.

b. The face value of the stock share is NT$10.

**SAMPLE STOCK SHARE OF THE TAIWAN PULP AND PAPER CORPORA-
TION ISSUED TO LANDLORDS IN PARTIAL PAYMENT FOR THE LAND
COMPULSORILY PURCHASED FROM THEM BY THE GOVERNMENT
UNDER THE LAND-TO-THE-TILLER PROGRAM**

FIGURE 10

a. The total capital value of the Corporation, as finally refixed, is NT$300 million, which is divided into 30 million
shares.

b. The face value of the stock share is NT$10.

SAMPLE STOCK SHARE OF THE TAIWAN INDUSTRIAL AND MINING CORPORATION ISSUED TO LANDLORDS IN PARTIAL PAYMENT FOR THE LAND COMPULSORILY PURCHASED FROM THEM BY THE GOVERNMENT UNDER THE LAND-TO-THE-TILLER PROGRAM

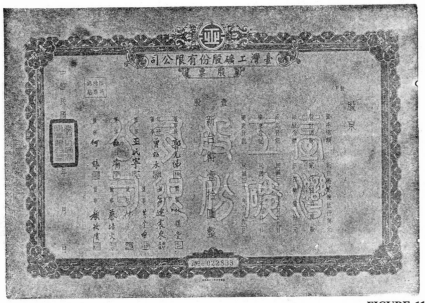

FIGURE 11

a. The total capital value of the Corporation, as finally refixed, is NT$250 million, which is divided into 25 million shares.

b. The face value of the stock share is NT$10.

SAMPLE STOCK SHARE OF THE TAIWAN CEMENT CORPORATION IS-
SUED TO LANDLORDS IN PARTIAL PAYMENT FOR THE LAND COM-
PULSORILY PURCHASED FROM THEM BY THE GOVERNMENT UNDER
THE LAND-TO-THE-TILLER PROGRAM

FIGURE 12

a. The total capital value of the Corporation, as finally refixed, is NT$270 million, which is divided into 27 million
shares.

b. The face value of the stock share is NT$10.

INDEX

Augsburg College
George Sverdrup Library
Minneapolis, Minnesota 55404